MEMORIES & MEMENTOES OF SUNDERLAND

THROUGH TIME

Keith Cockerill

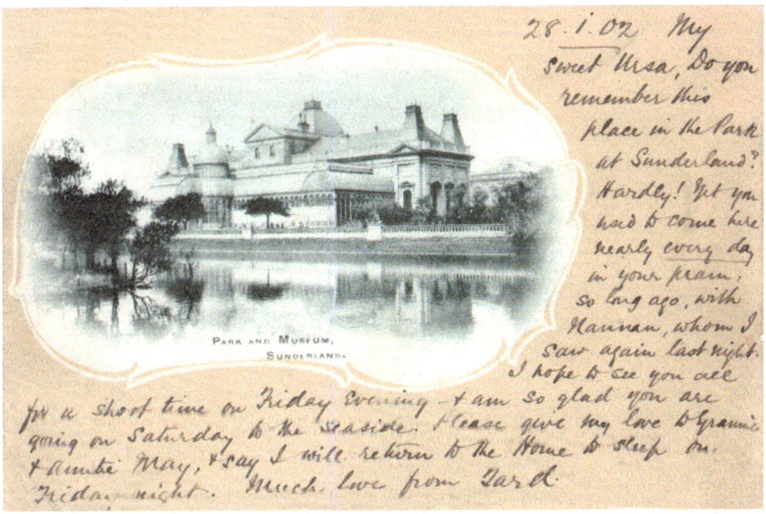

Memories

"My sweet Ursa, Do you remember this place in the Park at Sunderland? Hardly! Yet you had to come here nearly every day in your pram, so long ago with Nannan"

28/1/1902

AMBERLEY

Acknowledgements

Alan and Judy Henderson, Chris Hobdell, Brian Hubbard, Robert Moon, Marjorie Murray, Douglas Scrafton, Peter Searle, Peter Smith, Dennis and Joan Stafford, Mick and Wyn Wilson, David Wood, Peter Wynn.

Sunderland Echo, Sunderland Old Township Heritage Society, Sunderland Antiquarian Society, Friends of Sunderland Old Parish Church, the Rector Gray Society.

These images kindly supplied by Beamish Museum Limited, copyright Beamish Museum Limited; 57, 65, 66, 68 ,69, 71.

Mementoes

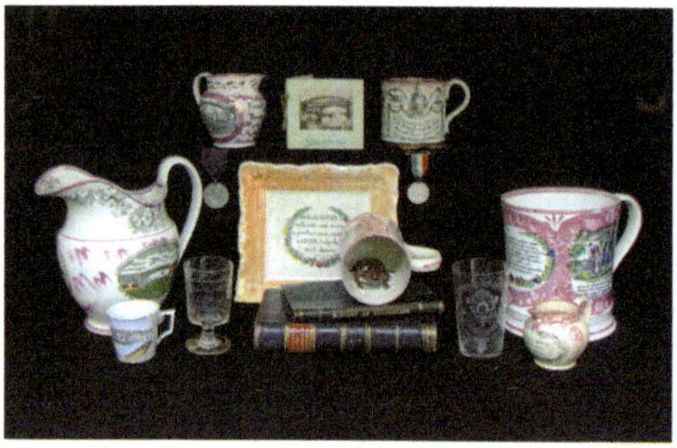

Remembrance

The sun shall loose its splendour,
The tides shall cease to flow,
And tyrant's hearts grow tender,
And melt at others woe.
Thy frosty breath December,
Shall blight the flower of May,
Ere I cease to remember,
The friends now far away.

Verse on an old Sunderland jug

First published 2010

Amberley Publishing Plc
Cirencester Road, Chalford,
Stroud, Gloucestershire, GL6 8PE

www.amberley-books.com

ISBN 978 1 4456 0216 5

British Library Cataloguing in Publication Data.
A catalogue record for this book is available from the British Library.

Typeset in 9.5pt on 12pt Celeste.
Typesetting by Amberley Publishing.
Printed in the UK.

Introduction

The many fascinating artefacts on display in our local museums well represent the rich and absorbing history of Sunderland, but some items closely associated with the city's long and illustrious past are kept elsewhere. The Codex Amiatinus or *Wearmouth Bible* for example – an early eighth century work of major international importance is housed in the Laurentian Library in Florence, Italy. In recent years an excellent facsimile copy of this unique bible has been exhibited locally.

Many Sunderland related mementoes lie privately in the hands of enthusiastic collectors, who often specialise in a single collecting category such as postcards or pottery. Countless more items, however, lie long forgotten in the backs of drawers or cupboards waiting to be rediscovered once more. The advent of internet auction sites has recently brought an abundance of interesting objects to the attention of Sunderland memorabilia collectors and the market is vibrant.

The underlying theme of this book is to match and display a range of mementoes of Sunderland with associated local views – an approach that I hope will awaken memories for the reader and stimulate their interest in the absorbing history of our city.

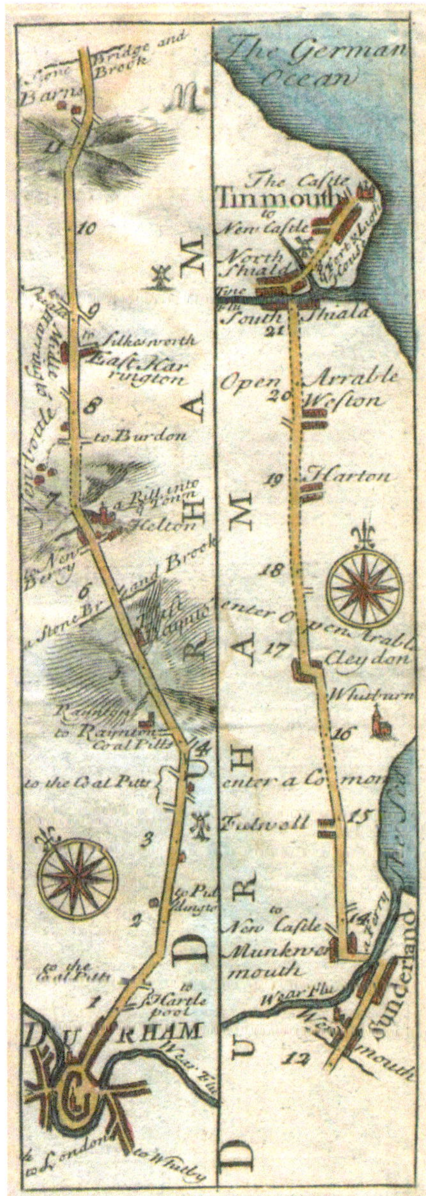

Right: Detail of a mid eighteenth century road map of Whitby to Tynemouth thought to have been created by Emmanuel Bowen. This portion shows the road from Durham to Tynemouth. The journey from Sunderland to Monkwearmouth required the use of the river ferry at this time. Wearmouth Bridge was not erected until 1796. The villages of Newbottle, East and Middle Herrington, Silksworth, Fulwell, Whitburn and Cleadon are also shown.

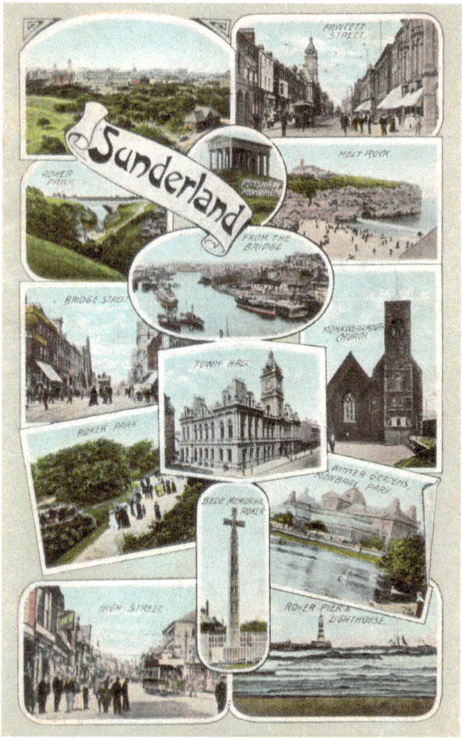

Sunderland: a Multi-View Postcard
A 1907 postcard of Sunderland, featuring many popular scenes of the day.

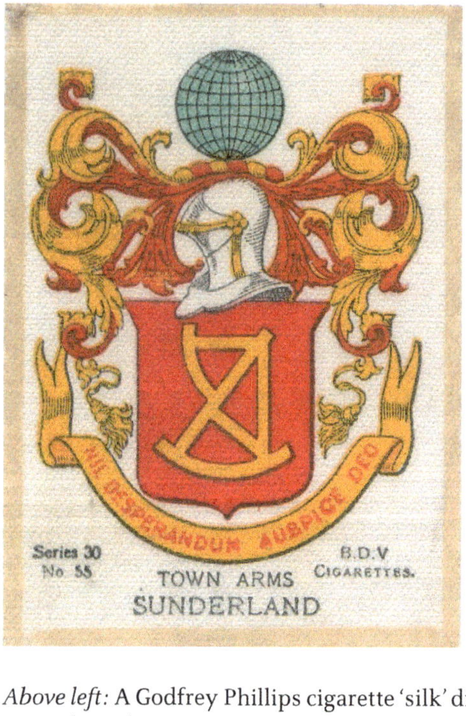

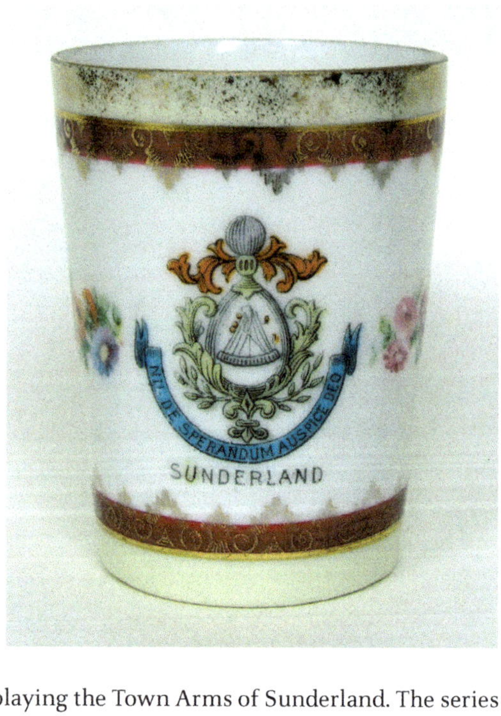

Above left: A Godfrey Phillips cigarette 'silk' displaying the Town Arms of Sunderland. The series was released in 1918.

Above right: A 'Gemma Ware' miniature beaker with a Sunderland crest.

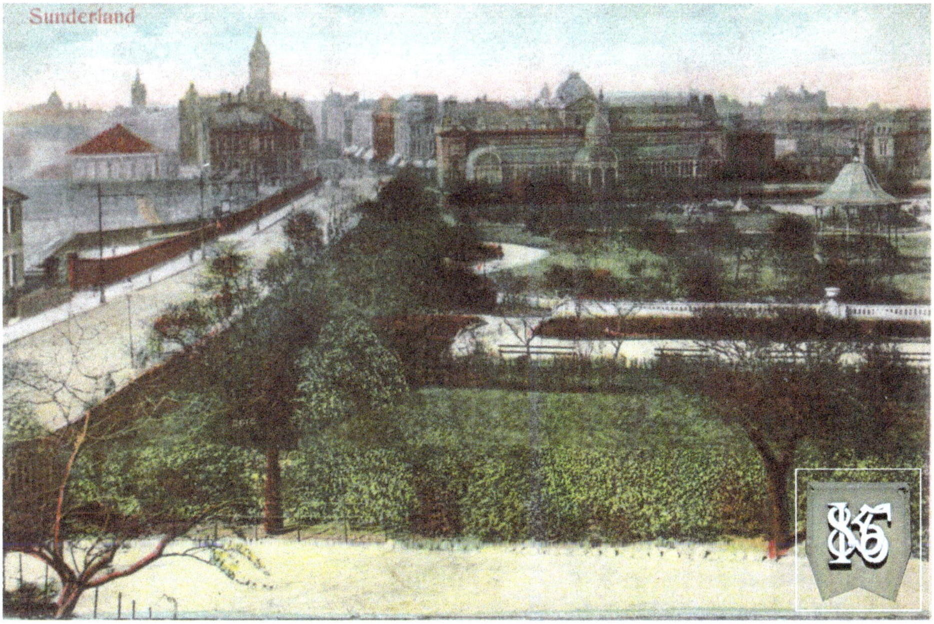

Mowbray Park 1905

A photograph of Mowbray Park taken around 1905 from the knoll upon which the Jack Crawford memorial stands. The park was created in two phases, the first section around Building Hill opening on 12 May 1857. Work had started some two years previously and the old park lodge adjacent to Toward Road bears a date stone of 1856 (inset). The park extension to Borough Road followed in 1866.

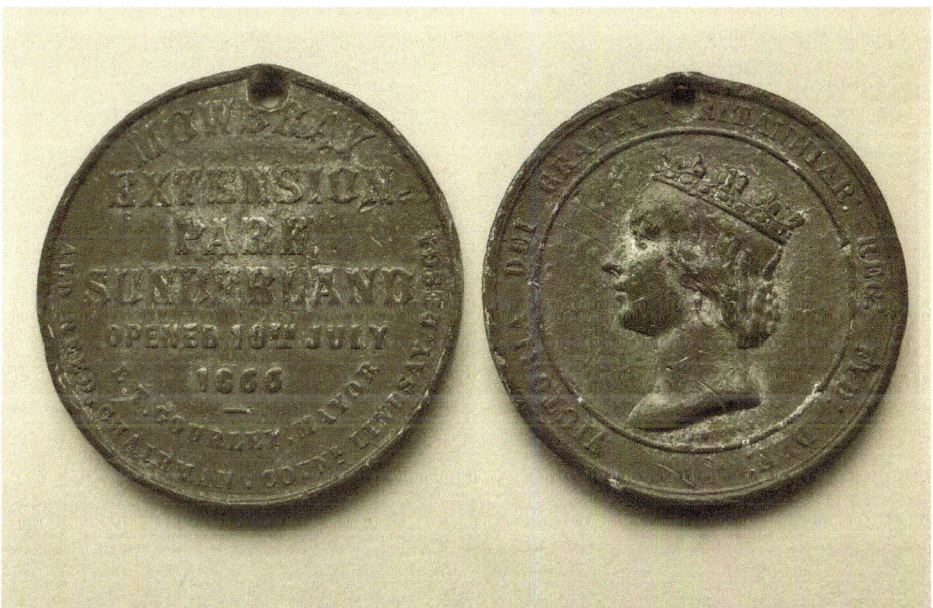

A medal struck in 1866 to commemorate the opening of the 'Mowbray Extension Park' on 10 July of that year.

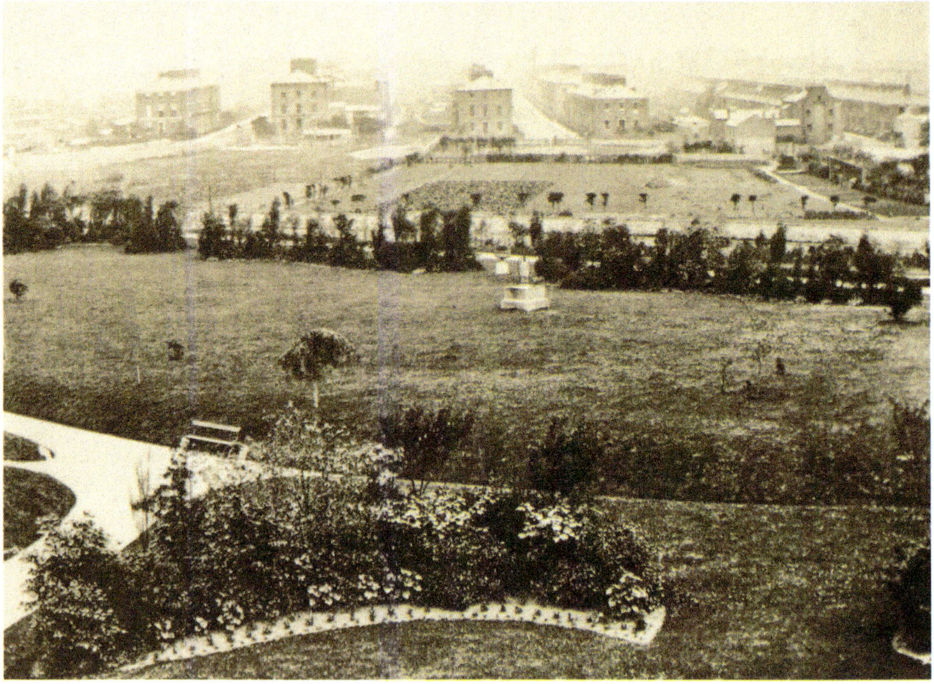

Mowbray Park 1860s
This rare, early photograph of Mowbray Park precedes the building of the Museum and Winter Gardens. The Extension Park of 1866 seems to be far from established, with much of the old Mowbray Garden still intact. A small lake adjacent to Borough Road appears to be present at this time. The picture comes from an extraordinary 'stereo view' of the park.

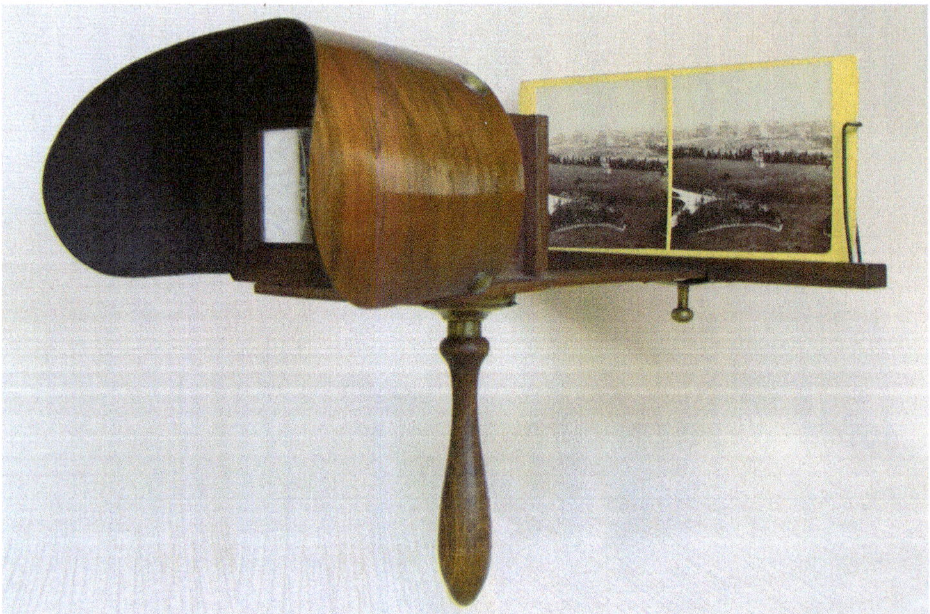

Viewing the Mowbray Park 3D image though a Victorian 'stereoscope'.

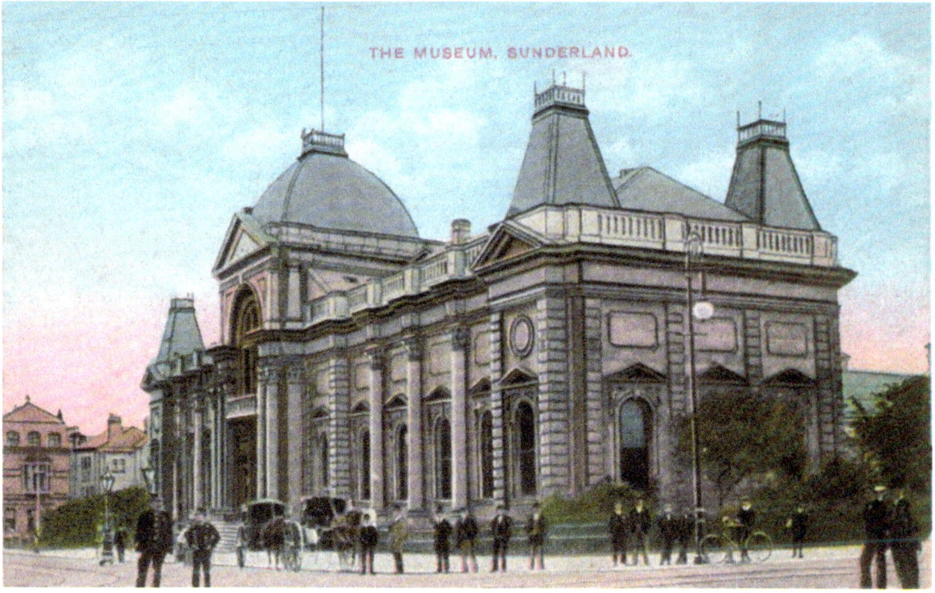

The Museum and Library – 1913

This postcard view of the Museum and Library on Borough Road dates to just before the First World War. The Mayor of Sunderland laid the foundation stone on 24 September 1877 in the presence of General Grant, ex-president of the USA and the building opened on 6 November 1879. The town centre library stayed within this building until 1995, before relocating to Fawcett Street.

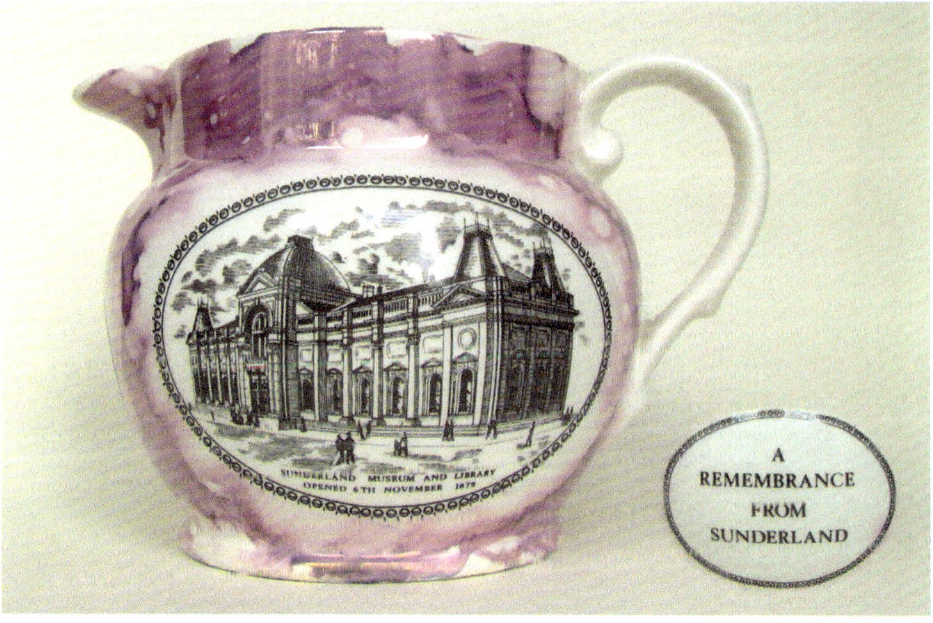

In 1989, Tyne and Wear Museums Service commissioned an attractive reproduction commemorative jug 'in the style of' Sunderland's nineteenth-century lustreware pottery. Both the Museum and Library (above) and Monkwearmouth Railway Station appear on the jug.

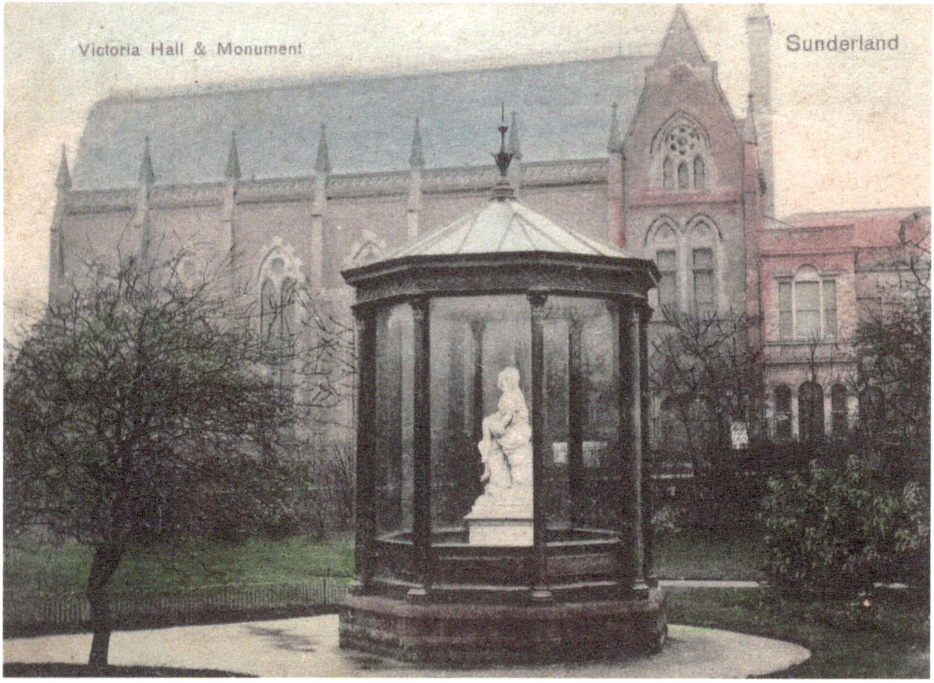

Victoria Hall and Memorial

The Victoria Hall, which opened in 1872, is primarily remembered for the terrible calamity that unfolded there on 16 June 1883 when 183 children lost their lives. The monument in the foreground of the picture commemorates this frightful catastrophe.

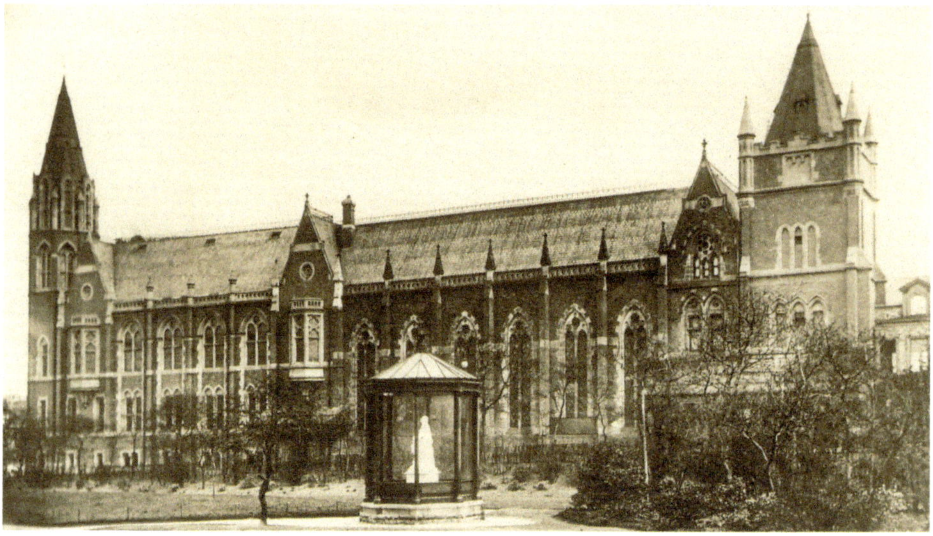

The council purchased the building in 1903 and the Alexandra Hall extension was completed three years later. It was the largest public venue in Sunderland and was the location for many prestigious events, such as the 'Monkwearmouth Pageant' held between 18 and 21 June 1924. The hall fell victim to the first German parachute mine dropped on the town on 16 April 1941.

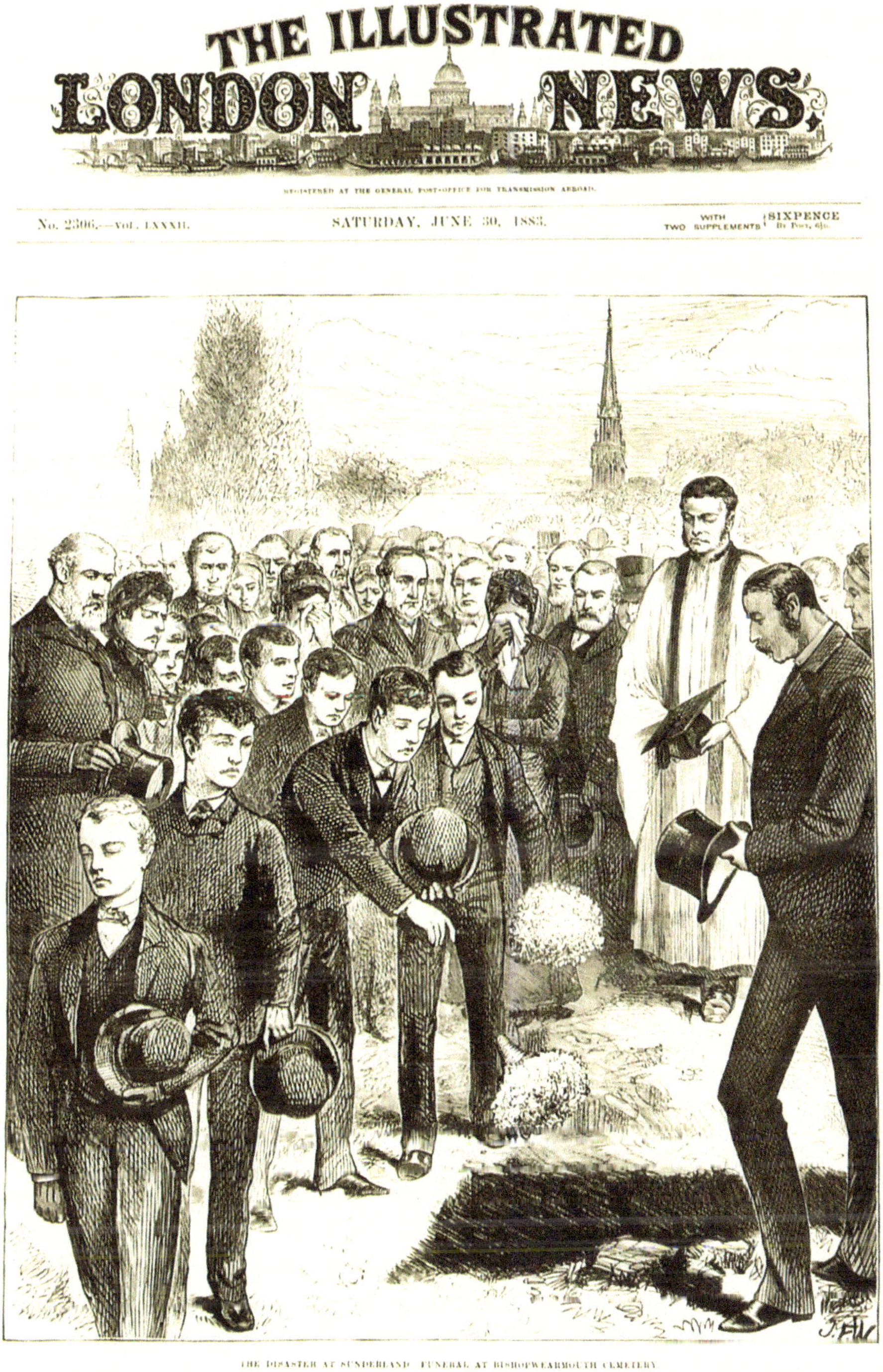
THE ILLUSTRATED LONDON NEWS

REGISTERED AT THE GENERAL POST-OFFICE FOR TRANSMISSION ABROAD.

No. 2306.—Vol. LXXXII. SATURDAY, JUNE 30, 1883. WITH TWO SUPPLEMENTS SIXPENCE By Post, 6½d.

THE DISASTER AT SUNDERLAND: FUNERAL AT BISHOPWEARMOUTH CEMETERY.

Three Days of Sorrow in Sunderland

How *The Illustrated London News* of 30 June 1883 reported the burials of the Victoria Hall Disaster victims. It took three days to lay all of the children to rest. This scene is at Bishopwearmouth Cemetery.

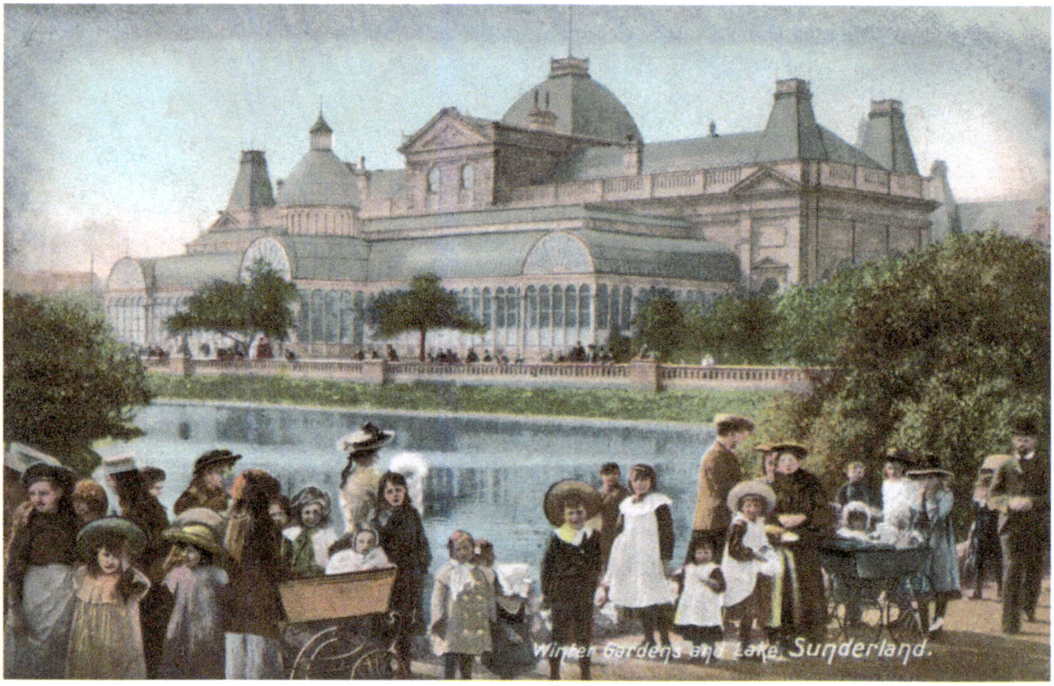

The Winter Gardens – 1905

The original Winter Gardens, pictured here in this very lively early twentieth century postcard, were erected at the same time as the Museum and Library in 1879.

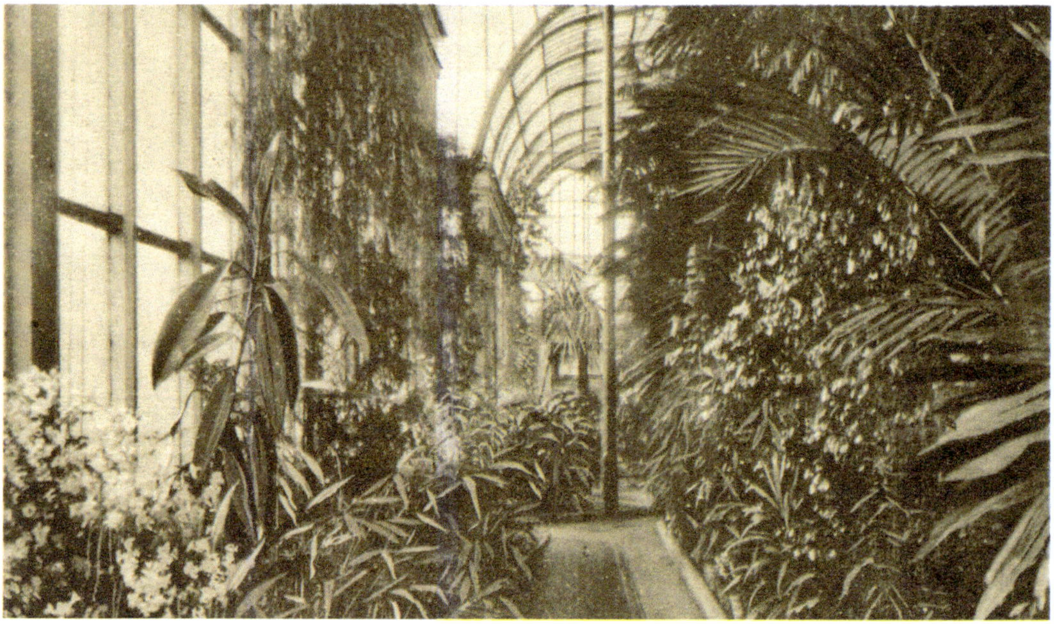

A 1905 view of the interior of the Winter Gardens. They must have been a truly captivating place for both children and adults to visit. Unfortunately, the same German parachute mine that severely damaged the Victoria Hall in April 1941 also destroyed the Winter Gardens.

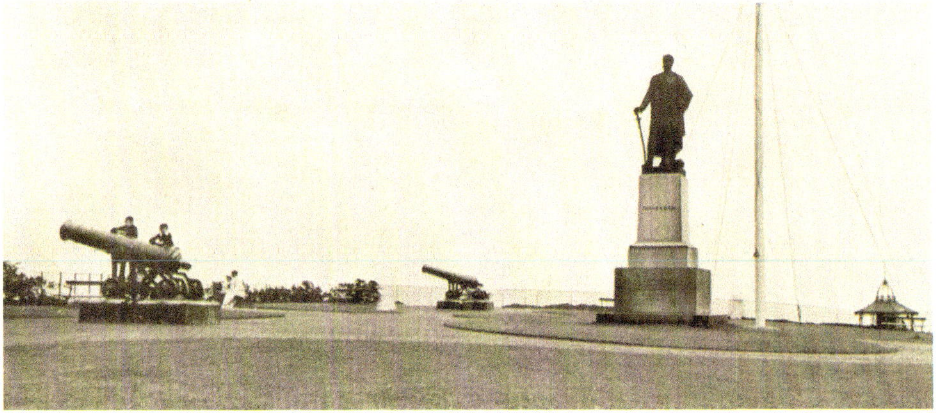

The Russian Guns on Building Hill

The Crimea War was a consequence of Russia's expansionist plans in the Balkans. Britain, France and the Ottoman Empire opposed them, with the war culminating in the year-long siege of Sebastopol and the battles of Balaclava and Inkerman. In early 1857, an application was made to the then Secretary-at-War, Lord Panmure, for two Russian guns captured at Sebastopol on 9 September 1855 to be placed on permanent display on 'Bildon Hill' in Mowbray Park. On 5 May of that year, a London trader *The Linton* berthed alongside Holmes Wharf with the guns on board. The guns were mounted on carriages manufactured at the ironworks of Mr. Ald. Stainton of South Shields. A half-day holiday was declared for the people of Sunderland to attend the ceremony. On 11 May 1857 at 1.30 p.m. six horses drew each gun to the summit in the park and a royal salute was fired by two small pieces of cannon. Mr De Lacy's Band then played the National Anthem. Following an address by the Mayor and Mr Alderman Allison, chairman of the public grounds committee, the assembled thousands dispersed. The statue of General Havelock was not raised here until almost four years later.

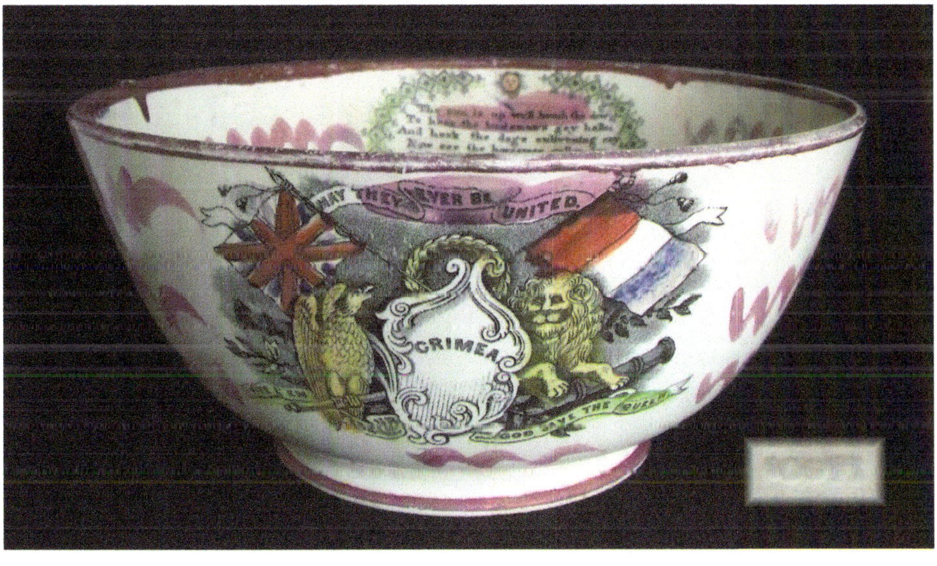

A Crimea commemorative bowl manufactured by Scott's Pottery of Southwick, Sunderland. It reads 'Vive L'Empereur', 'God Save the Queen' and 'May They Ever Be United'. Two cannons are incorporated into the transfer print on the bowl.

RUSSIAN GUN

TAKEN AT

SEBASTOPOL,

9th SEPTEMBER, 1855,

PRESENTED BY

LORD PANMURE,

Secretary-at-War,

TO THE

BOROUGH OF SUNDERLAND,

Placed here 11th May, 1857.

GEORGE SMITH RANSON, ESQ.,

Mayor.

WILLIAM SNOWBALL ESQ.,

Town-Clerk.

RANSON.

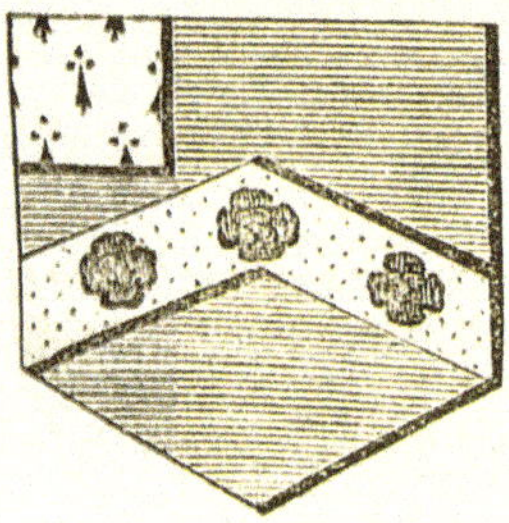

SNOWBALL.

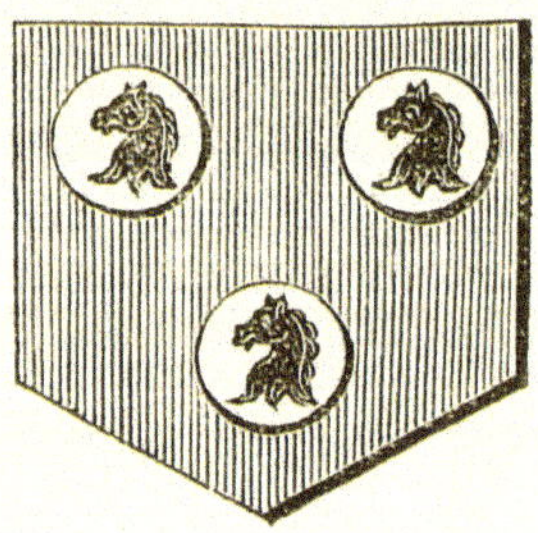

Stone Pedestal Inscription

A record of the inscription on the stone pedestals on which the two guns were placed, as transcribed in 1858 by local historian Jeremiah William Summers.

General Havelock

This is how the statue of General Havelock in Mowbray Park looks today. The nearby cannon in the park are now replicas, the old Russian guns having been melted down during the last war. Major General Sir Henry Havelock, KCB was born at Ford Hall, Bishopwearmouth on 5 April 1795 and became famous as the hero of Cawnpore and Lucknow. He died of dysentery in India on 24 November 1857 just a few days after the relief of Lucknow. Two statues were erected to his memory, both designed by William Behnes – one in Trafalgar Square London, and this one in Mowbray Park on 5 April 1861.

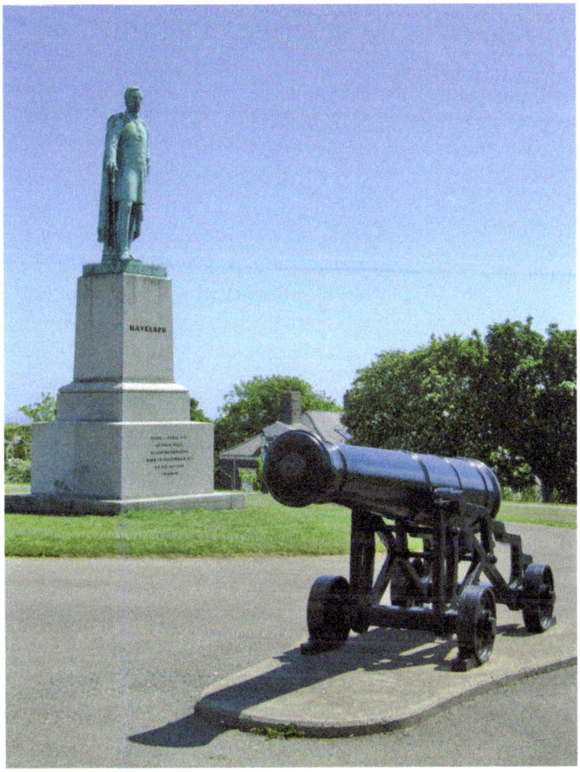

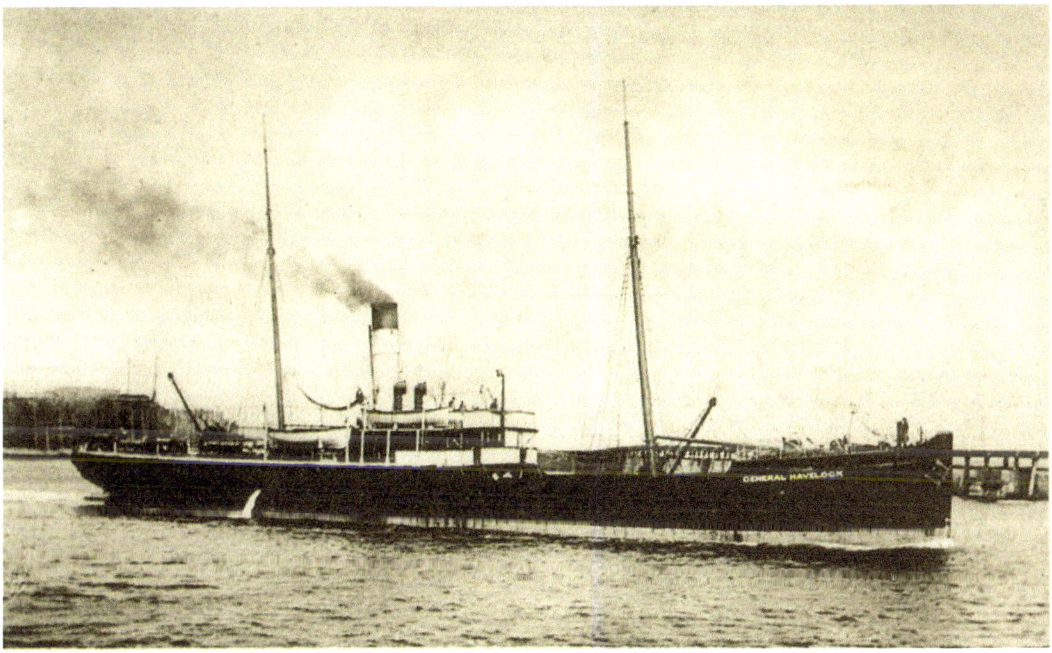

We normally associate the naming of pubs and buildings after General Havelock, but here is a picture from the early 1900s of the S.S. *General Havelock*. The passenger steamer operated along the coast between Sunderland, Scarborough and London.

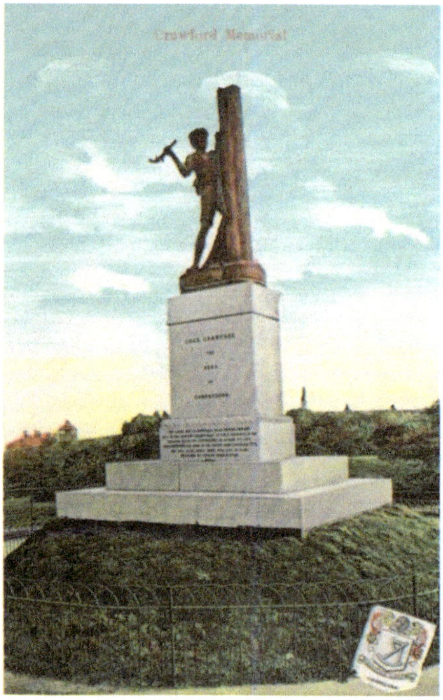

Jack Crawford Hero of Camperdown

The statue of Jack Crawford, which was raised in Mowbray Park in 1890. Local lad Jack was born the son of a Wear keel man on Pottery Bank. He became a national hero when he nailed the colours of Admiral Duncan's ship *The Venerable* back to the mast after they were shot away by the Dutch fleet at the Battle of Camperdown on 11 October 1797.

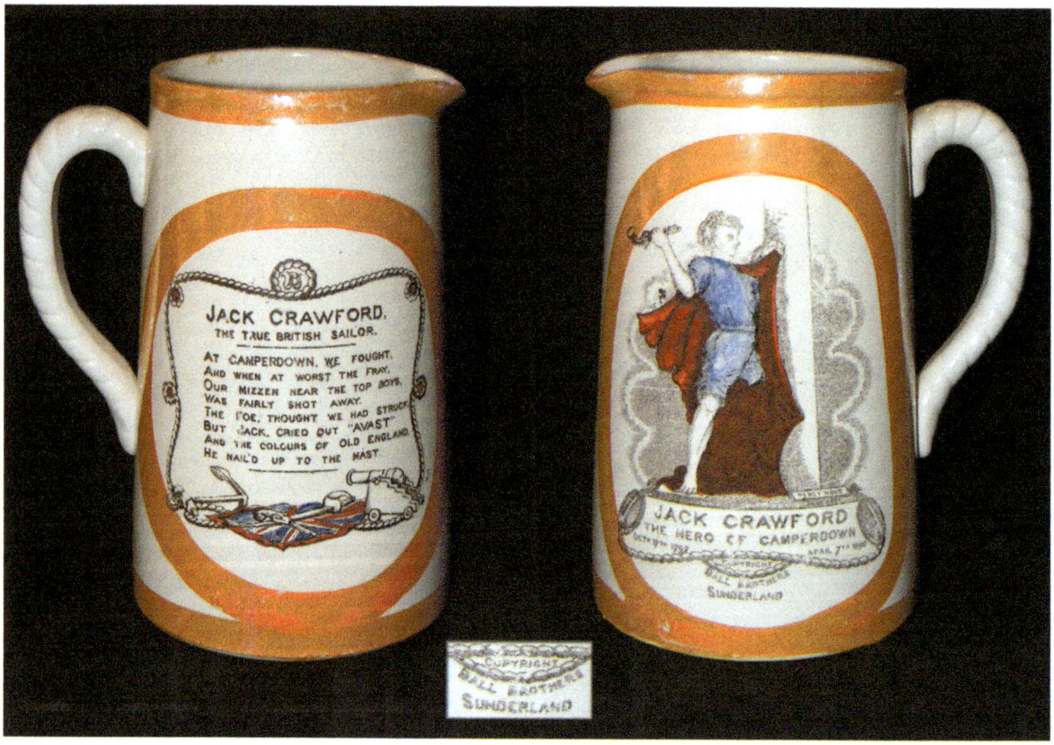

A fine 'orange lustre' Jack Crawford jug produced by Ball's Pottery of Sunderland. By 1884, the pottery was being managed by brothers William Richard and Thomas Lees Ball and was trading as 'Ball Brothers' (see inset).

Jack Crawford and the Battle of Camperdown.—An old chronicler of bygone events sends us the following:—The battle of Camperdown, between the English and Dutch fleets, was fought, as is well known, on the 11th October, 1797. The first intimation of the success of our fleet was received in due course by post in Sunderland about eleven o'clock on a Sunday morning, by the mail gig from Durham, and, as usual on such occasions, the horse and driver were decorated with ribbons. The postman hastened to the Market-cross, near the foot of Union-lane, where he announced the victory to the great joy of the inhabitants, one of whom, whose name we unfortunately forget, was so elated with the news that on passing St. John's Chapel he opened the door, and, with stentorian voice, shouted out, "Admiral Duncan has defeated the Dutch fleet at Camperdown!" This exclamation forthwith touched the loyal heart of the organist, and he immediately struck up "Rule Britannia," and the congregation, determined to be no less loyal, notwithstanding they were at prayer at the time, thereupon rose and stood during its performance. On the morning of the above day, before the arrival of the glad tidings, the Loyal Sunderland Volunteers, commanded by Major Robert Hayton, marched to South Shields, to repay a visit which they had had from the volunteers of that town. It was dark when the heroes of the "Battle of Hendon" returned to Sunderland—at which battle, by-the-bye, it used to be coolly asserted that the *gallant* major, a man of small stature, crept into a rabbit hole for safety, though the greatest injury to any of the combatants was the loss of an eye to Private Sinclair—and they immediately proceeded to the Barracks, where they got a supply of powder, and fired a *feu de joie* in honour of the event, the band playing the national anthem. The barrack-yard was crowded with citizens, who testified their joy at the victory by their enthusiastic cheering. Admiral Duncan was rewarded with a peerage and a pension, and our townsman, poor Jack Crawford, had the honour of being presented to his Majesty King George the Third. Crawford, unfortunately, was a very illiterate man, and greatly addicted to intemperance; this barred his promotion in the navy, from which he was ultimately discharged with a pension of £30 per annum. On the first visitation of cholera in this town poor Jack was one of its earliest victims. His remains were interred in Sunderland churchyard, and "there sleeps the brave," without a stone having been placed to mark the spot where his ashes rest. This is scarcely creditable to a place like Sunderland, for, with all Crawford's failings, his name is imperishably associated with the annals of the town. It is gratifying to know that the flag of the Venerable, which our hero nailed to the mast, has been carefully preserved by Lord Duncan's descendants, as, on her Majesty paying a visit to the Earl of Camperdown's seat, in Scotland, a few years ago, his lordship's eldest son waved the veritable piece of bunting which had so triumphantly floated on the top-gallantmast of the Venerable, over the head of her Majesty as she alighted at his father's residence.

When News of the Battle Reached Sunderland

The above account was discovered incorporated into the binding of a copy of *The History of the Town and Port of Sunderland and the Parishes of Bishopwearmouth and Monkwearmouth* by James Burnett – a book that was published in 1830.

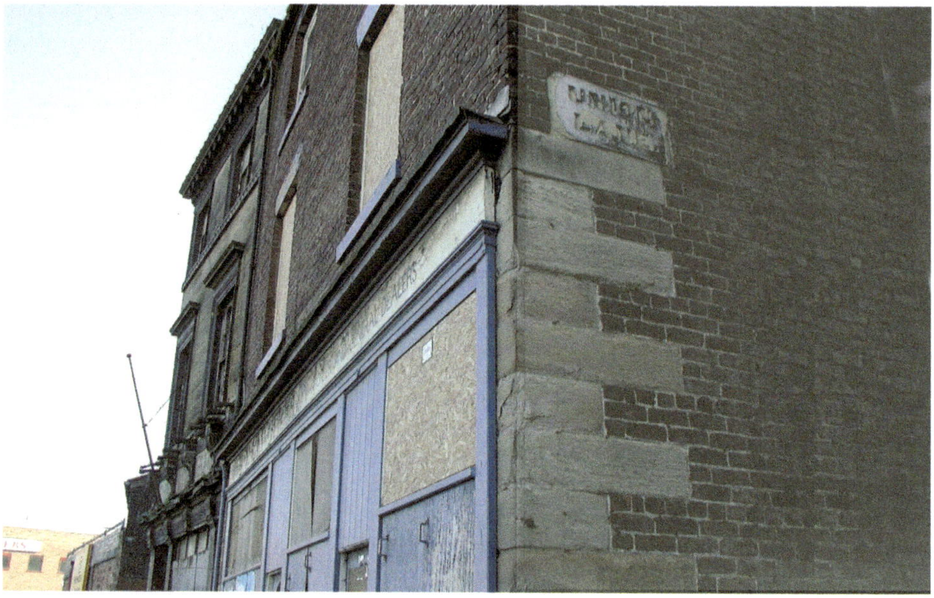

The Battle of Camperdown Victory
The foot of Union Lane at its junction with High Street, where the mail gig from Durham arrived to break news of the great victory (photographed in 2003).

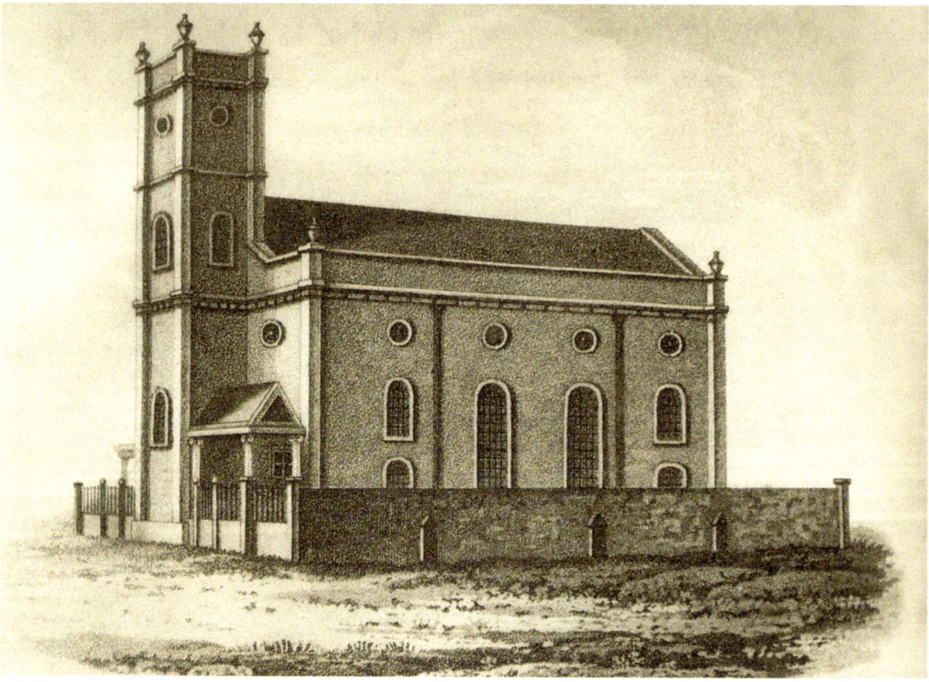

An early nineteenth-century print of St John's Chapel. After hearing news of the battle an inhabitant on passing the chapel opened its door and shouted "Admiral Duncan has defeated the Dutch fleet at Camperdown". The organist immediately struck up *Rule Britannia* and the congregation although in prayer rose and stood throughout its performance!

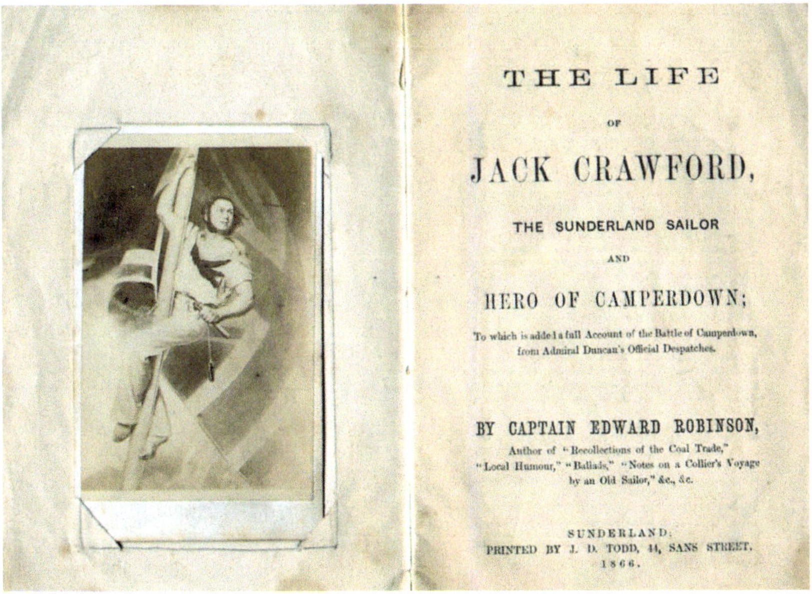

The Lift of Jack Crawford

The first pages of a locally printed book that recounts the life of Jack Crawford. It was written by Captain Edward Robinson in 1866. Jack died on 9 November 1831, a victim of the cholera outbreak of that year, but by 1866 his grave in Holy Trinity churchyard was still without a headstone.

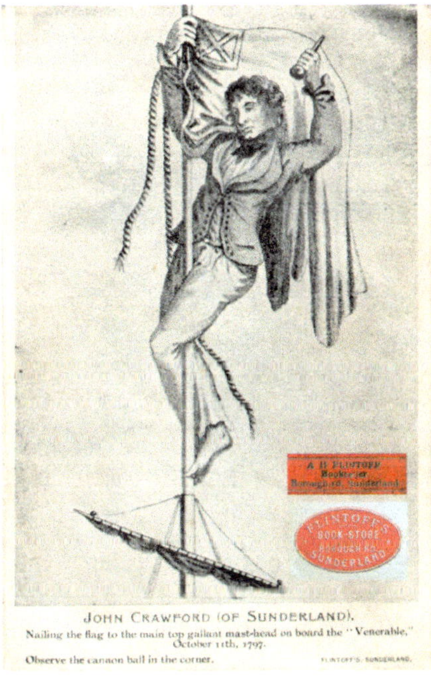

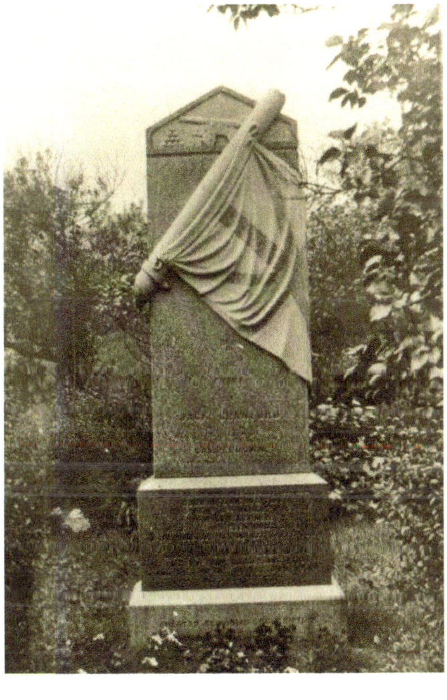

Two Flintoff prints – one a postcard depicting Jack's glorious deed and the second a photograph of his tombstone, which was eventually erected in 1888. Flintoff was a bookseller in Borough Road throughout the nineteenth century. (See postcard insets left).

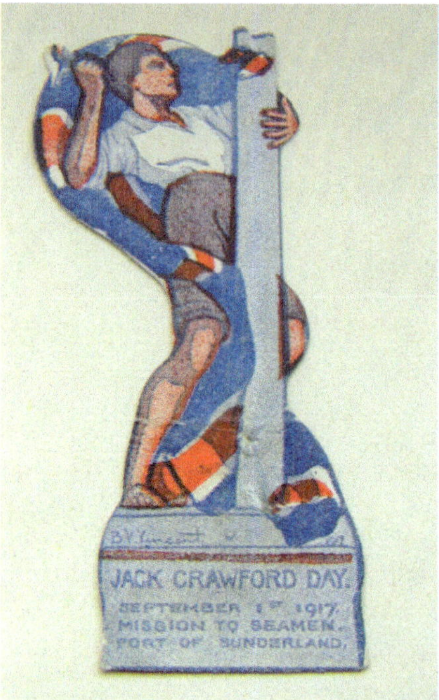

Jack Crawford Day
A lapel badge sold on 'Jack Crawford Day' 1st September 1917 on behalf of the Mission to Seamen, Port of Sunderland.

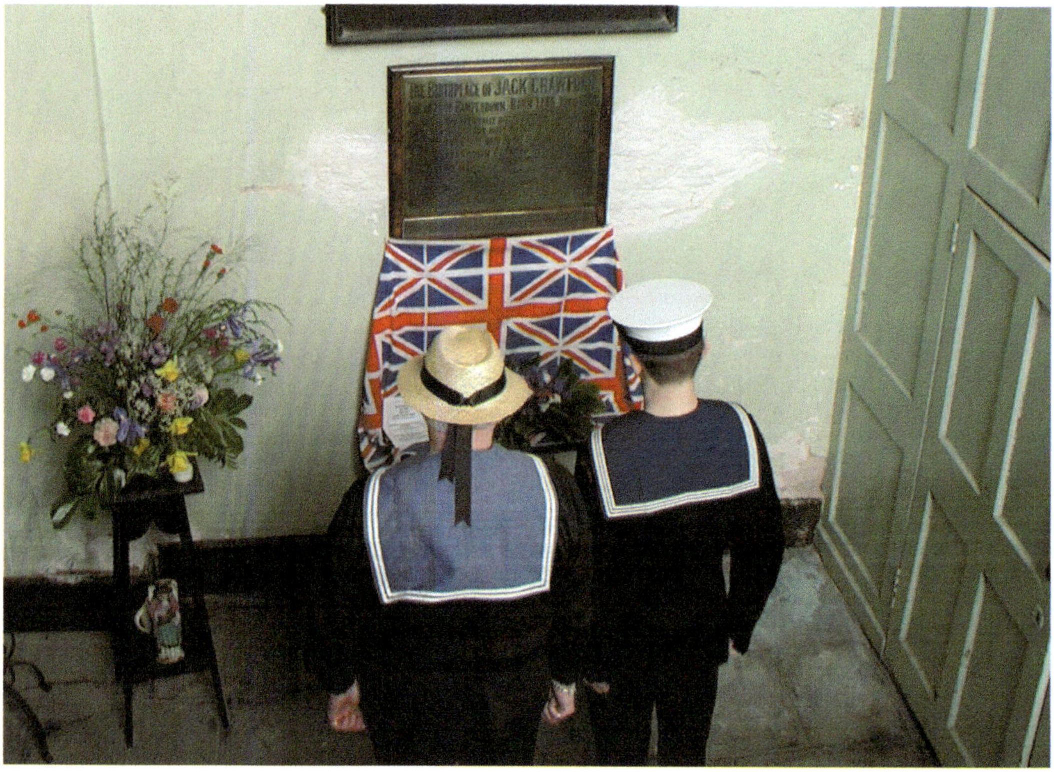

A celebration of the life of Jack Crawford was held at Sunderland Parish Church on Saturday 20 March 2004, when a wreath was laid in his memory.

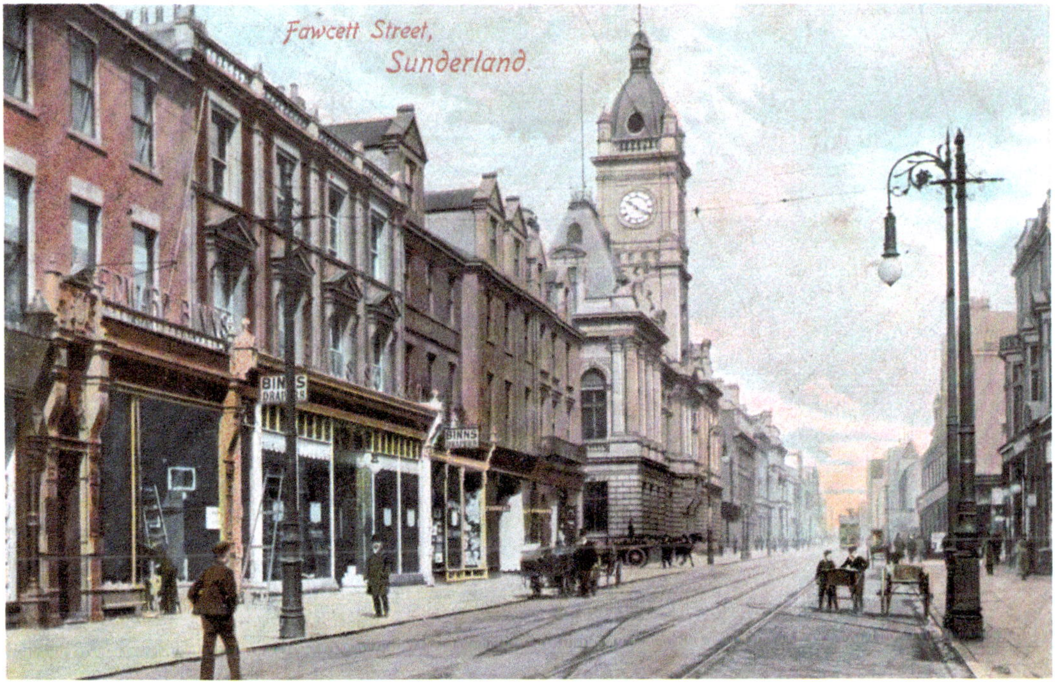

Fawcett Street and Binns'

A general postcard view of Fawcett Street at the start of the twentieth century. Henry Binns' drapery store can be seen to the left of the picture. A dramatic expansion of the business was to take place over the following twenty years and by 1921, the store was trading on both sides of Fawcett Street.

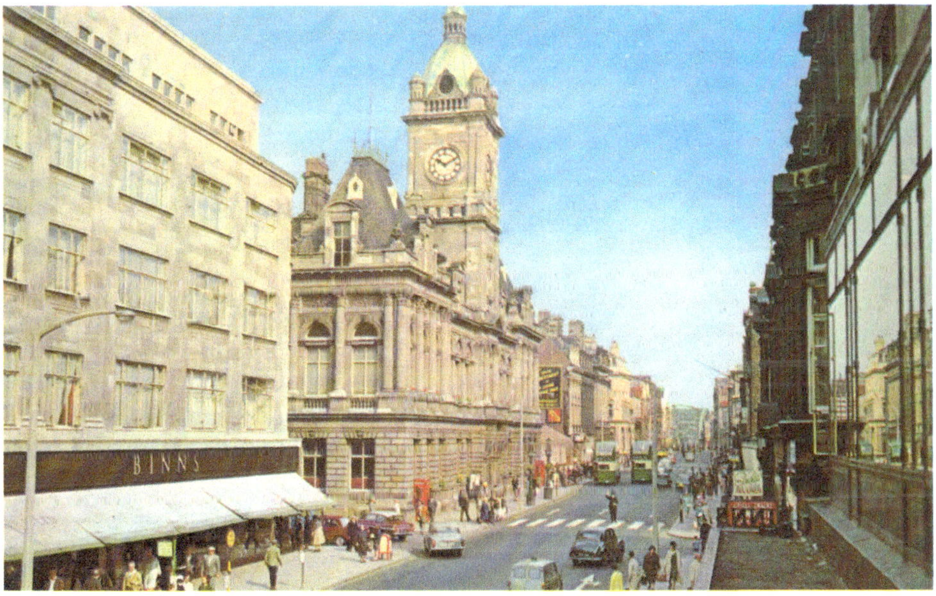

A similar viewpoint in around 1960. A new Binns' store (left) was opened in 1953, the older premises having been destroyed in the bombing raids of April 1941.

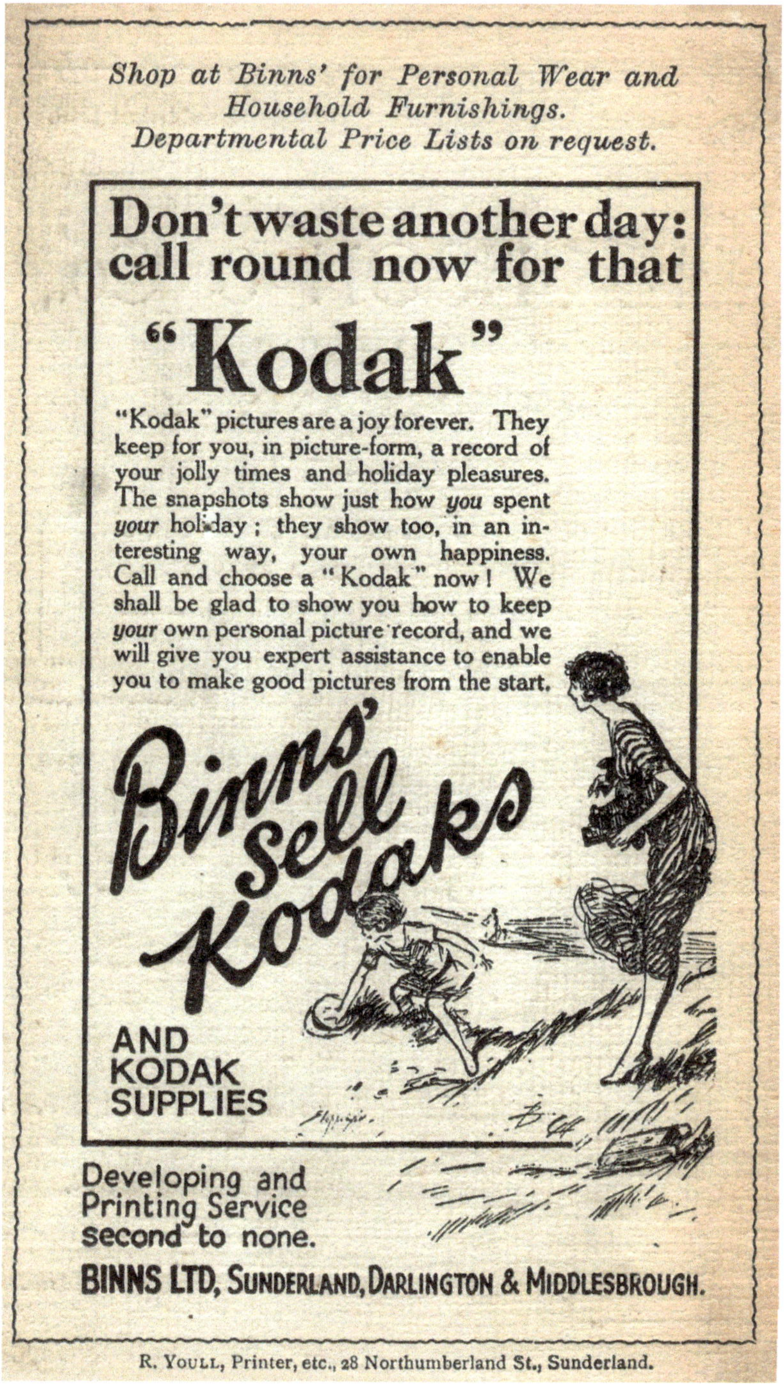

Binns' Sell Kodaks

This Binns' advertisement dates to 1924 and is from an age when photography for the masses was in its infancy. Your pictures could show you "your own happiness"! Note the reluctance of the advert to call the photo-imaging device a camera. It was a 'Kodak'!

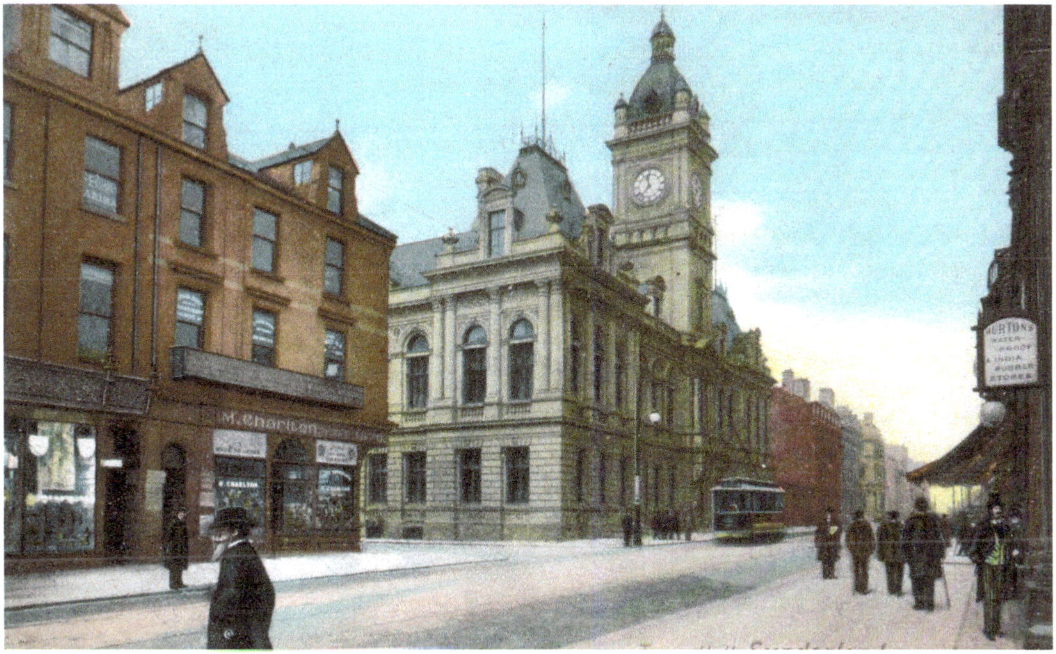

The Town Hall

Sunderland Town Hall in Fawcett Street around 1903, which was designed in an Italianate style by Ipswich architect Brightwen Binyon. The foundation stone was laid on 20 September 1887 and the building opened on 6 November 1890. Earlier plans to build a Town Hall in Mowbray Park had failed to materialise.

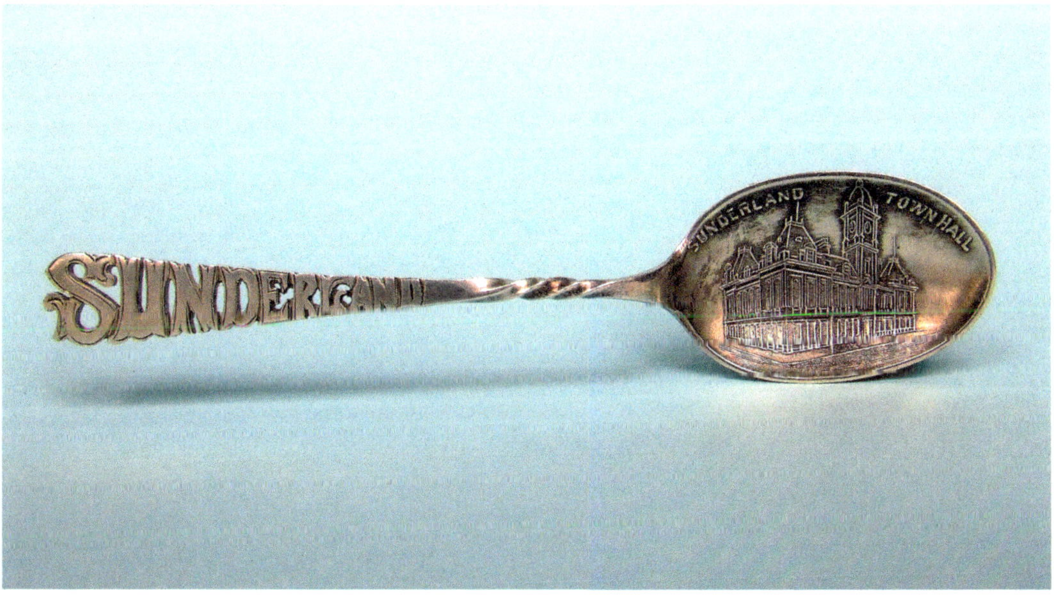

A silver teaspoon made to match in every way the elegance of our old Town Hall. It is hallmarked for Birmingham 1903. The Town Hall itself was controversially demolished in February 1971 when the new Civic Centre was erected in Burdon Road.

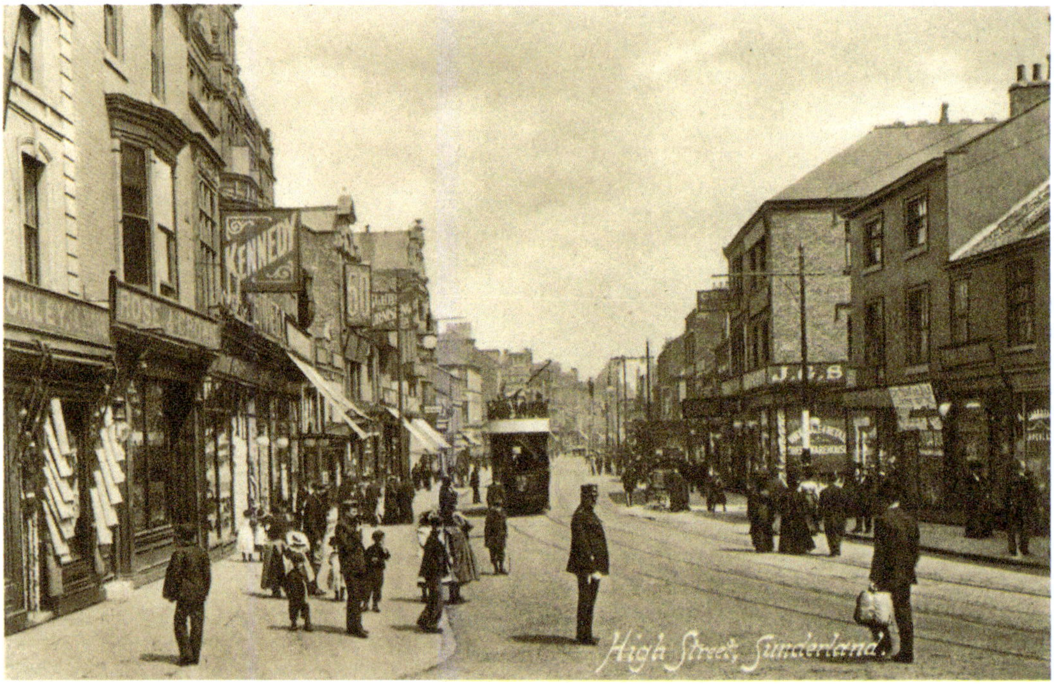

High Street West and J. A. Kennedy
A view of High Street West around 1912. To the left is the department store of J. A. Kennedy, which was trading at this time in the Cobden Exchange. Kennedy's took over the premises from Thomas Beardall who ran a drapery business there.

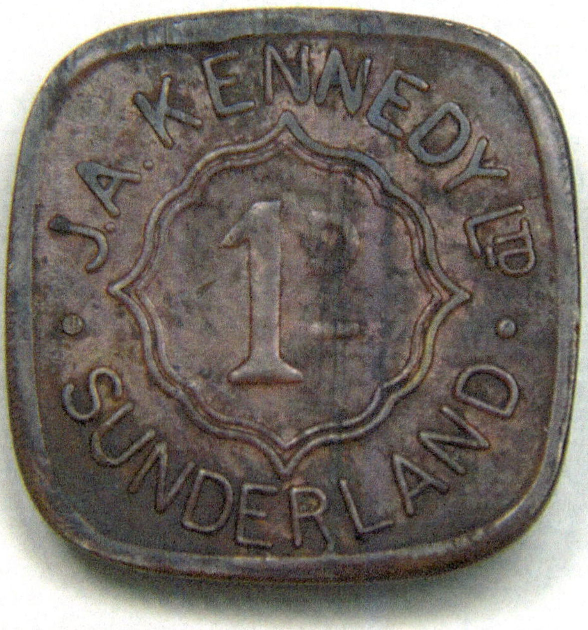

A J. A. Kennedy penny token. 'Shop money' was issued by the store for customers to spend there. The money could later be repaid to the shop over an agreed period of time.

High Street West to Mackies Corner

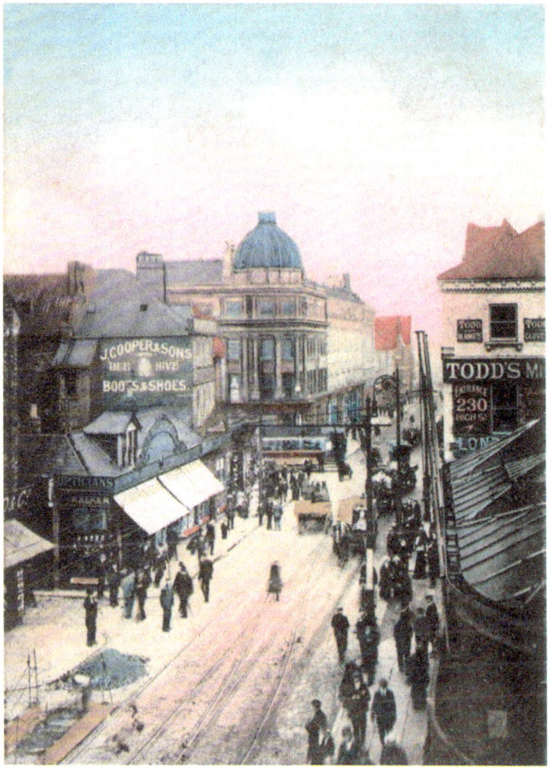

A wonderful postcard view along High Street West to Mackies Corner, which dates to around 1903. The photographer seems to have taken the picture from an upper window of Blacketts Store! The card writer informs us that the two ladies in white hats walking past the north entrance of the Central Railway Station (lower centre right) are called Carrie and Janet.

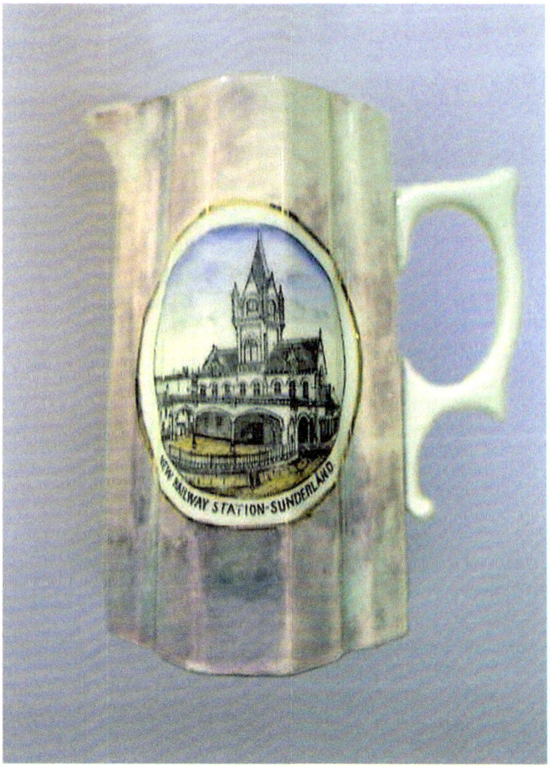

A ceramic jug of German manufacture, which dates to around 1879 – the year that the new Central Railway Station opened. The north end of the station, showing the Gothic clock tower designed by William Bell is featured on its front.

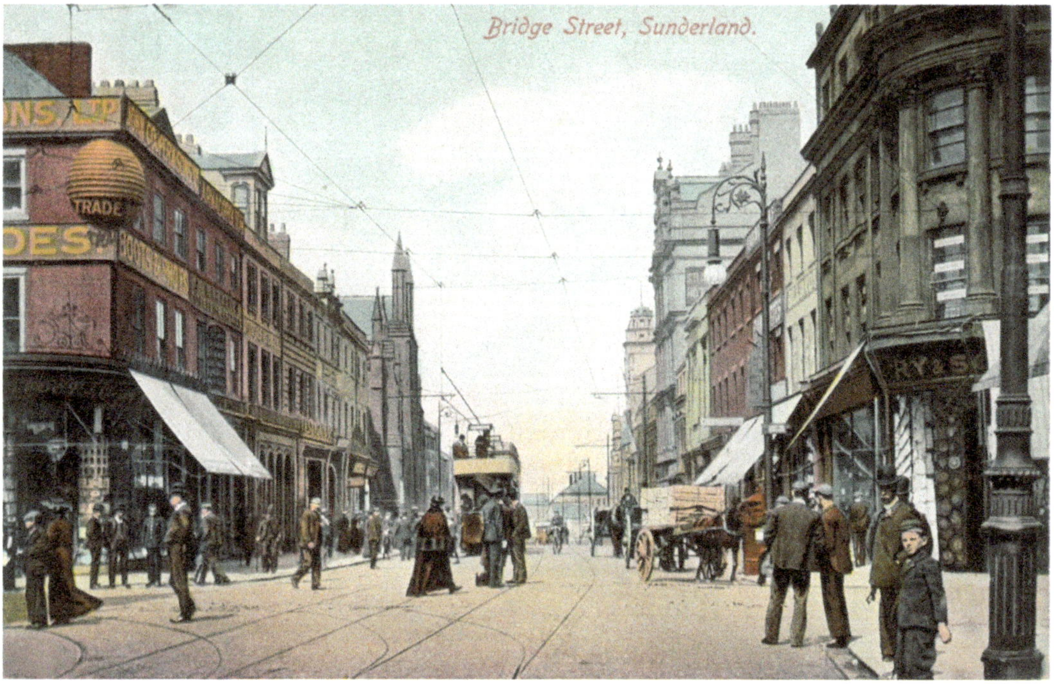

Bridge Street

Bridge Street in the early 1900s. The tall building centre right is Sunderland's eminent Grand Hotel, which opened around 1885. It closed in 1969 and was demolished a year or so later for ring road improvements.

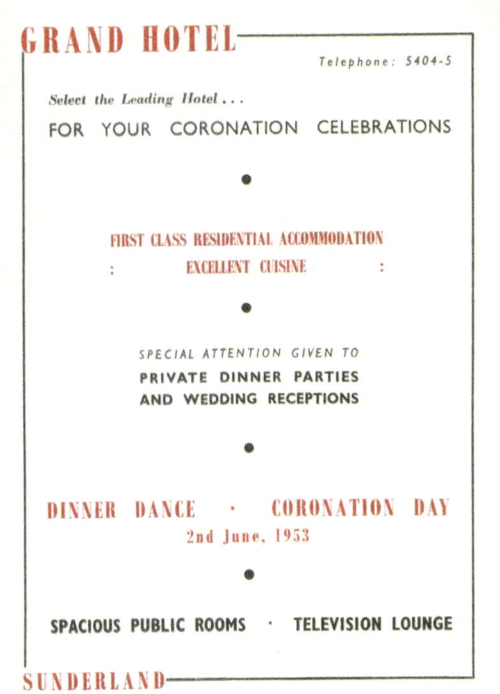

Fifty years after the above photograph was taken, the Grand Hotel was advertising its facilities for the forthcoming 1953 Coronation.

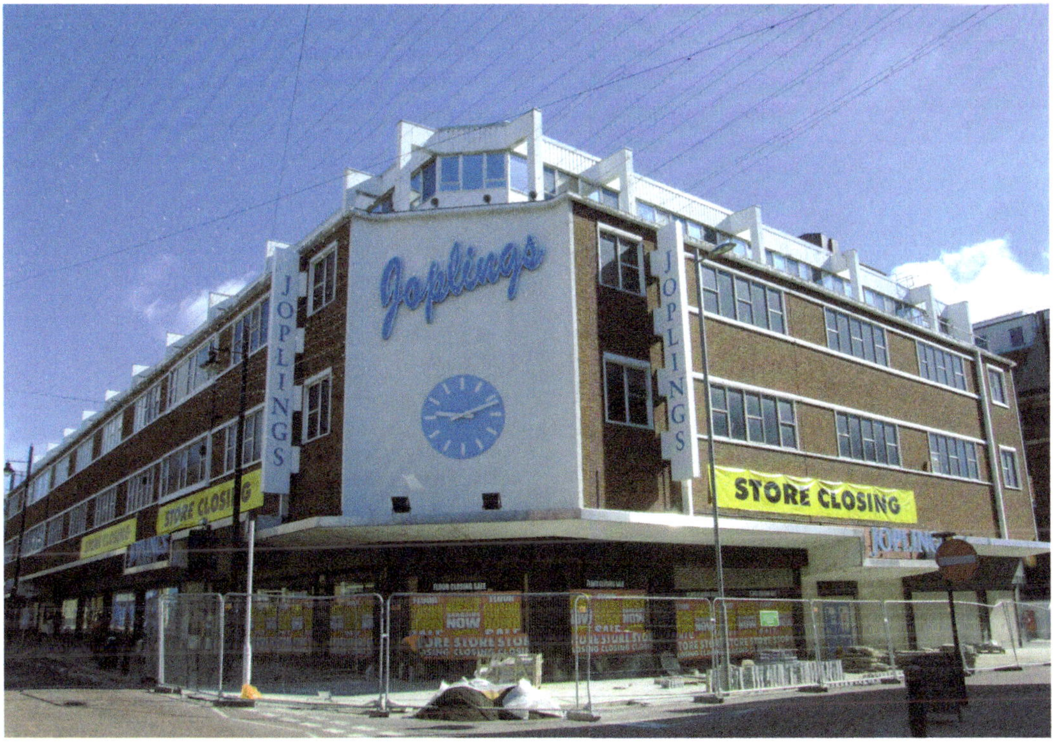

John Street and Joplings

A sad sight indeed for patrons of one of Sunderland's oldest and best-loved stores, as the 'store closing' signs come into view in May 2010. Thomas Jopling and Joseph Tuer first opened a drapery business in High Street East in 1804, which expanded and thrived for many years under successive generations. It came under the ownership of Stephen Moriarty Swan and Robert Hedley in 1882 and traded as Hedley and Swan, but customers always knew the store as 'Joplings'. The business relocated to High Street West in 1919, but a fire destroyed the premises in 1954. They returned briefly to High Street East, then finally to their home in John Street (pictured above) in 1956.

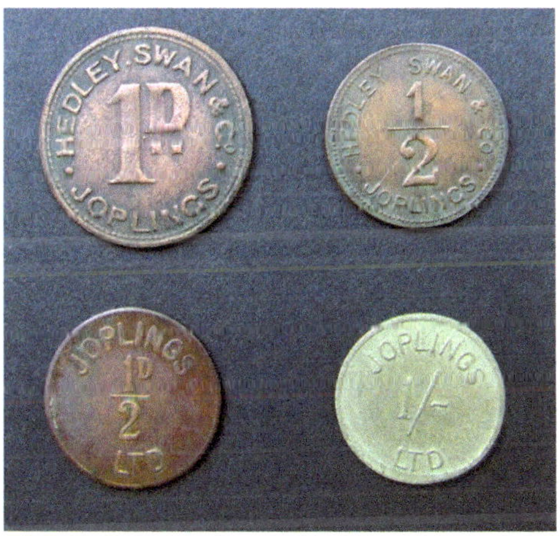

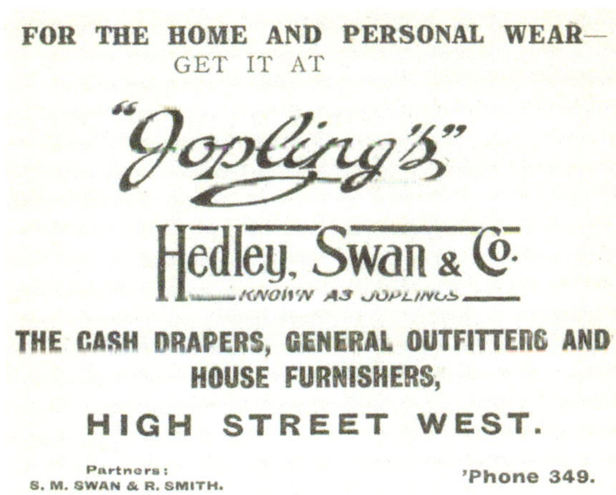

Left: Hedley Swan and Joplings shop tokens. *Right:* An advertisement from 1924.

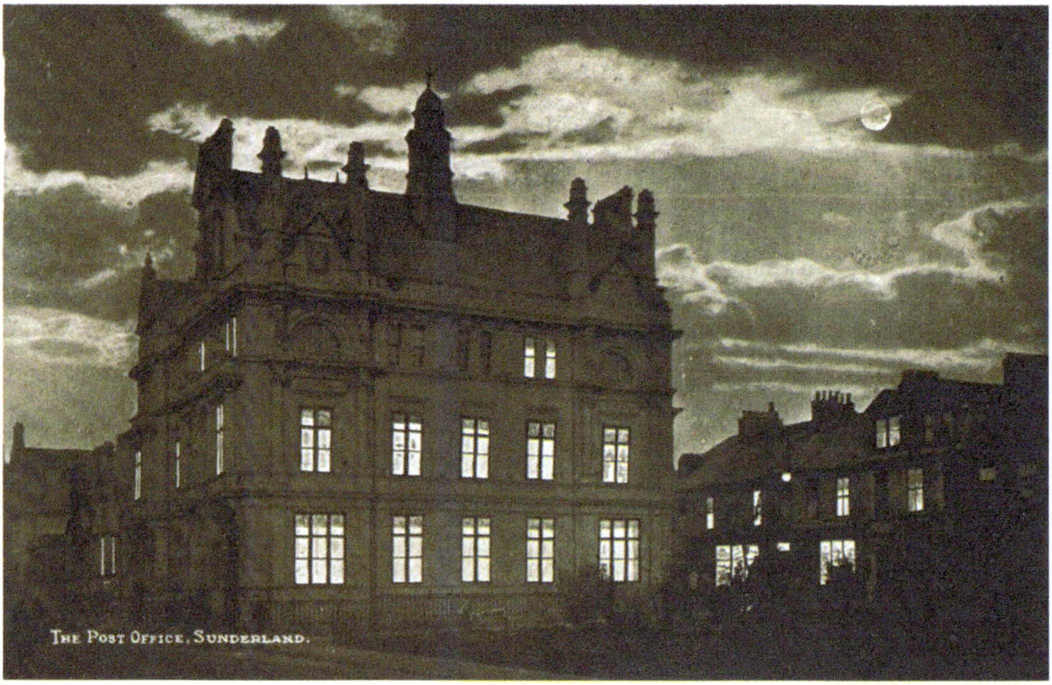

The General Post Office, West Sunniside

An unusual 'hold to the light' postcard view of the General Post Office in West Sunniside that dates to a period just after the completion of the structure in 1903. The architect of the building was Sir Henry Tanner.

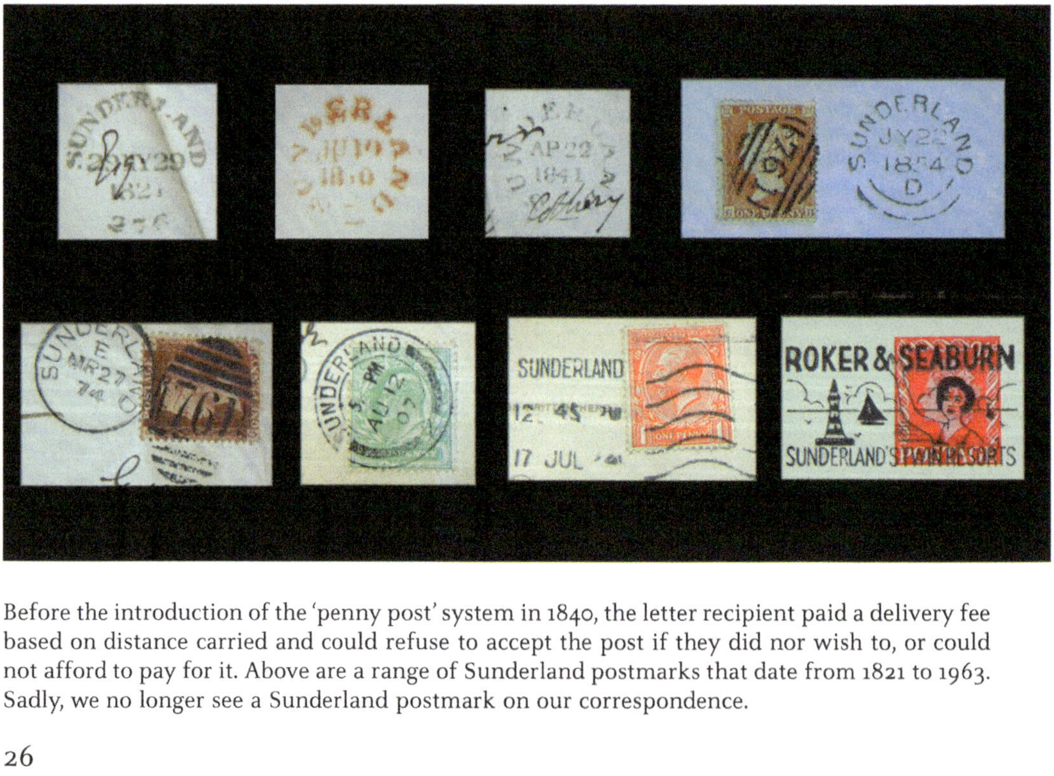

Before the introduction of the 'penny post' system in 1840, the letter recipient paid a delivery fee based on distance carried and could refuse to accept the post if they did nor wish to, or could not afford to pay for it. Above are a range of Sunderland postmarks that date from 1821 to 1963. Sadly, we no longer see a Sunderland postmark on our correspondence.

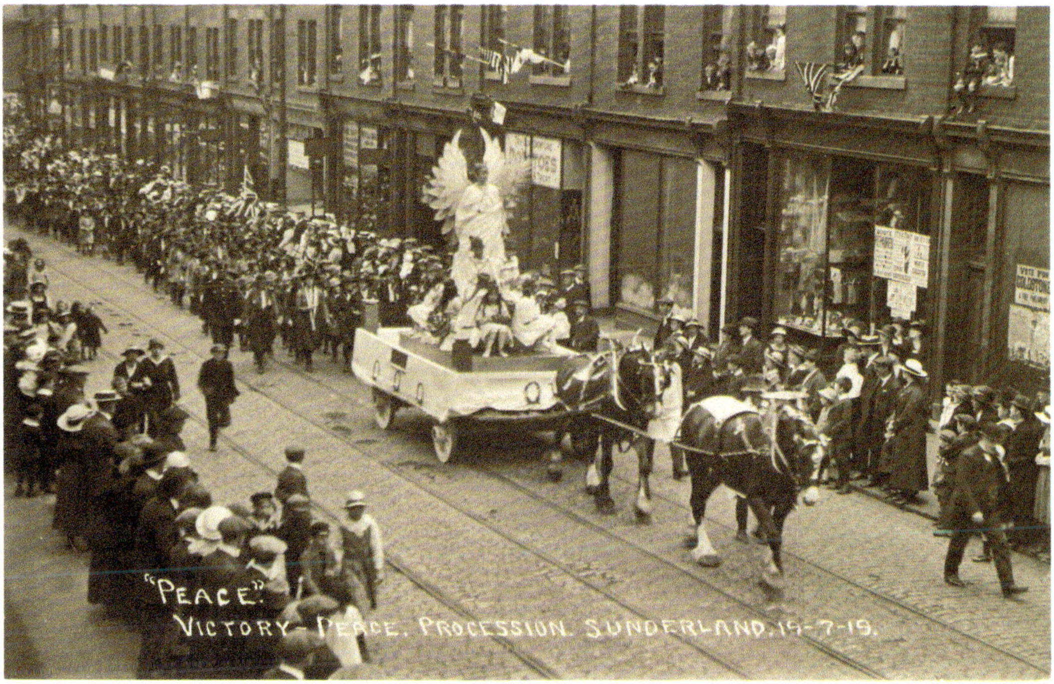

Victory – Peace Procession 1919

The peace procession in Sunderland on 19 July 1919. Children, eager to witness the march, sit precariously on outer windowsills above the shop fronts. No 'health and safety' laws in those days! A War Memorial was erected in Mowbray Park three years later.

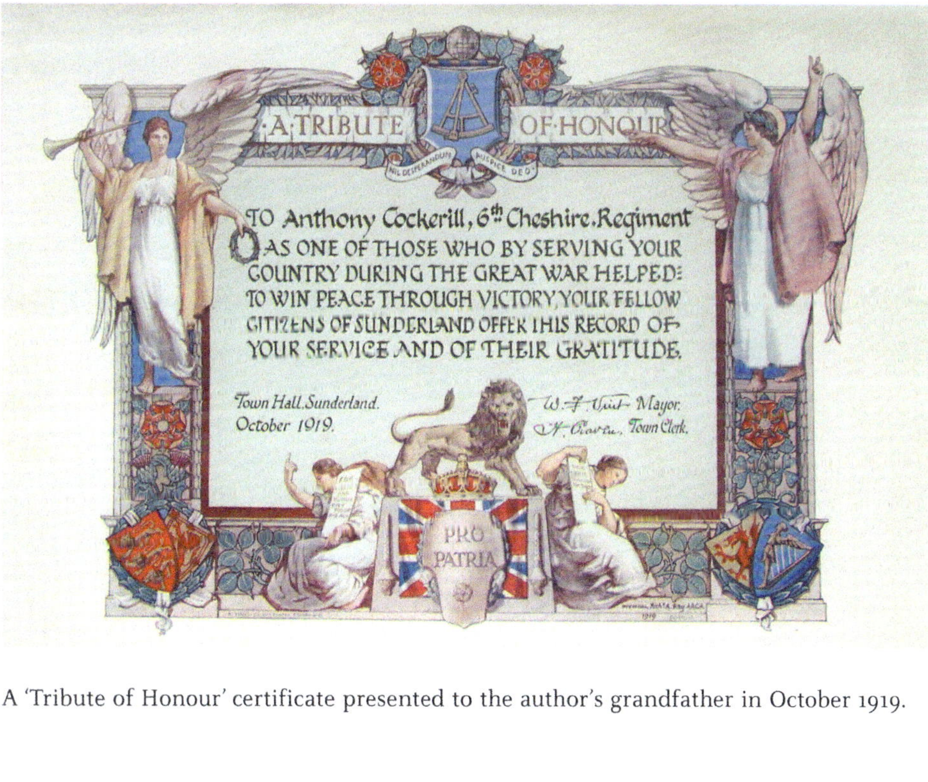

A 'Tribute of Honour' certificate presented to the author's grandfather in October 1919.

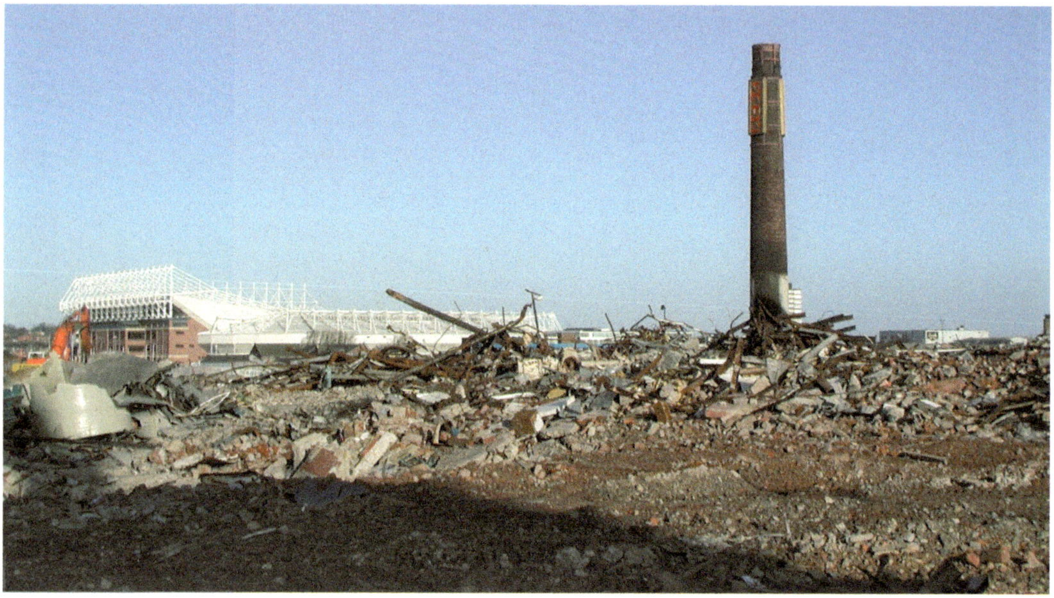

Vaux Brewery

A photograph taken on 25 January 2003, showing the demolition of the Vaux Brewery complex. The Vaux chimney fleetingly survives amid the debris, to honour a business alliance between town and brewery that lasted for 162 years. The company operated from the above Castle Street/ Gill Bridge Avenue site from 1875, but was first established in Sunderland in 1837. The family, however, had been involved in brewing since 1806.

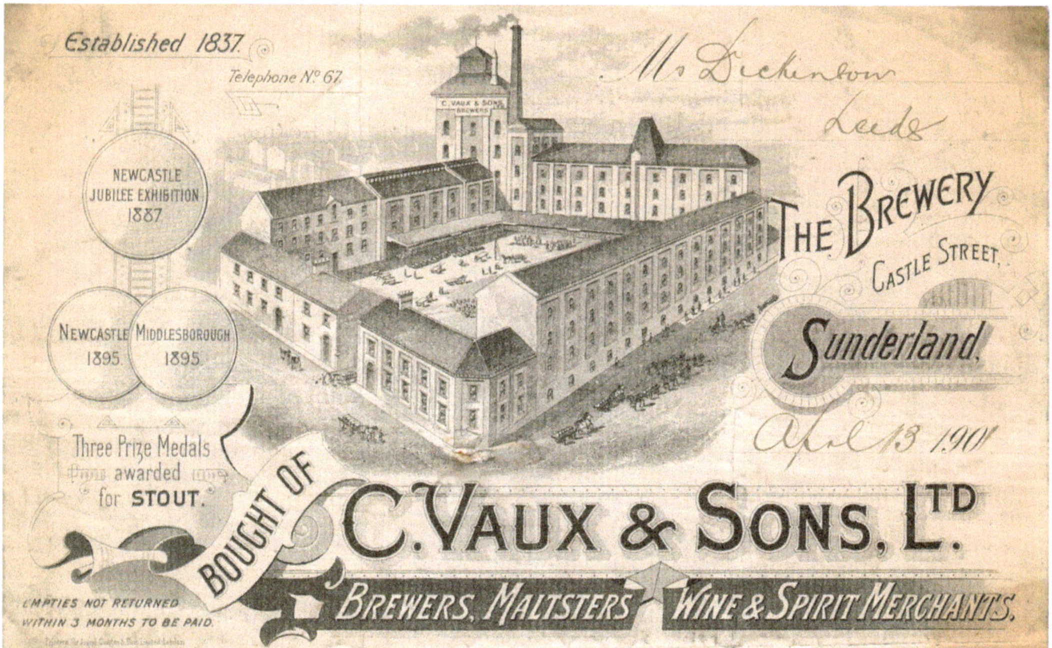

A Vaux billhead for 1901 – the year that Maxim Ale was first introduced.

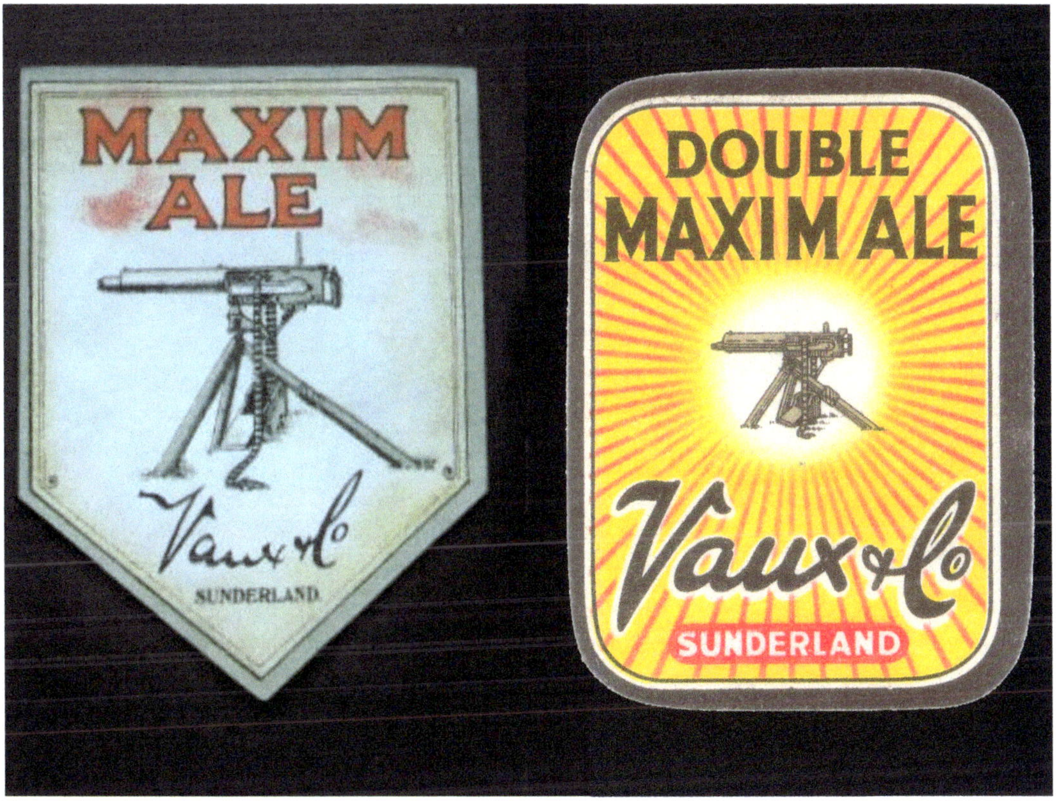

Beer and Breweries

Beer Labels from Maxim and Double Maxim Ales. Maxim Ale was introduced in 1901 to commemorate the return from the Boer War of the Maxim Gun Detachment, which had been commanded by Colonel Ernest Vaux. In 1938 the ale was increased in strength and rebranded as 'Double Maxim'.

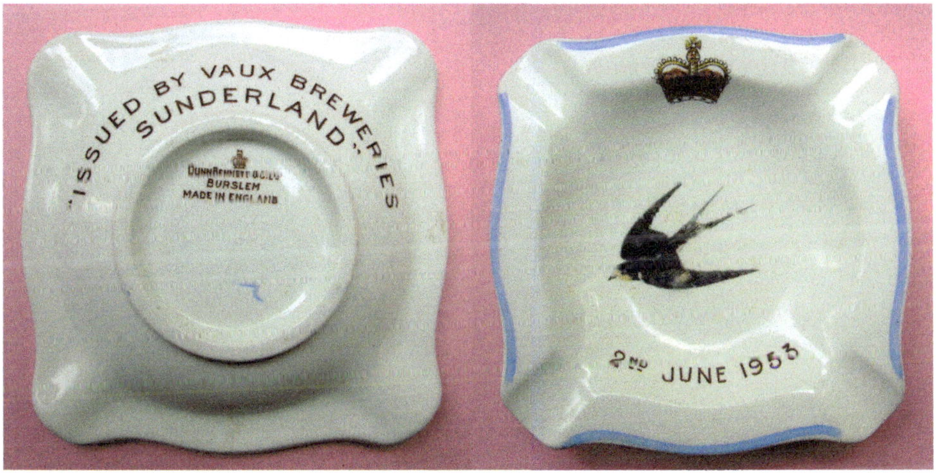

An ashtray commissioned by Vaux Breweries to celebrate the Coronation of Queen Elizabeth II on 2 June 1953.

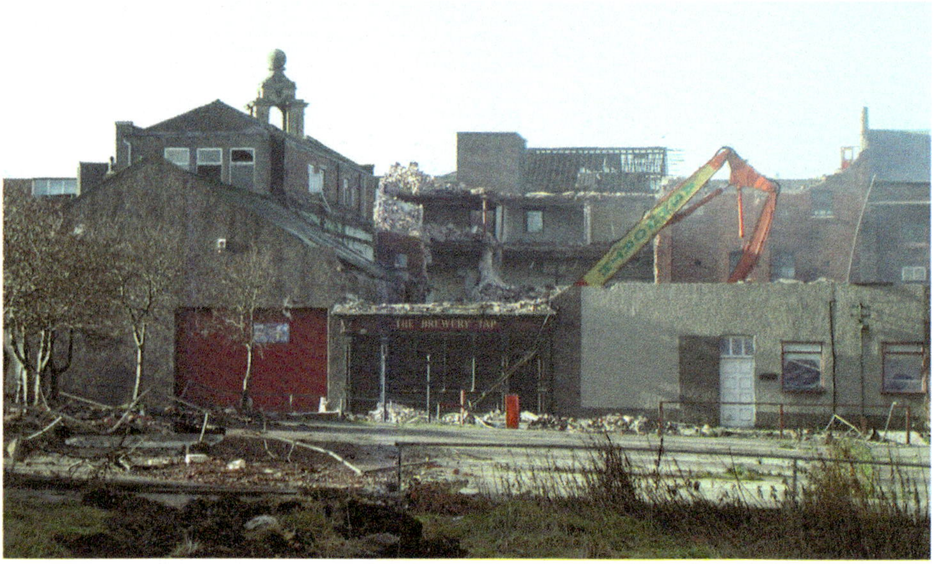

Changing Times

Another January 2003 view of the demolition process. The 'Brewery Tap' public house (centre), which was an integral part of the complex, also fell under the sledgehammer. Until 1974, this old pub had been called 'The Neptune'.

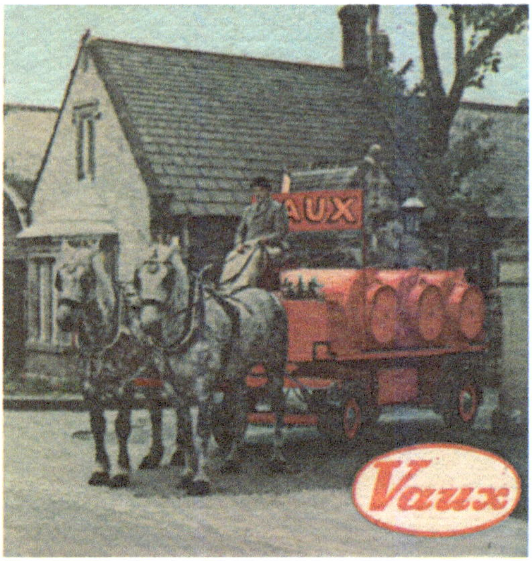

A beer mat showing one of the much loved horse drays that were used by Vaux to transport ales from brewery to pub. The location for the photograph appears to be Whitburn Hall Lodge.

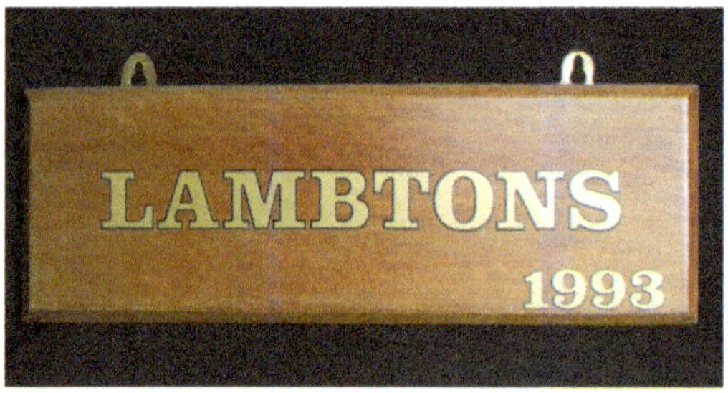

A dray horse 'nameplate' from the stables of Vaux, which was bought at auction in September 1999 following closure of the brewery.

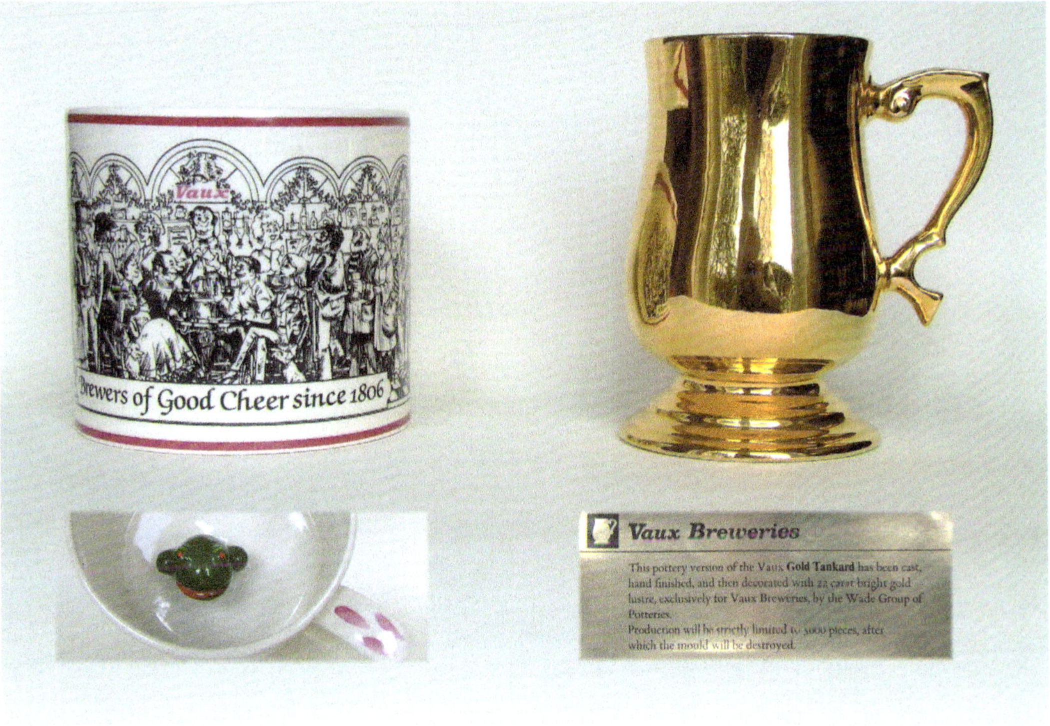

Vaux Breweries

Around thirty pottery tankards were commissioned by the brewery over a period of years and are much sought after today by collectors. Two of the rarest are shown above. The frog mug (left) was made in 1980 in a limited edition of 1,750 pieces. More on frogs later! The gold tankard (right) was decorated in 22-carat bright gold lustre. Its production was limited to 5,000 pieces, after which the mould was destroyed.

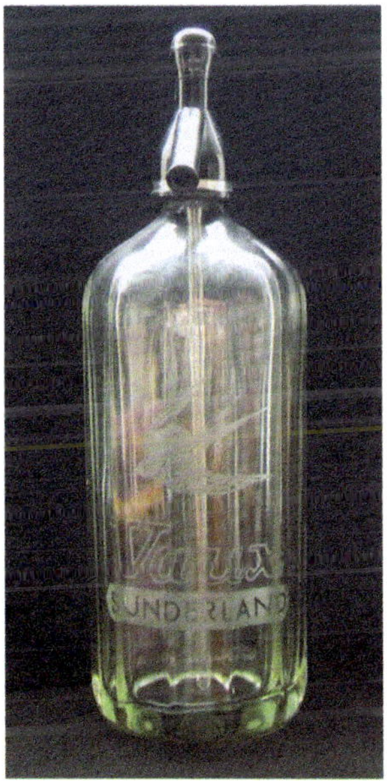

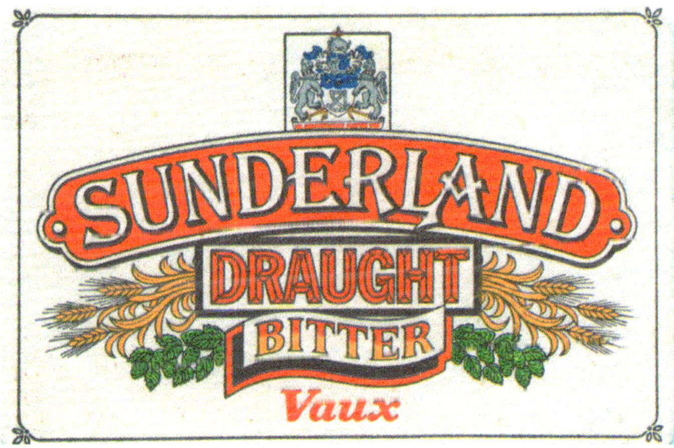

Above: A Sunderland Draught Bitter beer mat.

Left: Whisky drinkers will remember these soda siphons, which sat on every Vaux pub bar counter!

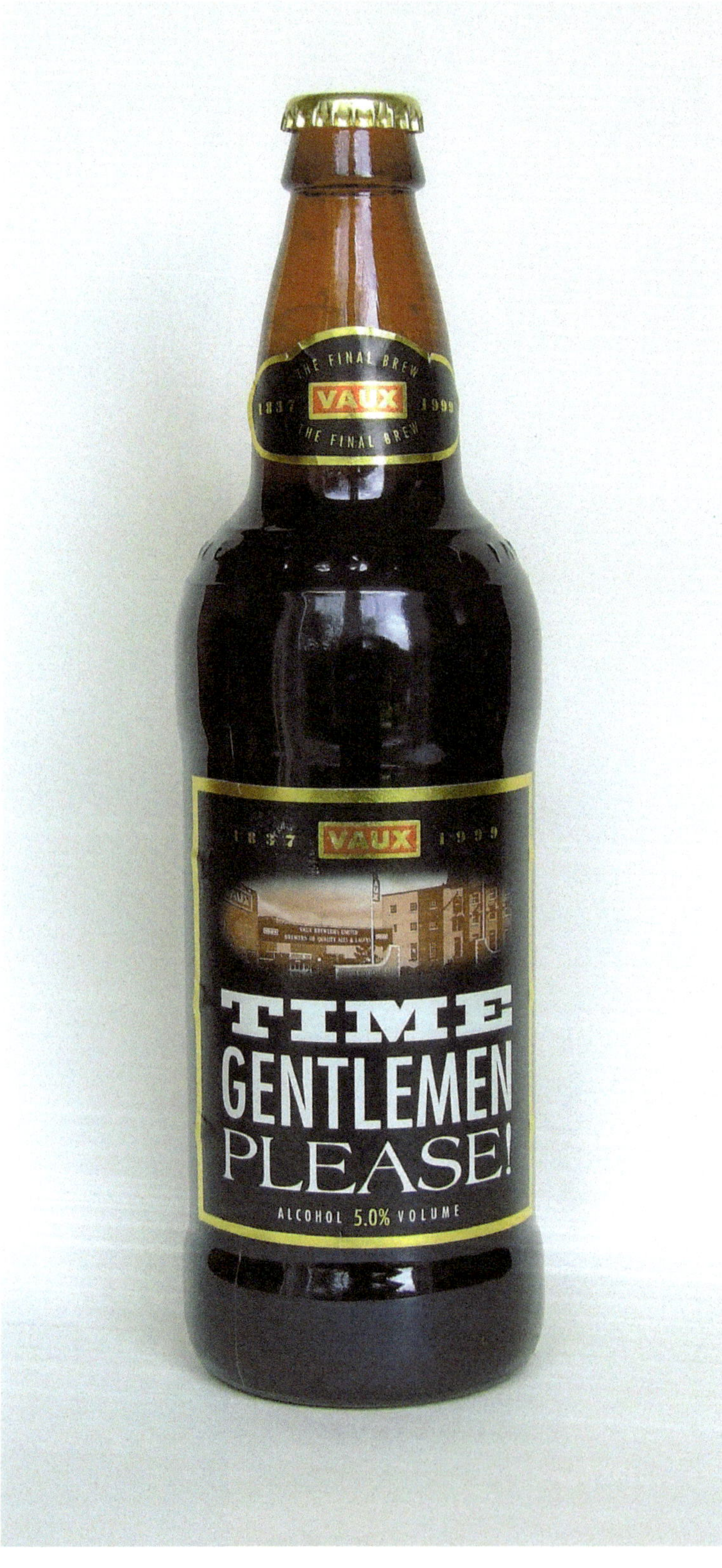

The Final Brew
The label on the rear of this bottle reads: "In 1999 the Vaux Brewery in Sunderland will close its doors on a long and distinguished brewing history. This premium ale is the very last creation from the Vaux master brewers. It is in the truest sense, a limited edition ale. Every drop should be enjoyed as a celebration of over 150 years of brewing excellence".

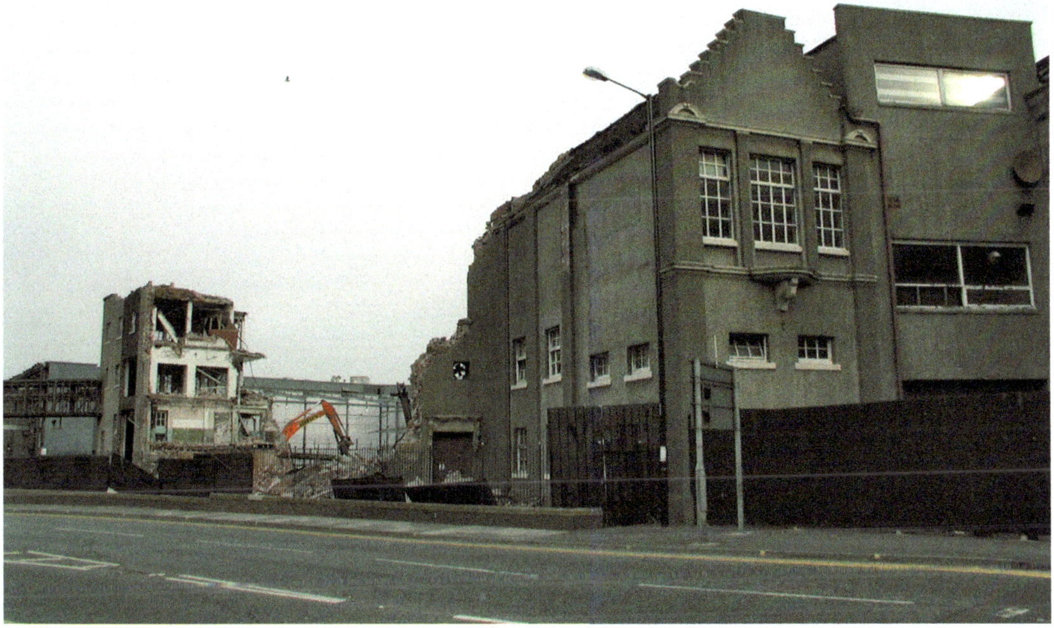

The Avenue Theatre

Demolition of the Avenue Theatre (right) on 4 October 2003. The theatre closed on 27 February 1932 after fifty years of entertainment and was afterwards absorbed into the adjacent Vaux Brewery complex.

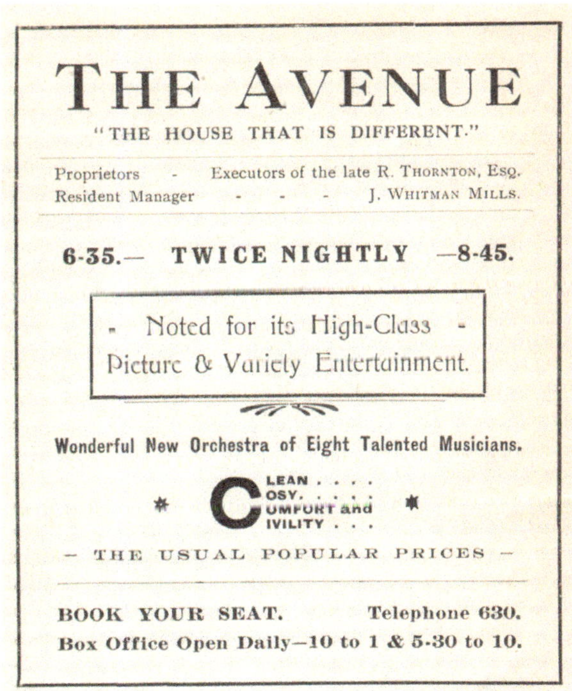

A 1924 advertisement for the Avenue Theatre. It was opened by Richard Thornton on 30 October 1882. When Thornton opened the nearby Empire Theatre in 1907, the viability of The Avenue suffered as a consequence and closed. It reopened in 1908 to show 'pictures' and present 'variety entertainment'.

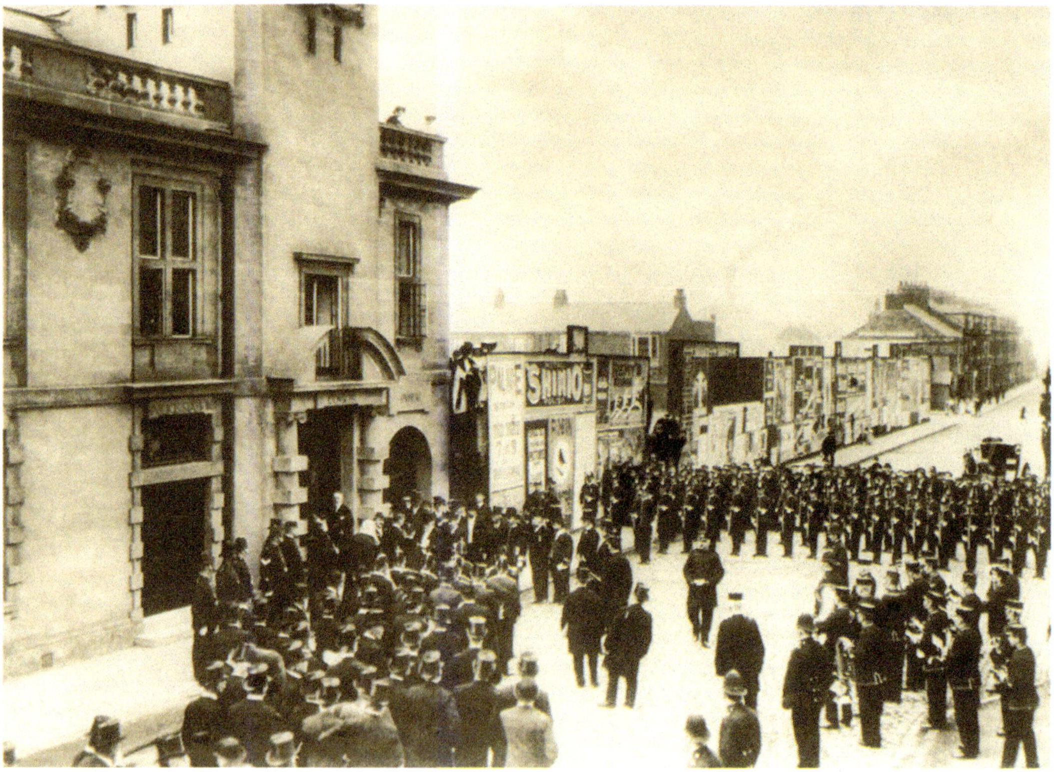

Gill Bridge Police Station
A lovely photograph that records the opening on 28 August 1907 of the new police station and courts in Gill Bridge Avenue. The stone built structure, which incorporated a large clock tower, was erected at a cost of over £40,000. *Photo courtesy of Sunderland Antiquarian Society.*

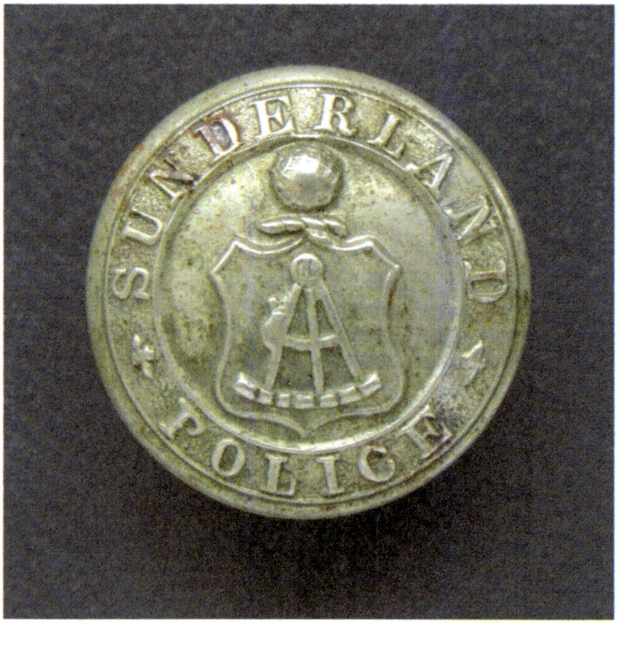

A Sunderland police button that dates from 1924. The button metal is nickel and it has a maker's mark for Briggs, Jones and Gibson of Manchester.

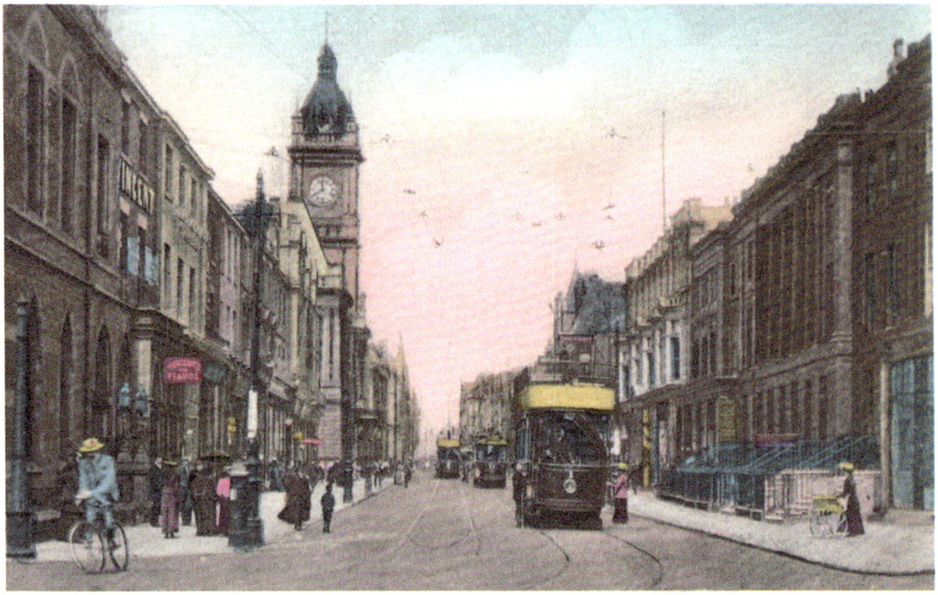

Local Transport in Sunderland

Electric trams travelling along Fawcett Street in around 1905, some five years after their introduction. Councillor Trewitt, Chairman of the Tramways Committee had taken the controls of the front electric tram in a seven car inaugural procession in August 1900, which terminated at the Town Hall. It was reported that one or two passing horses had disapproved, one so vigorously that a "cyclist was upset and his bicycle smashed".

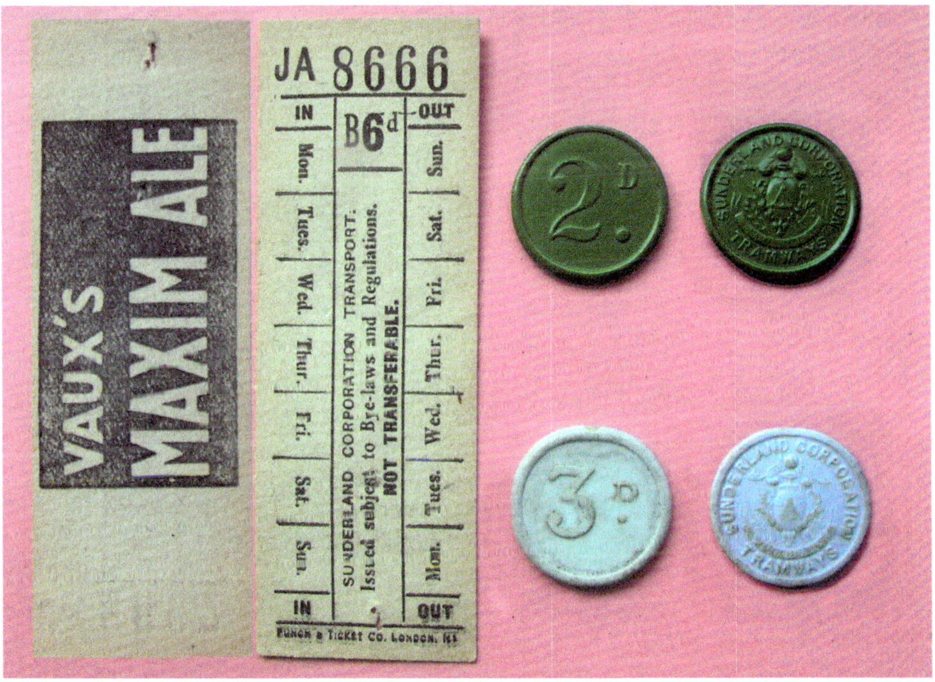

A Sunderland tram ticket and 2*d* and 3*d* tramways transport tokens.

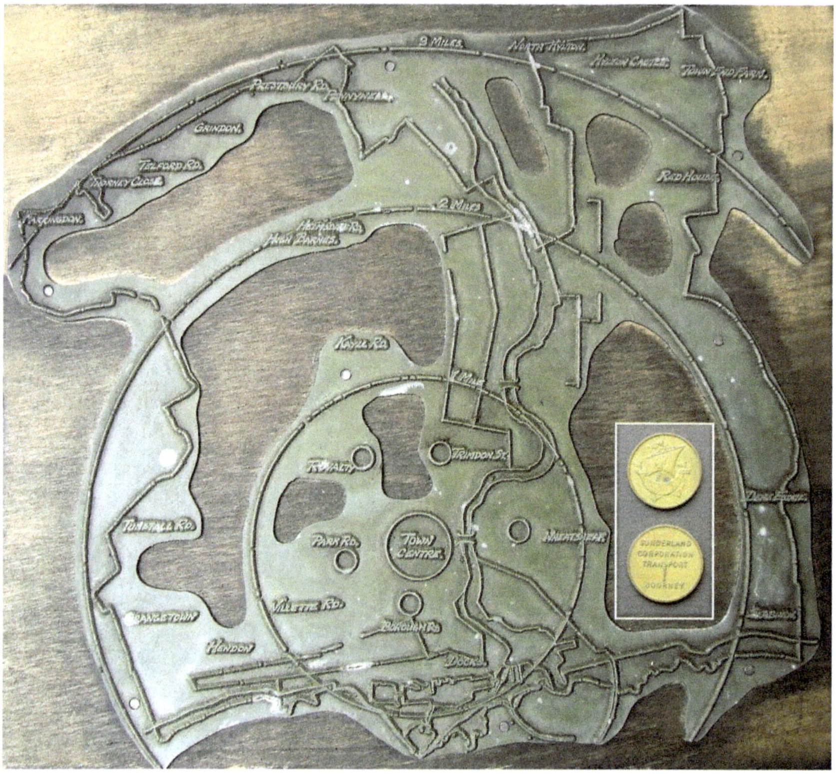

Transport Tokens

A printing block used to produce the radial zone maps for a new transport token system introduced for Sunderland Corporation buses in the 1960s. One of the transport tokens is also shown (inset). The printing block picture is presented in its 'mirror image'.

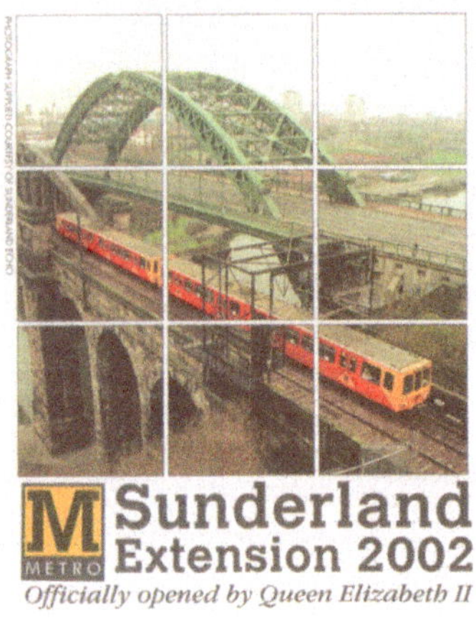

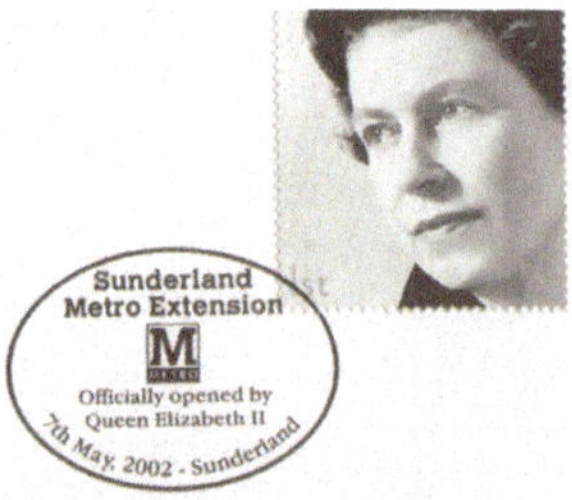

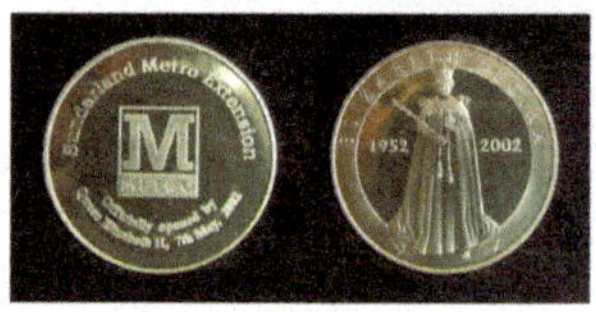

A first day cover commemorating the Metro extension to Sunderland, which was officially opened by Queen Elizabeth II on 7 May 2002. The first passengers had boarded their metro trains on Wearside on Easter Sunday 31 March 2002 to travel the new 18.5 km route. *Inset*: A medal struck to celebrate the Queen's Golden Jubilee and the Metro extension to Sunderland.

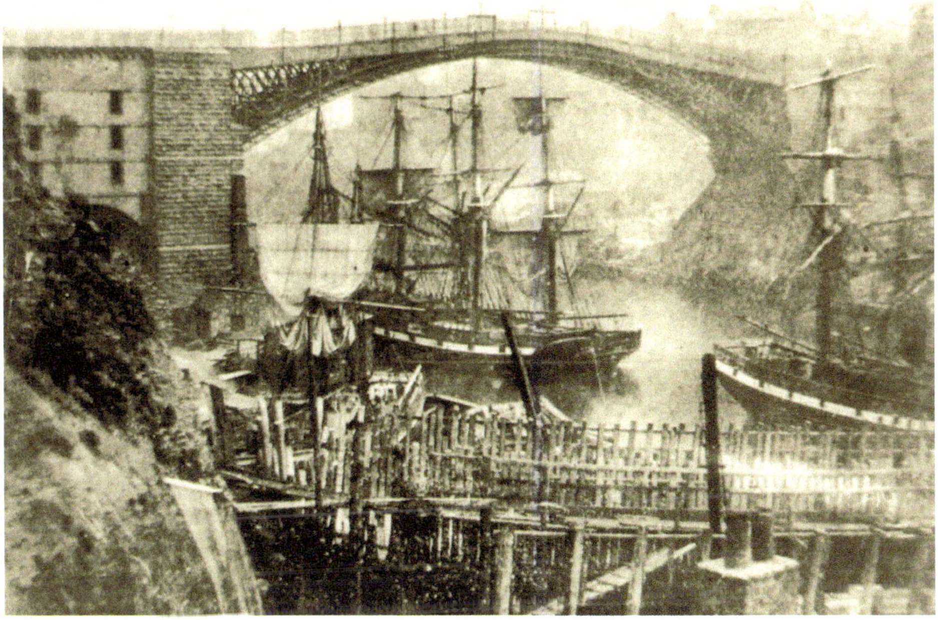

The 1796 Wearmouth Bridge

A mid nineteenth century photograph of, what at that time was, 'the largest single span cast iron bridge in the world'. County Durham MP Rowland Burdon had provided much of the £34,000 finance for the venture. The bridge opened in the presence of His Royal Highness the Duke of Gloucester on 9 August 1796 in front of 80,000 spectators.

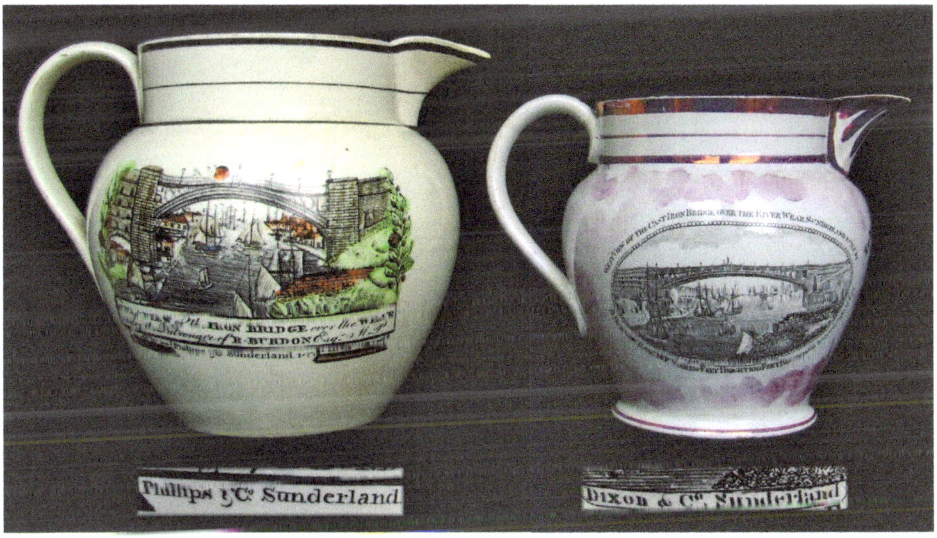

Two Garrison Pottery jugs manufactured to commemorate the erection of the 1796 cast iron bridge over the River Wear. Both jugs were made between 1813 and 1819. Interestingly, the two pieces illustrate the transition from simple 'creamware' (left) to the pink or 'Sunderland lustre' decorated wares (right) that the town became famous for. John Phillips and Robert Dixon were principal partners of the pottery at this time.

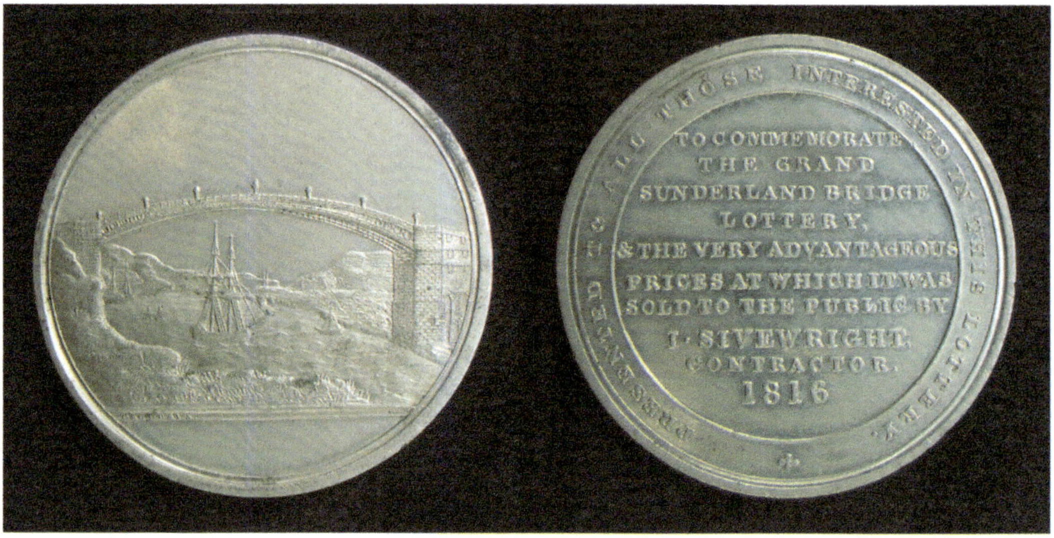

Lottery Medal

Bridge financier Rowland Burdon became bankrupt in 1806 when the bank of Surtees and Company failed. An Act of Parliament was obtained 'enabling his assignees and other persons therein named to dispose of the securities upon the tolls of the bridge and ferry boats by way of a lottery'. Each lottery subscriber was given a lottery medal shown above. The lottery was successful in that Burdon's debts were paid off in October 1816.

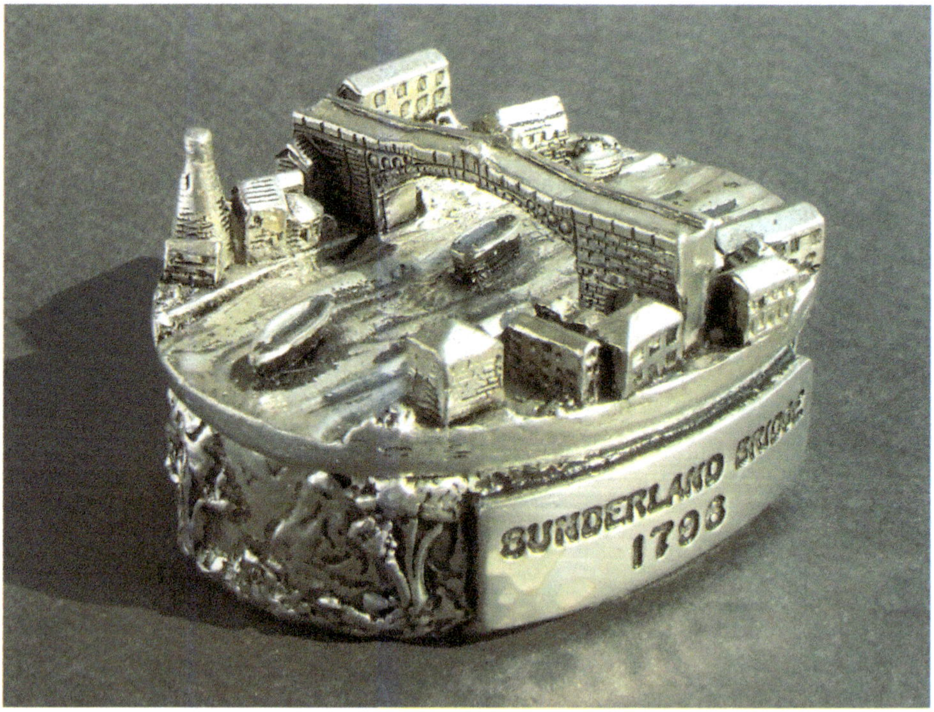

A lovely hand-cast small pewter pin box with superb modelling of the 1796 cast iron bridge by A. E. Williams of Birmingham.

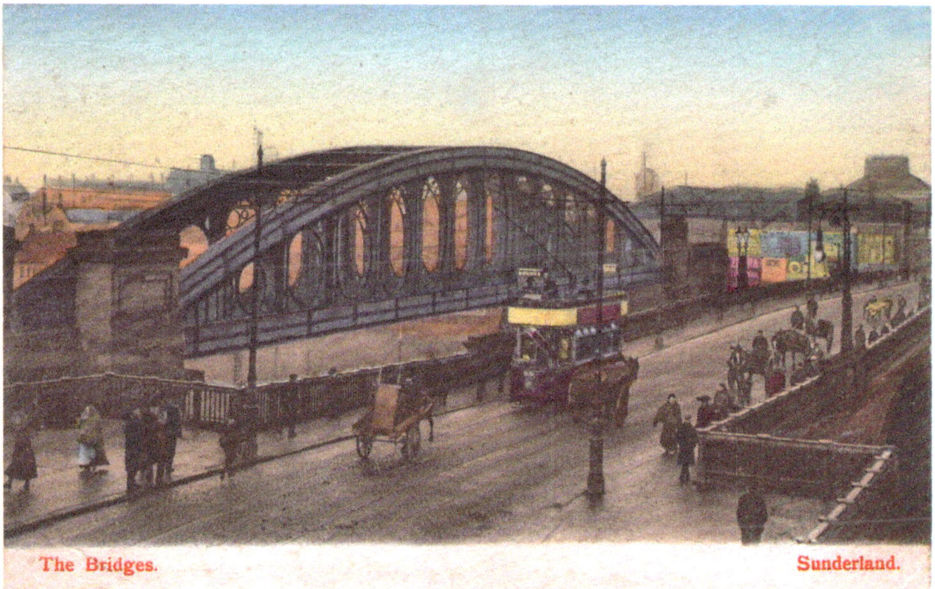

The 1859 Wearmouth Bridge and 1879 Rail Bridge

An early 1900s view of the 'flattened deck' of Wearmouth Bridge adjacent to the rail bridge of 1879. The road bridge underwent a major reconstruction by Robert Stephenson in 1857, when serious flaws in the 1796 bridge developed. Stephenson removed the 'hump' from the old bridge deck by raising the height of the abutments. He discarded the cast iron circular spandrel filling and created box girders for added strength. The reconstructed bridge opened on 5 March 1859.

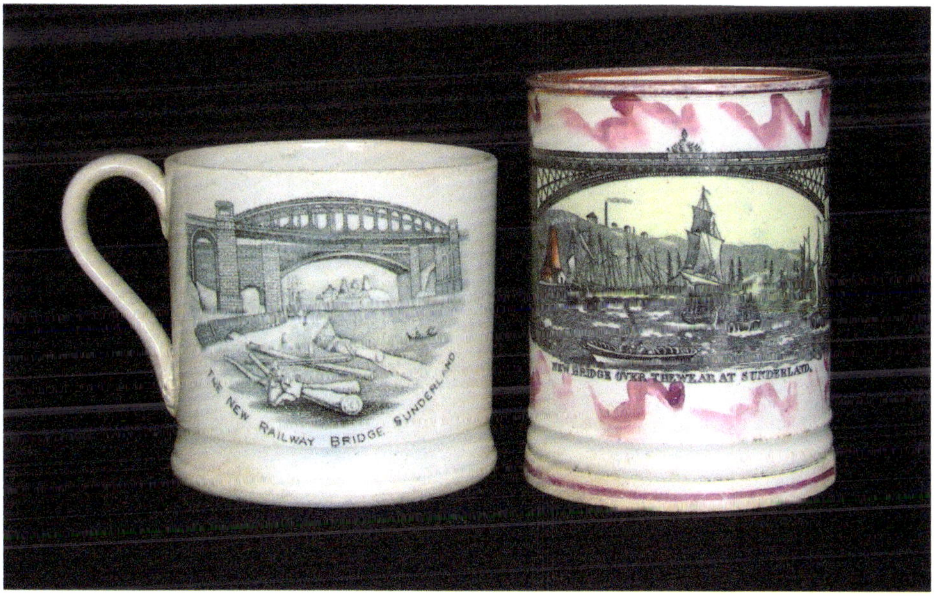

Locally made mugs commemorating the new railway bridge of 1879 (left) and the Stephenson reconstructed road bridge of 1859 (right). The pink lustre mug has a surprise for the user inside of it! (see over).

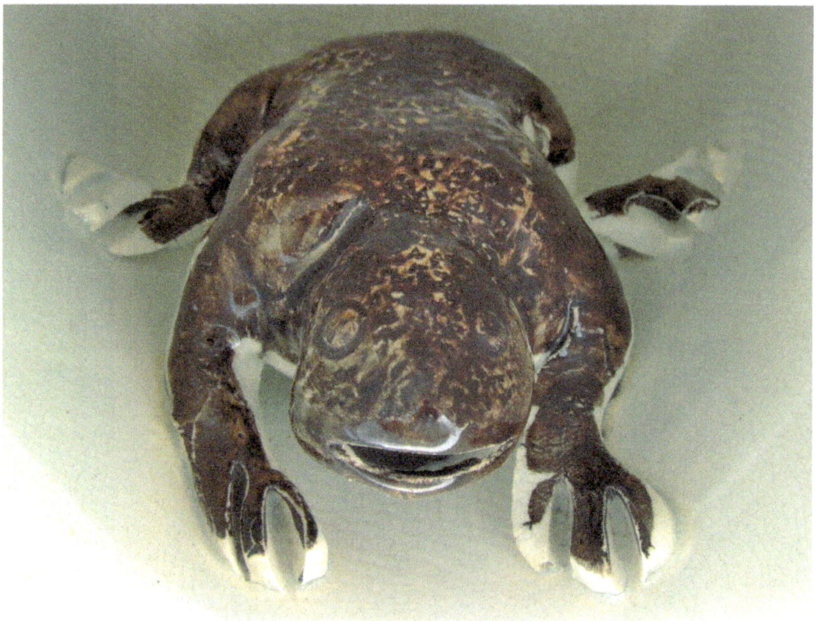

Sunderland Frogs
A frog in a Sunderland mug.

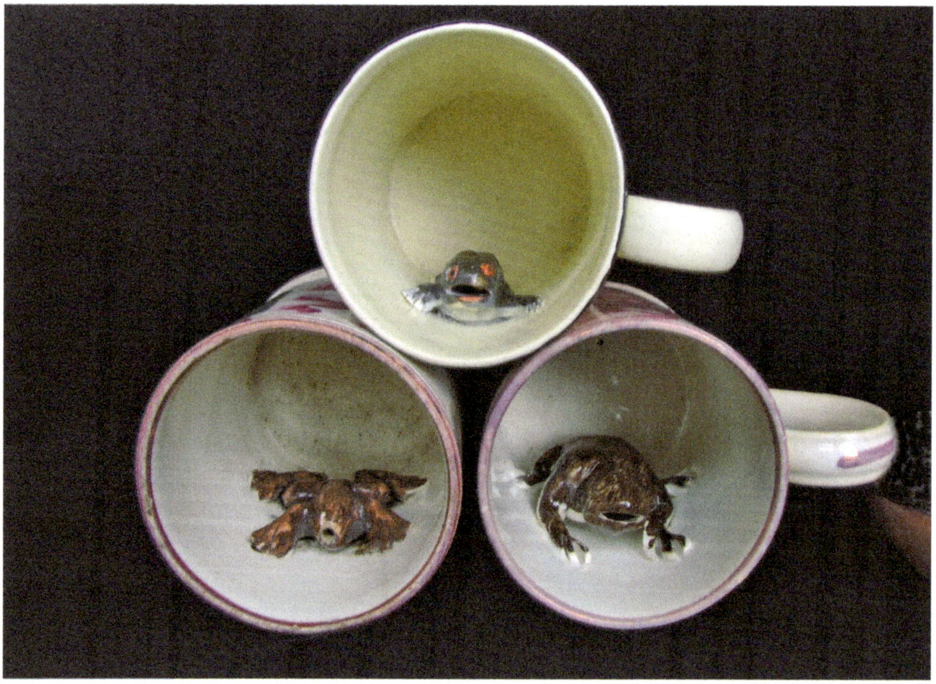

Sunderland frog mugs from the nineteenth century are now extremely collectable and make high prices at auction. The mugs rarely show a maker's mark, but as can be seen above, different potteries adopted their own frog designs. The frog therefore may often help identify the pottery that made the piece!

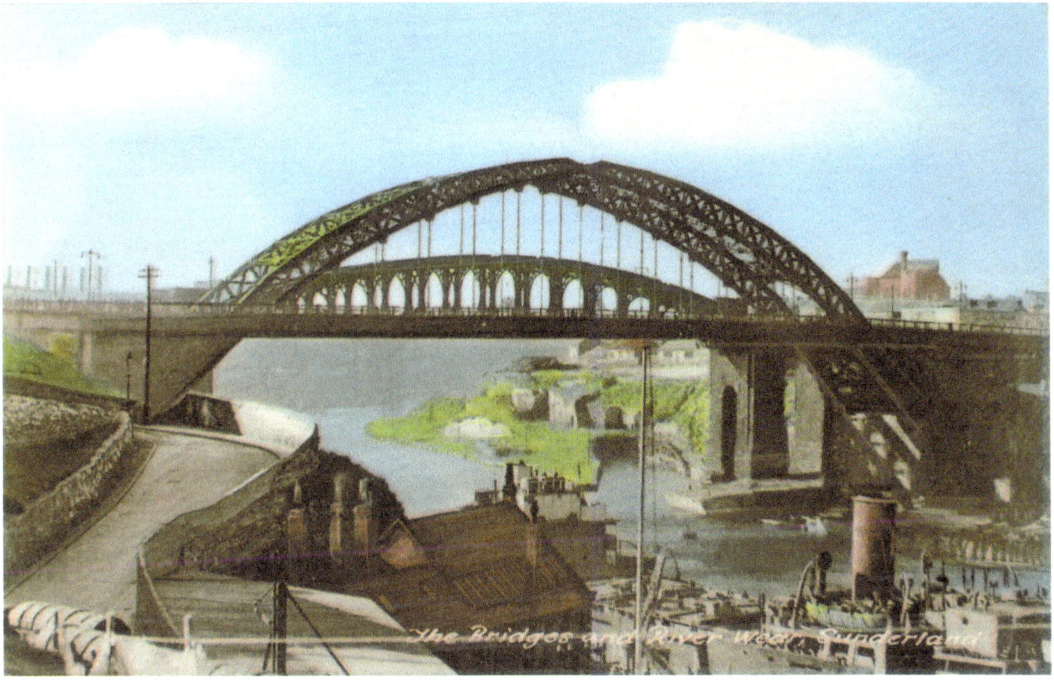

The 1929 Wearmouth Bridge

A postcard view of the existing Wearmouth Bridge erected between 1928/29. It was built around the old 1859 structure to avoid traffic disruption and was formally opened 31 October 1929 by the Duke of York – later George VI.

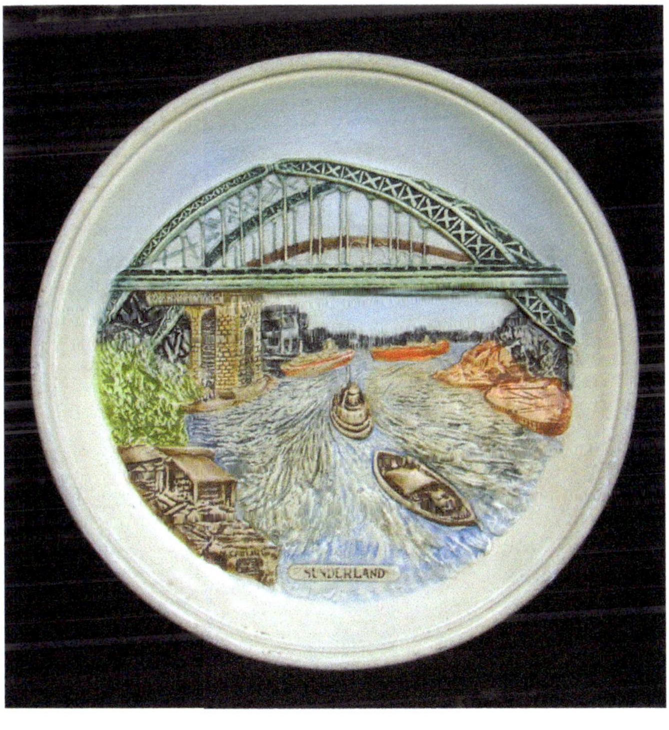

A plaster wall plaque of the current Wearmouth Bridge. Norman Carling, a former designer at the Maling Pottery on Tyneside, modelled the piece for the 'Plasta Crafts Company', probably in the early 1960s.

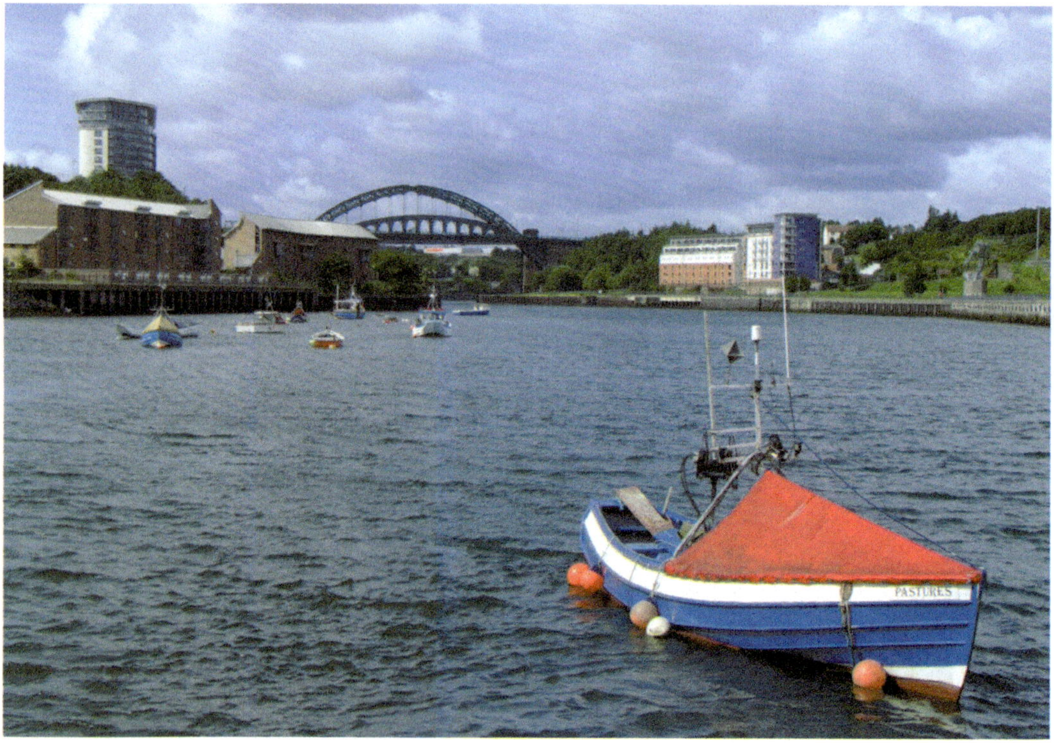

The Wear Bridges Today
How the Wear bridges look today, when viewed from the Fish Quay area. The rail bridge was renovated in 2007 – the first time since its erection in 1879.

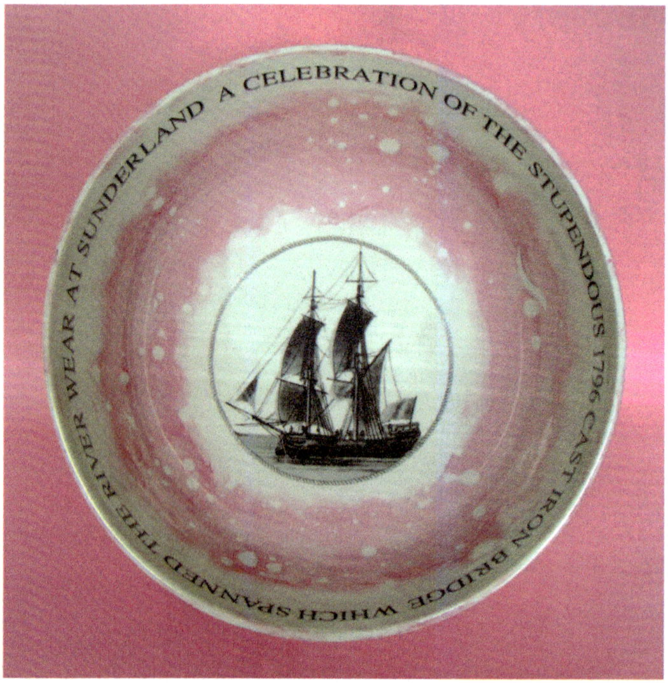

The bicentennial anniversary of the completion of the old cast iron bridge was appropriately commemorated in 1996, when Tyne and Wear Museums commissioned this limited edition bowl (left). It is made in the style of nineteenth century Sunderland lustreware. Around the rim, it reads; "A celebration of the stupendous 1796 cast iron bridge which spanned the River Wear at Sunderland".

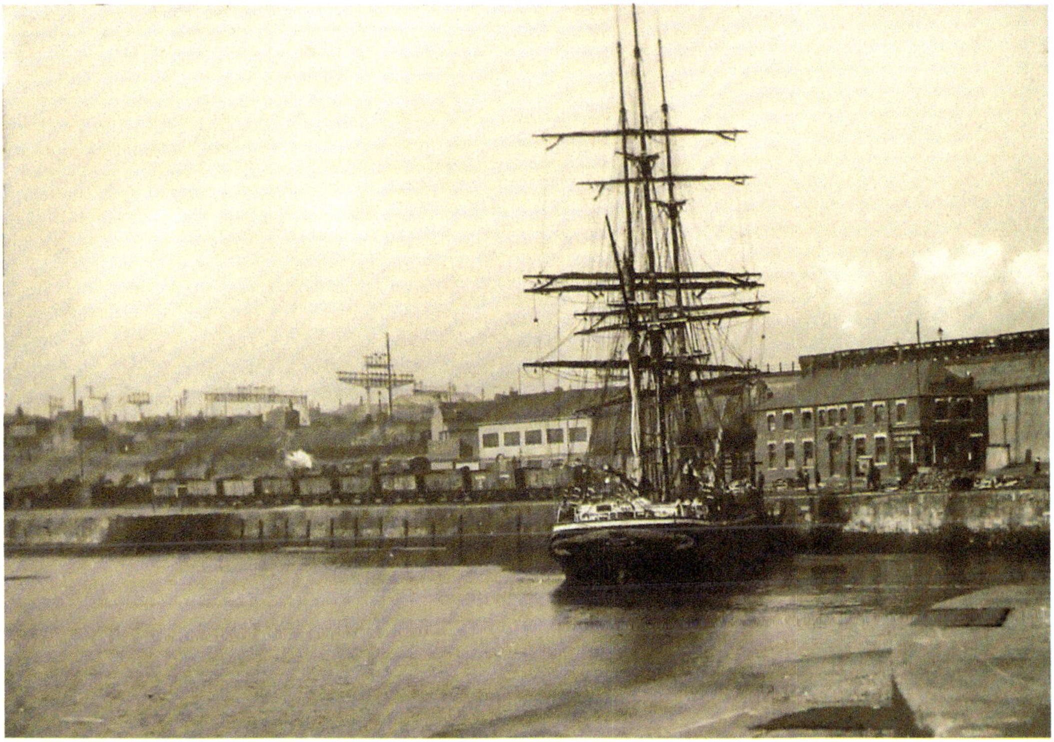

The South Docks, Sunderland
A rare view of the South Docks at Sunderland reproduced from an early lanternslide. The Hudson Dock opened on 20 June 1850 and the Hendon Dock followed in 1868.

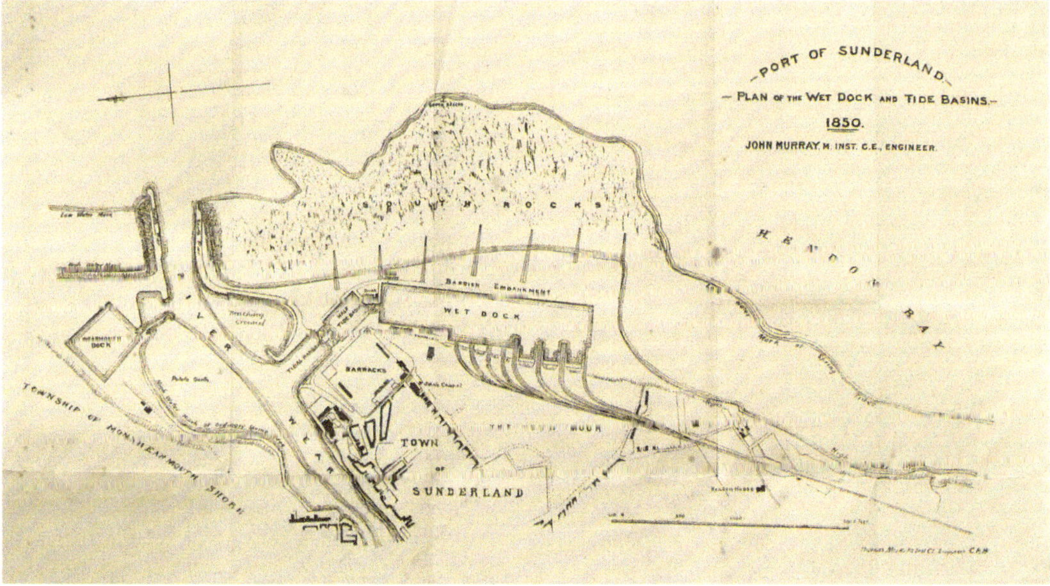

A copy of John Murray's 1850 plan of the Wet Dock and Tide Basins. The early rail lines running across the Town Moor to the coal staiths at the South Dock are shown.

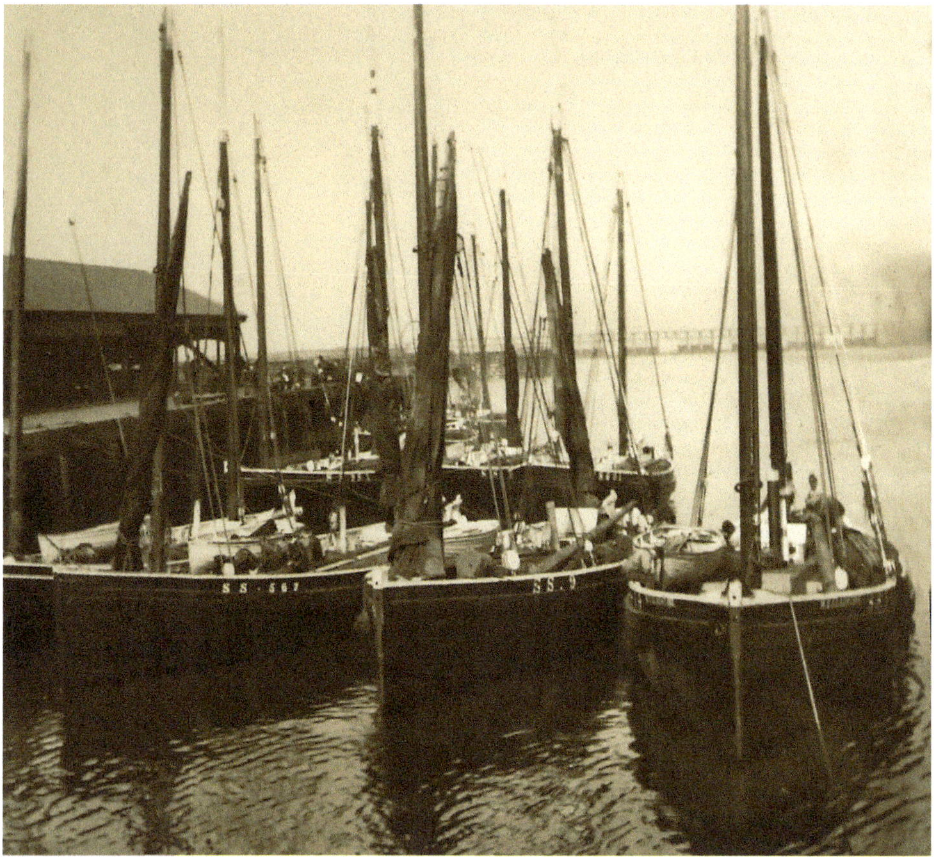

The Fish Quay

This old lanternslide is marked 'the Fish Quay, Sunderland', which at that time was situated in the South Dock.

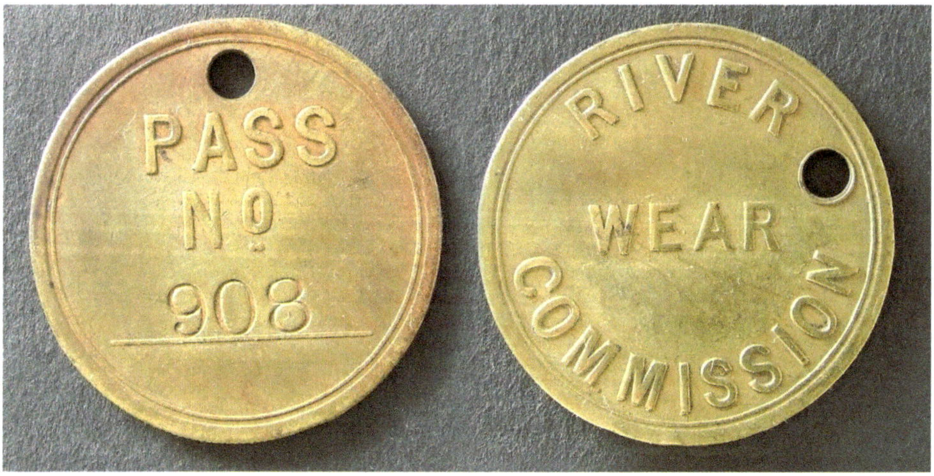

A River Wear Commissioners' dock pass. The Commissioners took over the Docks from the Dock Company in July 1859.

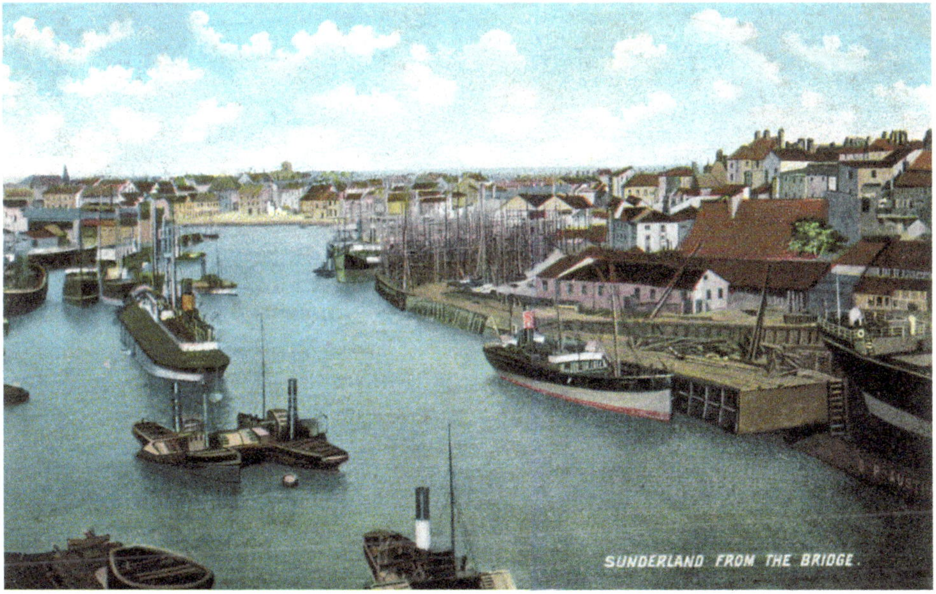

S. P. Austin & Son

An early twentieth century view looking eastwards from Wearmouth Bridge. To the right is the dockyard of S. P. Austin & Son, which operated at this site from 1846, although the business had been founded on the opposite riverbank in 1826. The yard closed around 1964, after having merged with Pickersgill's some ten years earlier.

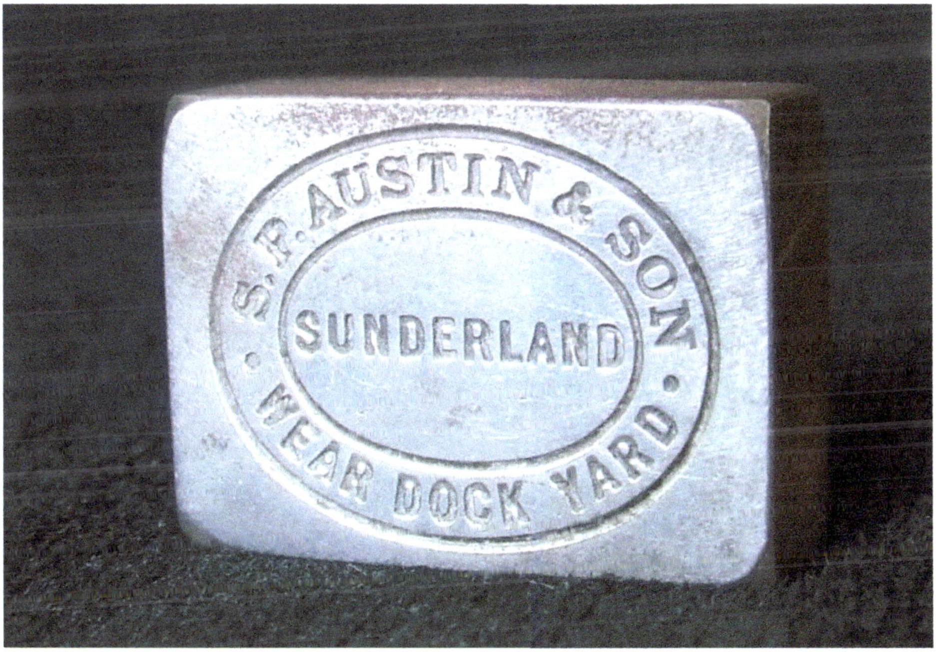

A die for transferring the S. P. Austin & Son logo onto company related documentation – possibly by printing, but more likely by embossing. Embossing would have required a matching set of 'male' and 'female' dies. This 'female' die is shown in its mirror image.

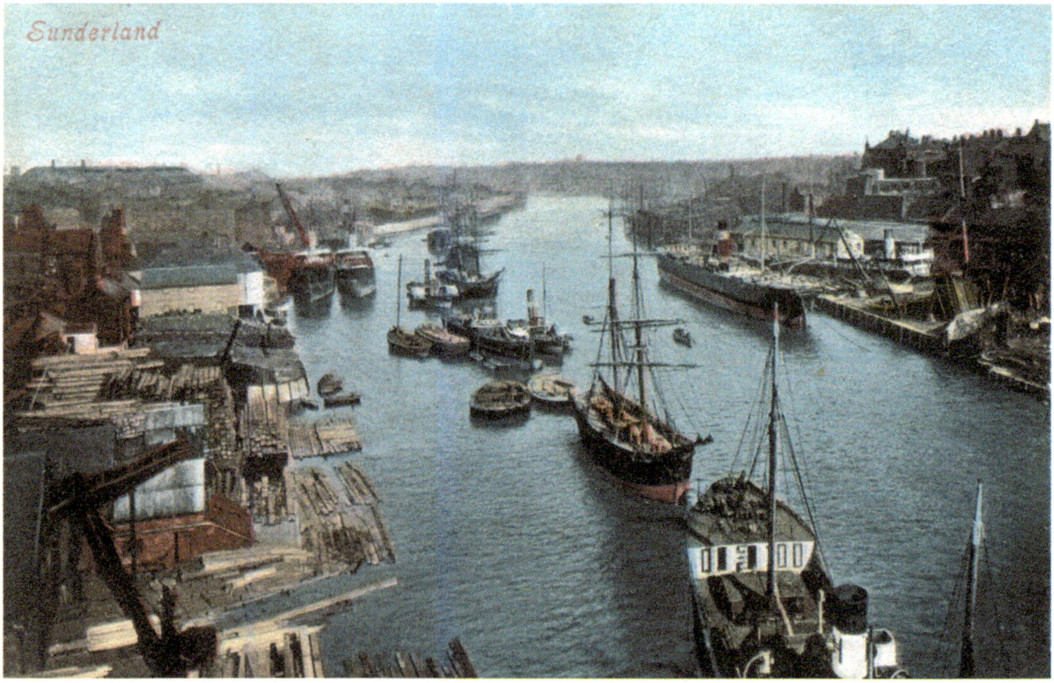

J. D. W. Wilson & Sons Sawmill

A 1905 postcard view from a similar viewpoint as the previous page, but displaying more of the north side of the river and showing the timber yard of J. D. W. Wilson & Sons, which was established in 1851. Huge quantities of timber were imported to meet the demand for the shipbuilding, coal mining and construction industries.

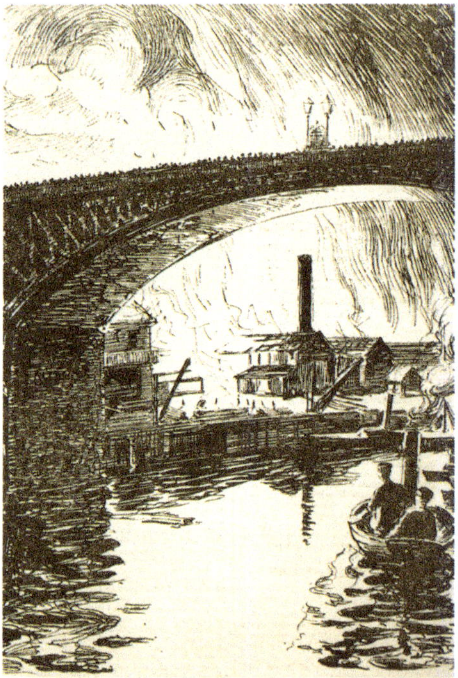

The Great Fire in Sunderland: The Bridge in Danger

An illustration depicting the great fire, which broke out in Sunderland on 'Friday night' at the timber yard of Messrs. J. D. W. Wilson & Sons.

"The yard was covered with great piles of timber of every description, but principally for mouldings and pitch pine. The damage was estimated at £18,000 to £20,000. The Wearmouth Bridge was in some danger and but for the fact that the wind blew away from it, it would not have escaped, as it has done, with a mere scorching, the house of the caretaker, however, being destroyed".

An exact date for these events is not disclosed in the account, but the existence of Stephenson's road bridge and the apparent absence of the rail bridge suggests sometime between 1859 and 1879.

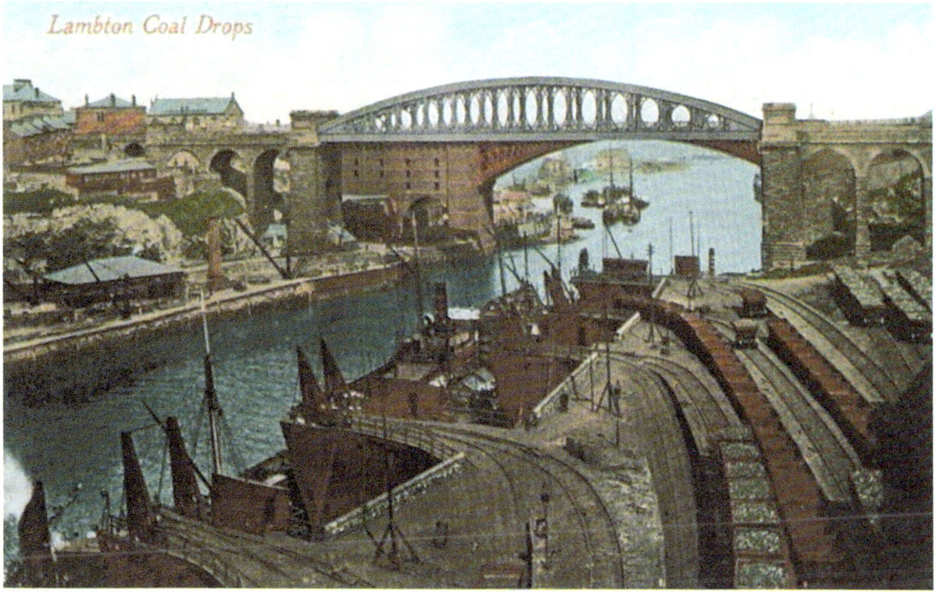

The Lambton Coal Drops
The Lambton Coal Drops photographed in the early twentieth century. The Nesham Family established staiths here as early as 1812/15 for the Newbottle Railway. By 1822, they were in the hands of John Lambton who amalgamated them with his existing Penshaw Line to create the Lambton Railway system.

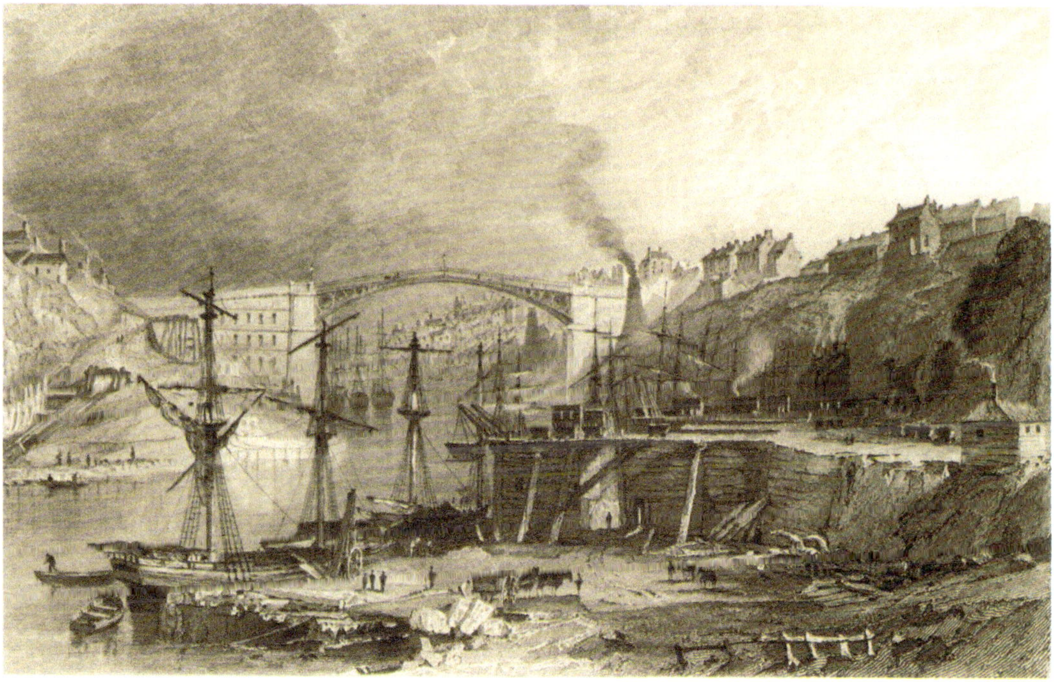

An 1833 steel engraving of the Lambton Coal Drops by William Le Petit after T. Allom. The cast iron bridge of 1796 can be seen in this early view.

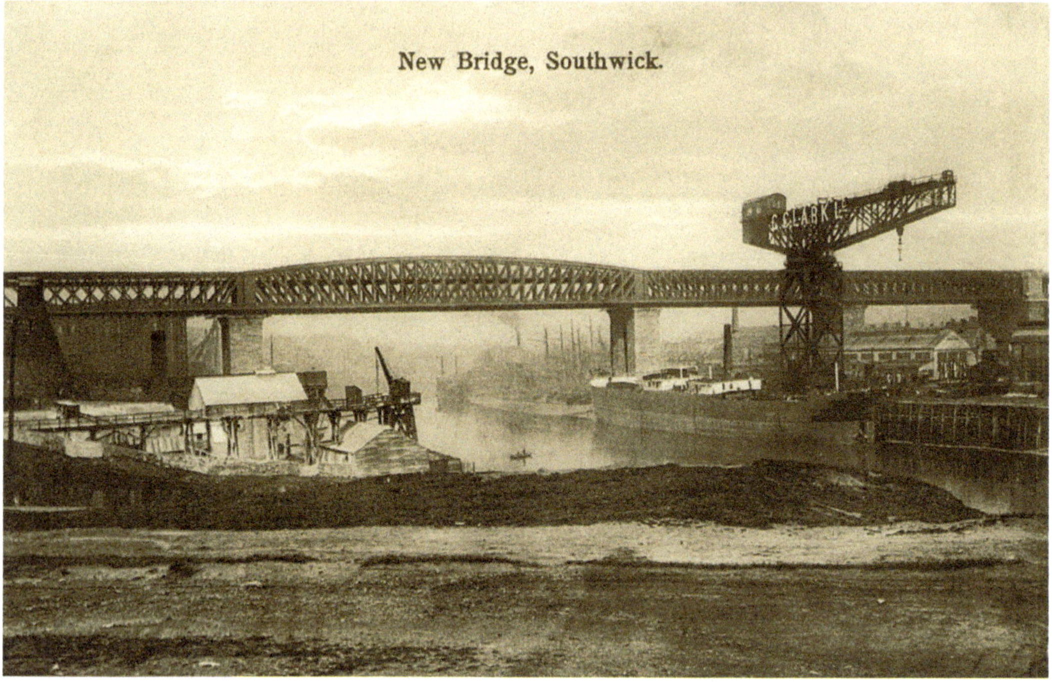

Queen Alexandra Bridge

The Queen Alexandra Bridge pictured just after completion in 1909. Its design as a double-decked 'rail and road' bridge was perhaps something of a misjudgement, as by 1920 the upper rail track was almost redundant due to a decline in the coal trade.

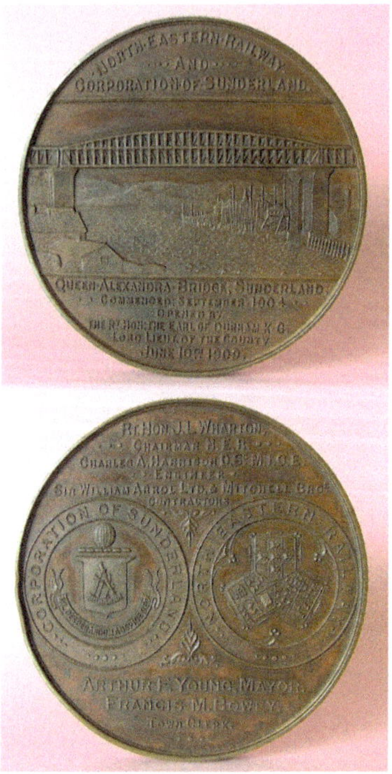

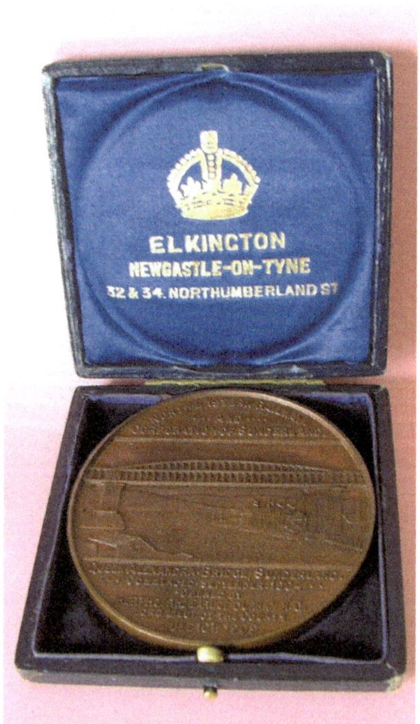

A medal struck to commemorate the opening of the Queen Alexandra Bridge on 10 June 1909 by The Rt. Hon: The Earl of Durham KG Lord Lieutenant of the County.

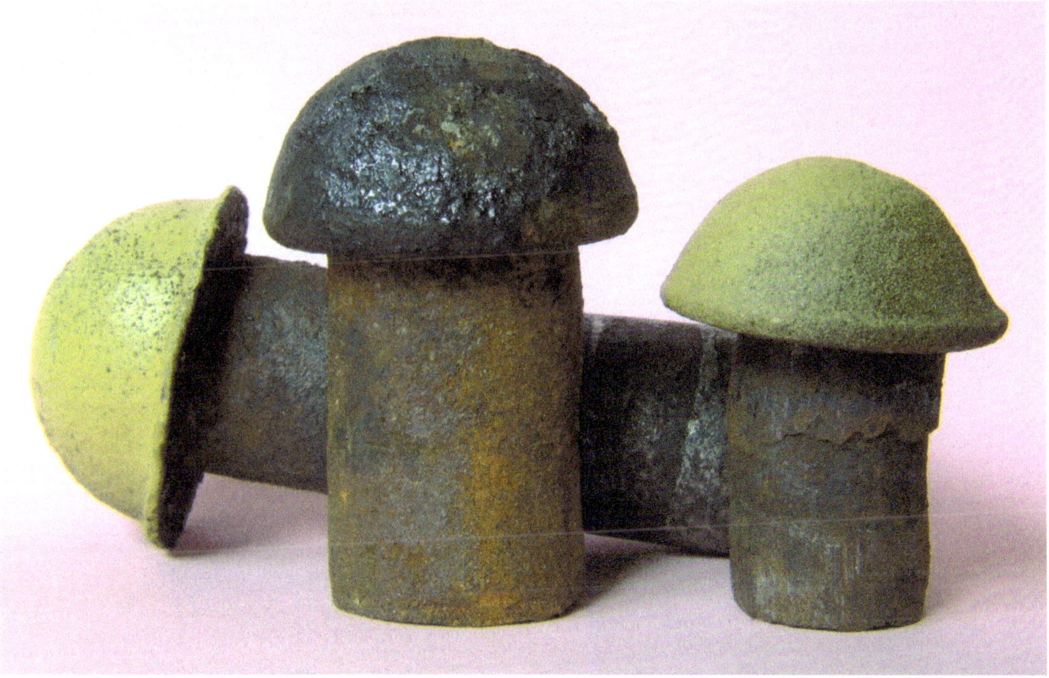

Bridge Refurbishments

In 2005/6 the bridge was given a £4.5 million overhaul. Above are old rivets removed from the structure during the renovation work.

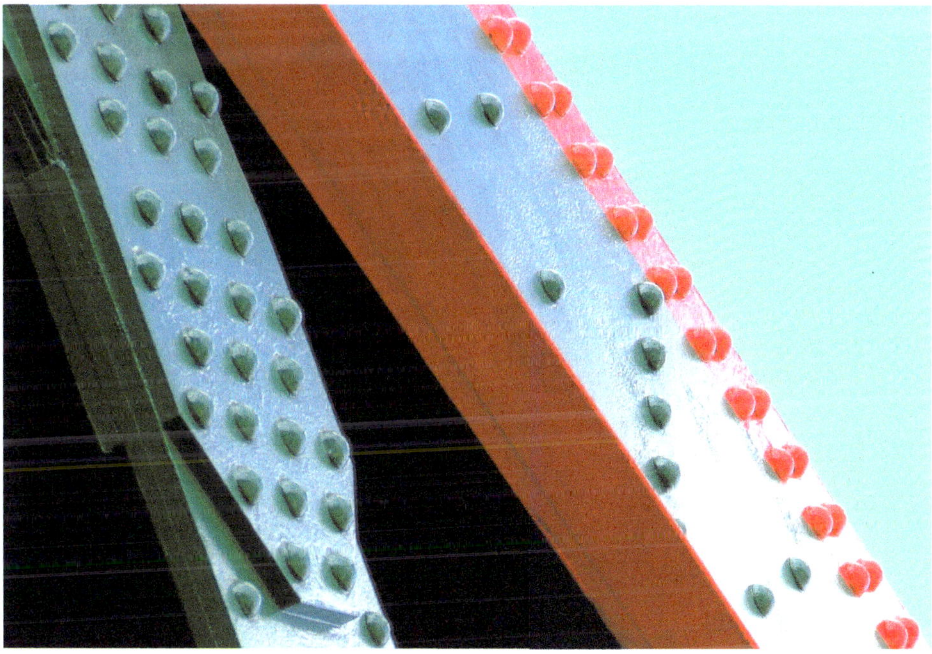

The striking new colours of the Queen Alexandra Bridge upon completion of the refurbishment, in 2006.

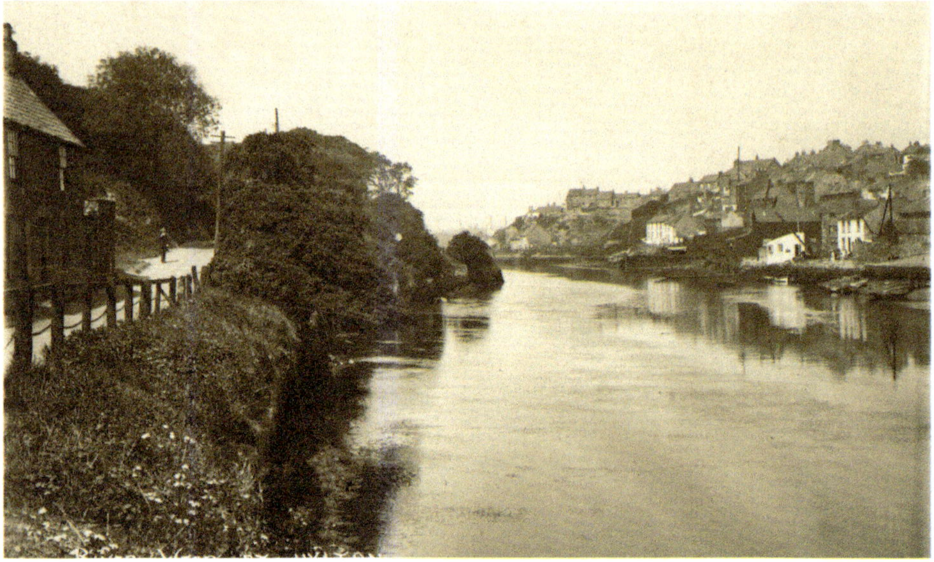

Hylton Riverside

A view from the north bank of the River Wear at Hylton looking eastwards. If this same scene had been recorded some 120 years earlier, the ancient river structure called 'Brigg Stones' would have been much in evidence in the foreground of the picture. The bulk of it was removed in the early nineteenth century following a campaign by the keel men, who said that it hindered their passage up and down the river.

The structure has been the source of much debate between antiquarians and archaeologists over the last 200 years. Was it a bridge or a paved ford? Was it a dam built to raise the level of the river upstream? Was it Roman or Medieval in date?

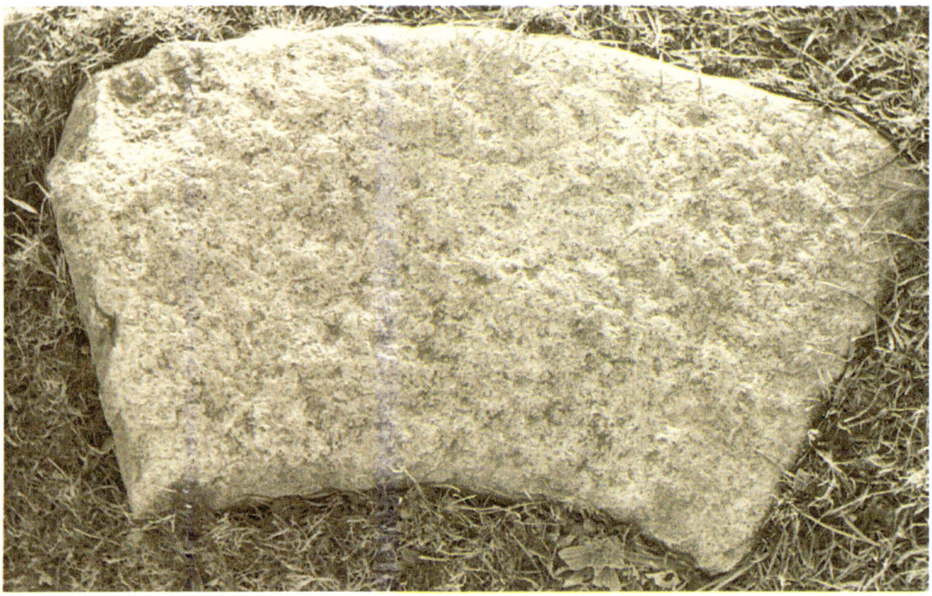

A photograph of a voussoir said to be from one of the arches of Brigg Stones. *Image courtesy of South Hylton Local History Group.*

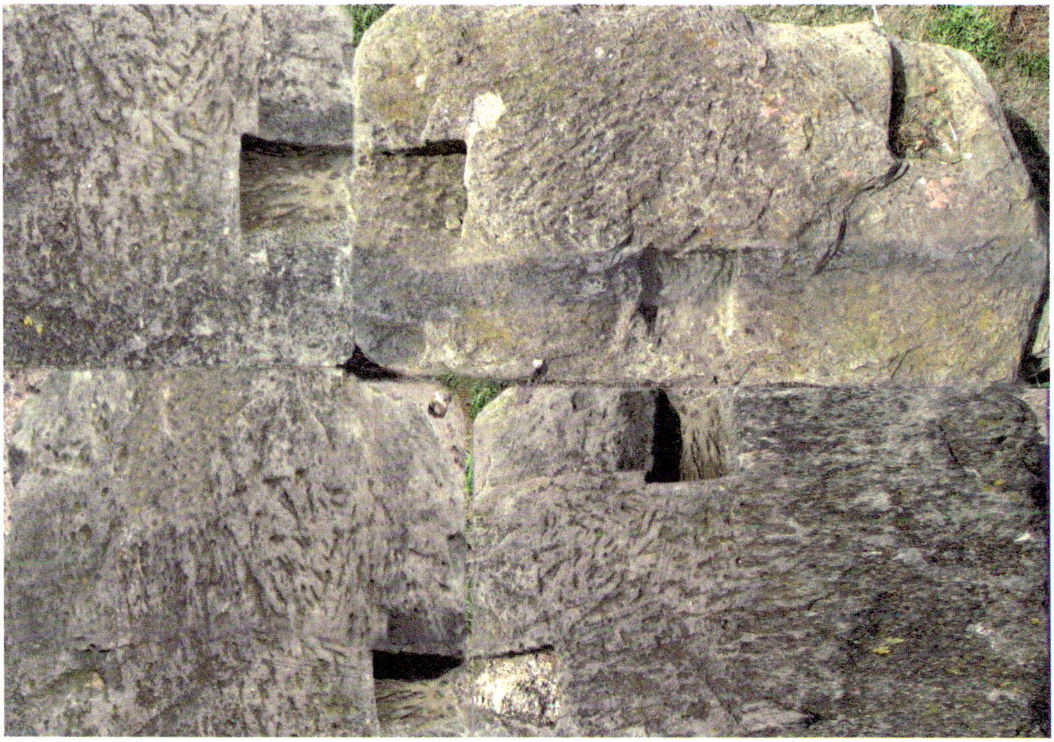

Opus Revinctum

When Brigg Stones was demolished in the early 1800s, huge quantities of its massive blocks were re-used as breakwater stones around the inner moles of the harbour at Roker. Others are scattered around the footpaths there. They can be recognised by their 'opus revinctum' dove-tailed holes and are comparable to stones from Roman structures identified elsewhere. The dove-tailed slots were cut into adjoining stones on the structure and metal butterfly cramps inserted and set in lead. This technique was common Roman practice where structures had to withstand the tremendous pressures of water.

In the above picture, the author has 'photographically reassembled' some of the individual blocks that he has photographed around the Roker area to demonstrate how 'opus revinctum' would have been utilised to strengthen the ancient structure.

As Brigg Stones was being dismantled, large quantities of lead were recovered by the apprentices from the cramp slots during their lunch breaks and sold by them for extra pocket money.

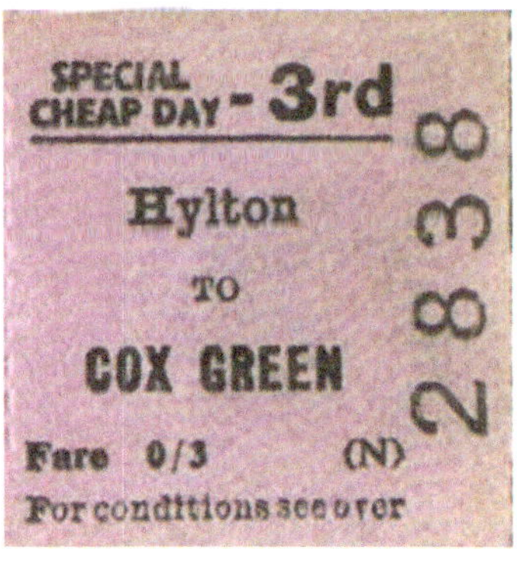

Let us temporarily re-open the LNER Penshaw Branch Line and make use of this 1950s train ticket to explore further upriver!

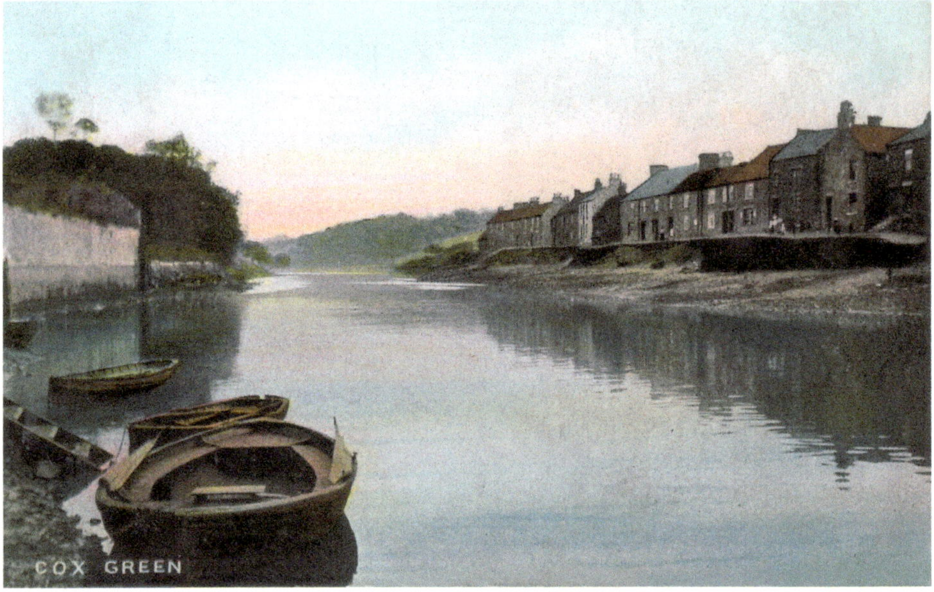

Coxgreen and Barmston

The ferry at Coxgreen and Barmston around 1911, which was run by members of the Frost family for many years. Only one of the old buildings to the right of the picture survives today – the local pub! The old quay to the left is identified on John Rennie's 1826 map of the River Wear as 'Orpeth Staith'.

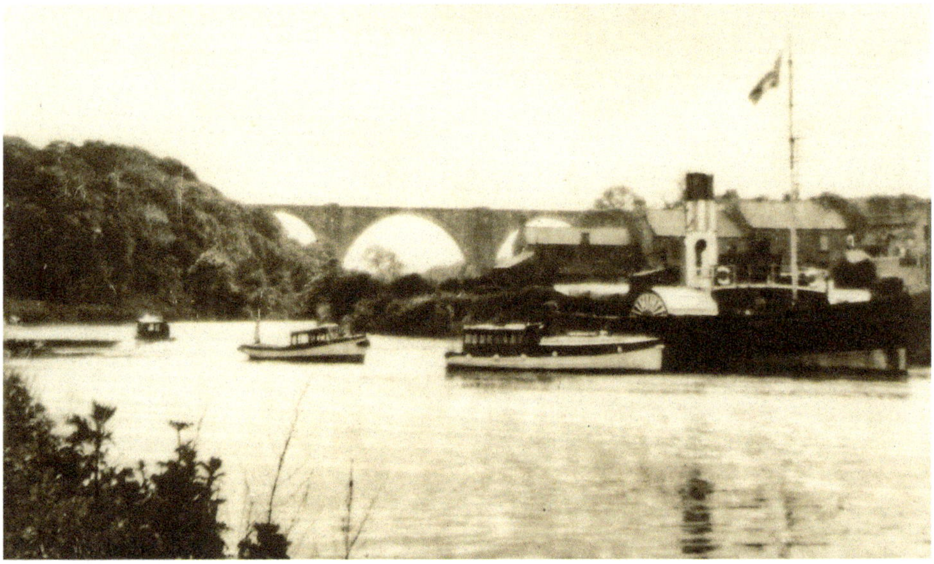

The steam paddle tug *Eppleton Hall* berthed slightly upstream from Coxgreen Ferry for a River Wear Commissioners' 'day trip' sometime before 1957. The tug was built in South Shields in 1914 and worked on the River Wear until 1964. Following restoration in 1970 she sailed from the North East to a new home in San Francisco Maritime Museum. The boat centre left is thought to be the *Sea Horse*. Beyond the vessels, stands the imposing Victoria Viaduct.

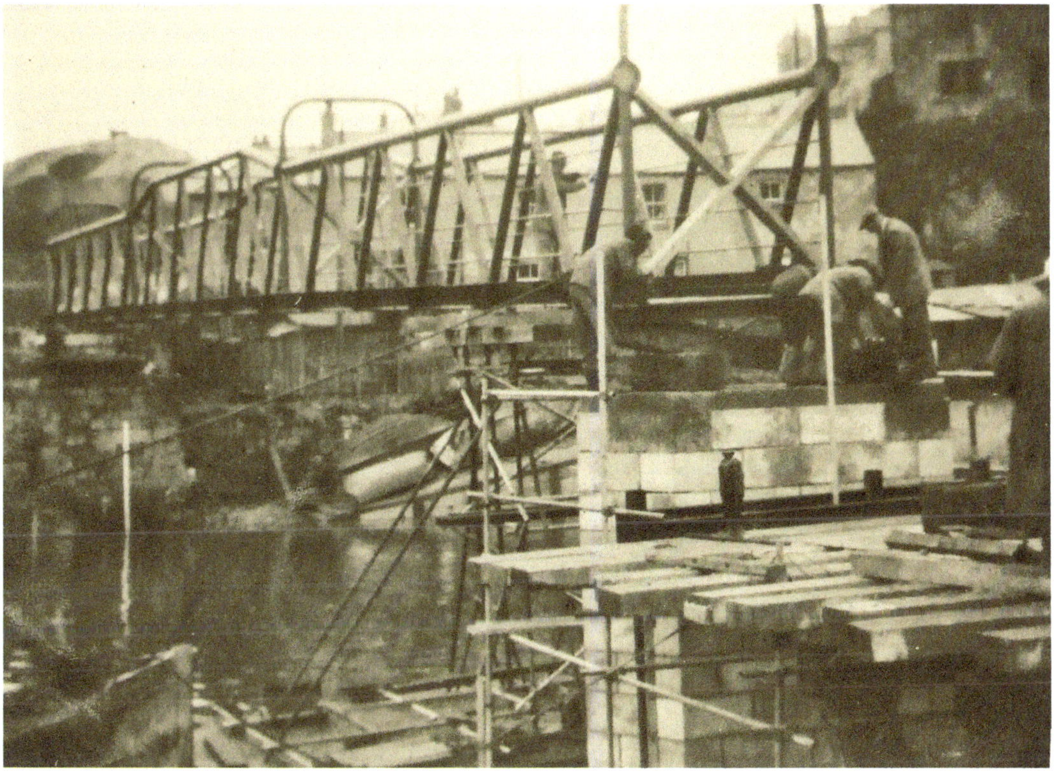

Coxgreen and Barmston Bridge

The Coxgreen and Barmston tubular steel footbridge under construction in 1957/58. The £7,500 expenditure to build the bridge was provided by Durham County and Washington Urban District Councils.

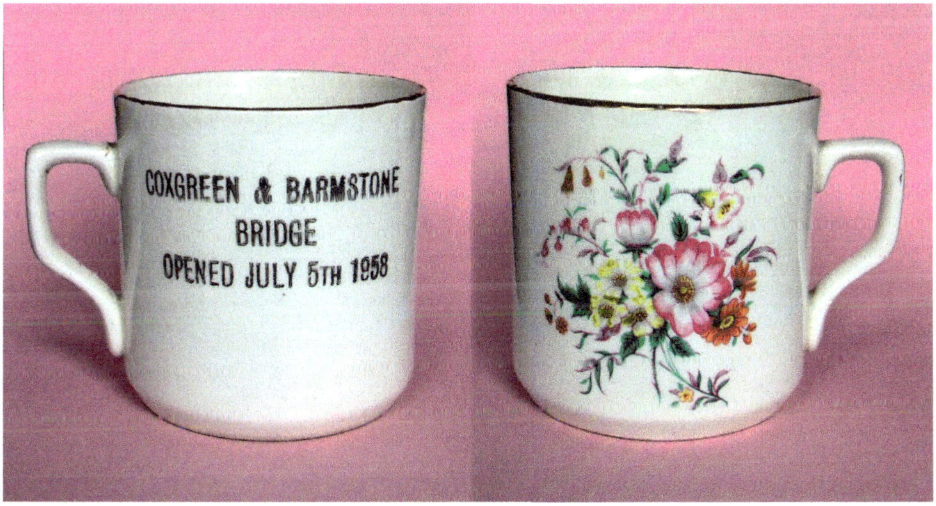

A mug issued to commemorate the opening of the Coxgreen and Barmston Bridge on 5 July 1958. (Note the misspelling of Barmston). The opening of the footbridge sounded the death knell for the local ferryboat service.

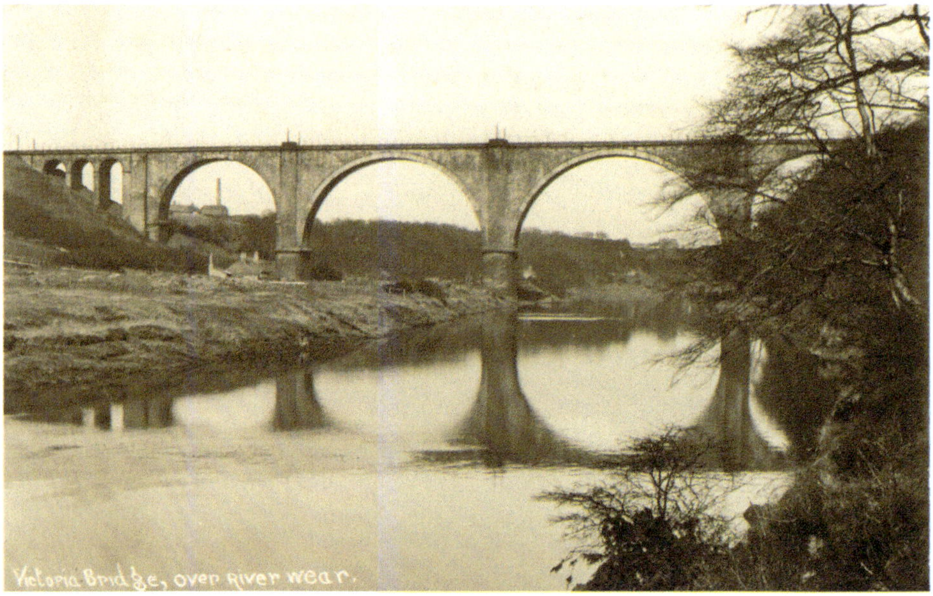

The Victoria Viaduct, Washington

The Victoria Viaduct pictured around 1912. The inspiration for its design came from a bridge built in Alcantara, Spain around 105 AD. Early plans for an iron rail, road and footbridge were rejected in favour of this magnificent stone structure. The final stone was set in place on Coronation Day 28 June 1838 and the bridge was consequently named the Victoria Viaduct. It opened to rail traffic on 24 August 1838.

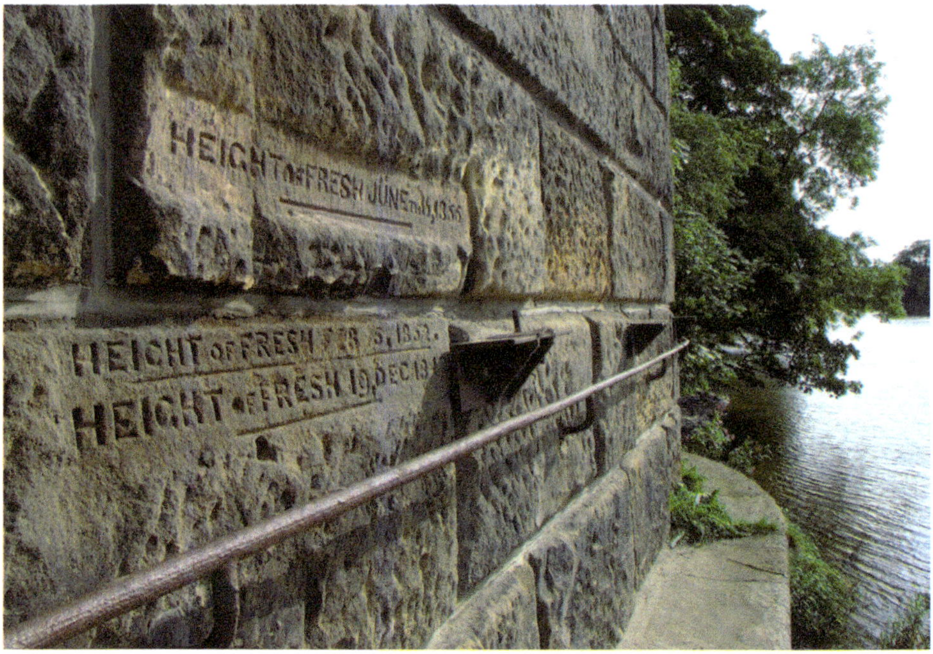

Nineteenth century 'heights of fresh' or flood markings chiselled into a pier of the Victoria Viaduct.

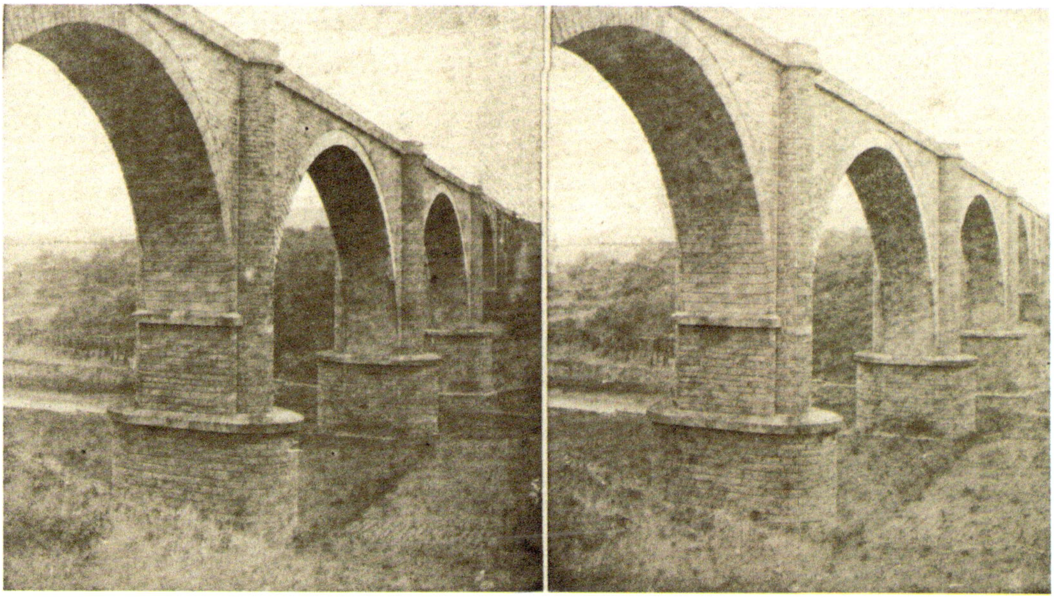

Low Lambton Staith

A very rare 'stereo view' of the Victoria Viaduct, possibly photographed as early as the 1860s. To the left of the viaduct is Low Lambton Staith. Here, coals were loaded into keelboats from adjoining waggonways for river transport to Sunderland, where they were transferred to the ocean going vessels of the port. By 1862, after 200 years of trade, keelboats no longer worked the tidal reaches of the River Wear.

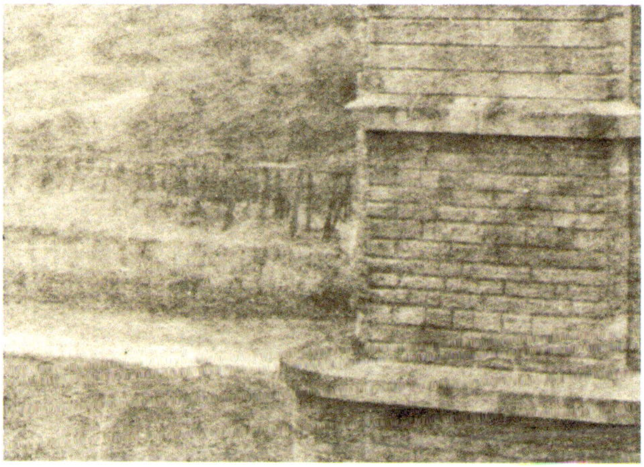

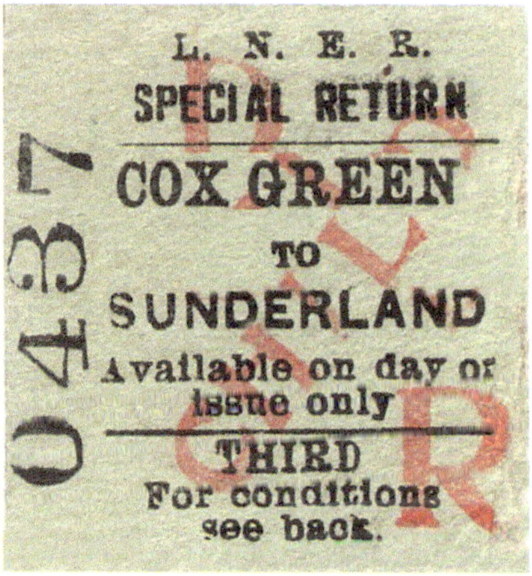

Above left: A partial enlargement of the old image showing Low Lambton Staith. Note the timber staging on the staith to take the coal waggons to the river's edge. A little further upstream at the *Dog Hole*, a gentleman called Will Paterson developed an improved method for transferring coals to the keelboats. He lowered the waggon down to the keel by use of 'the counter-balance and brake'. Such was the 'novelty' of his development that the Marquis of Londonderry took the Duke of Wellington there in 1827 to observe the process.

Above right: Time to catch the train again and return to town!

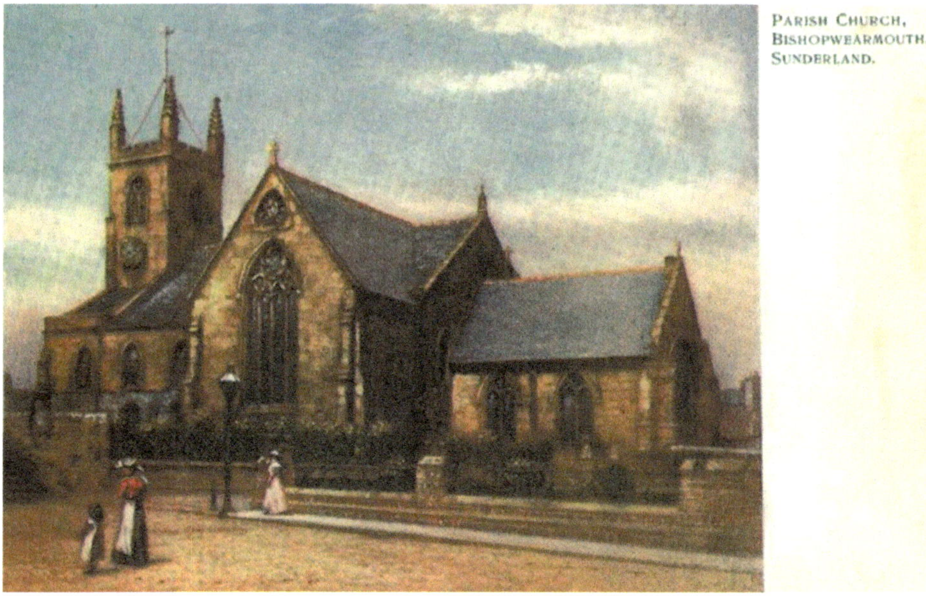

Bishopwearmouth Church

The ancient church here was said to have architecture "as old as the days of Athelstan". It became so ruinous and uncomfortable that St Michael and All Angels was rebuilt on its old foundations between 1806 and 1810. The church was altered four times throughout the nineteenth century and again in 1932. The Revd William Paley was appointed Rector here in 1795 and nearby Paley Street is named after him.

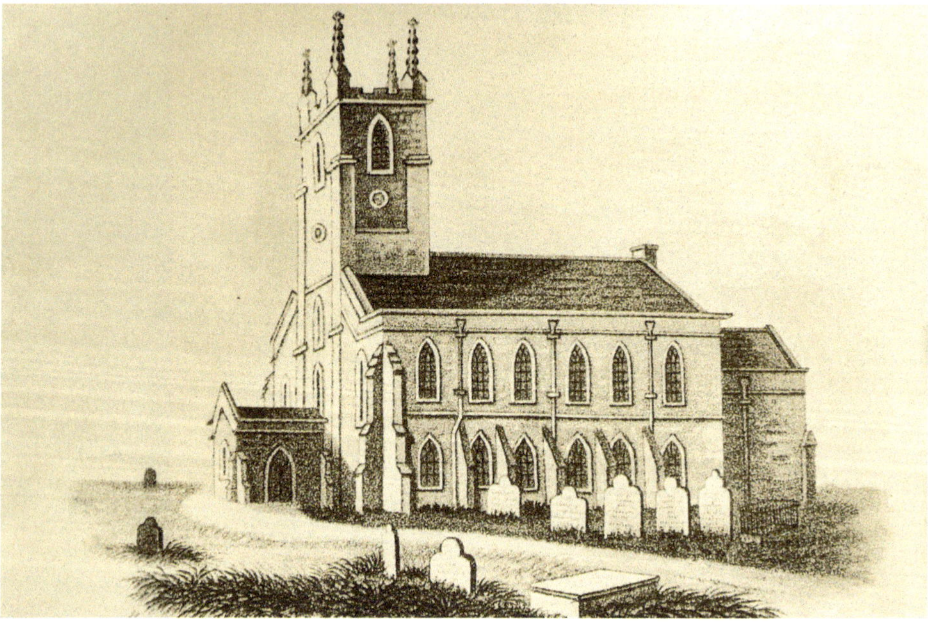

How the church looked in 1818, before the alterations that were undertaken throughout the last half of the nineteenth century. The print appears in George Garbutt's *History of Sunderland,* which was published a year later.

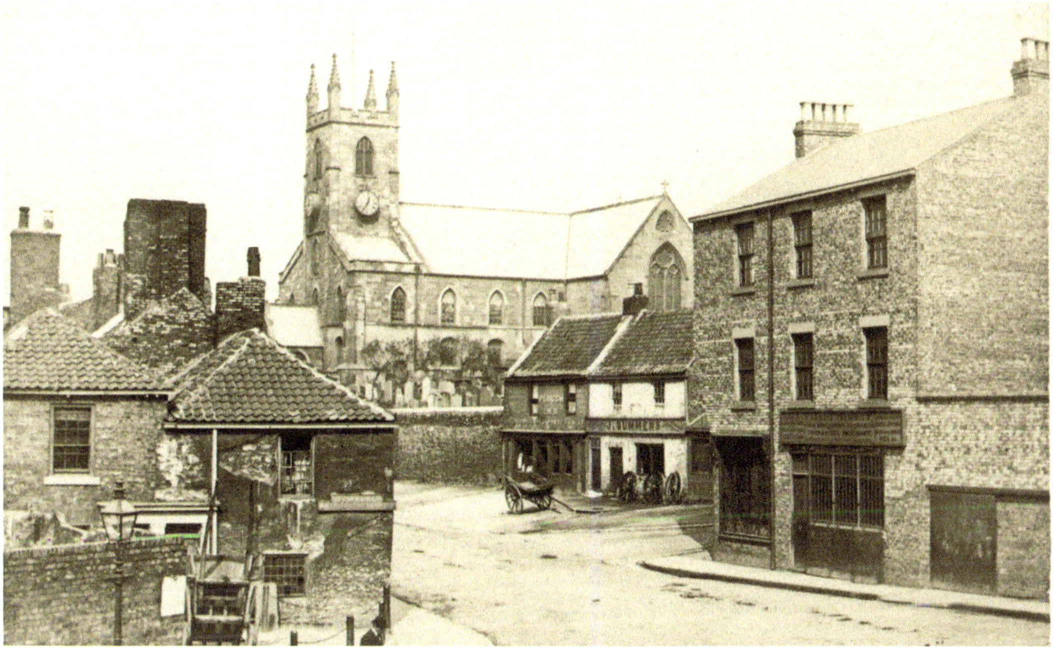

Bishopwearmouth Church

The Plough Inn and the premises of J. Summers, Francis Trewhitt and J. Walker can all be seen on this wonderful 1875 photograph of Bishopwearmouth Church and the surrounding village. *Image copyright Beamish Museum Ltd.*

Extract from a Codicil to the last Will and Testament of The Revd William Paley, DD. Rector of Bishopwearmouth Church

"If my life had been continued it was my intention to print in Sunderland a collection of sermons – five hundred copies to be distributed gratis in this parish – to deliver them to Mr Stephenson, to print and distribute one copy in a family – first to those who frequent the church, then to farmer's families in the country, then to such poorer families, as have a person who can read or are likely to read them – I would not have the said sermons printed for sale".

Right: One of five hundred copies of a book of sermons distributed free in Bishopwearmouth Parish after the death of Rector, Revd William Paley on 25 May 1805. James Graham printed the book in Sunderland in 1806.

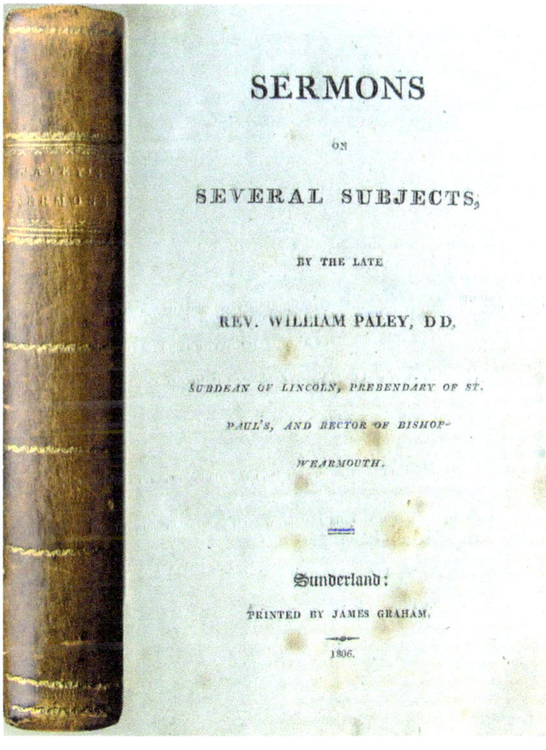

SERMONS

ON

SEVERAL SUBJECTS,

BY THE LATE

REV. WILLIAM PALEY, D D,

SUBDEAN OF LINCOLN, PREBENDARY OF ST. PAUL'S, AND RECTOR OF BISHOP-WEARMOUTH.

Sunderland:

PRINTED BY JAMES GRAHAM,

1806.

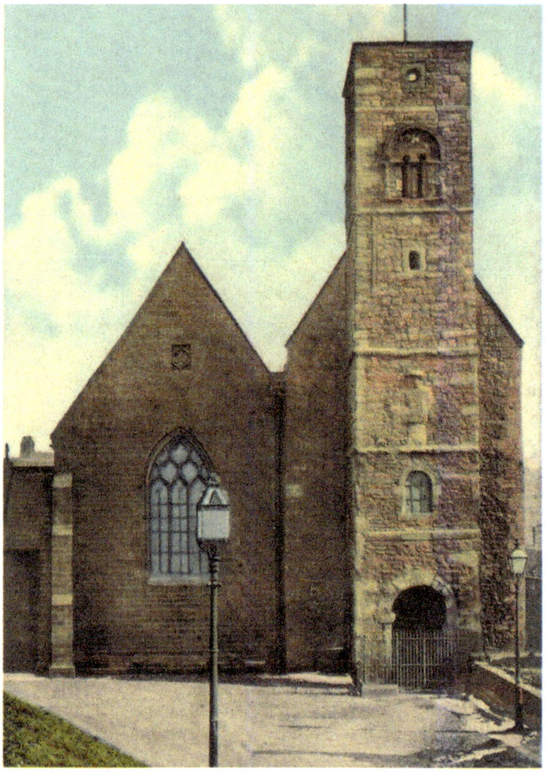

St Peters Church, Monkwearmouth
A view of St. Peter's Church and site of the ancient monastery built by Benedict Biscop in 674 AD on land granted to him by King Egfrid. The lower half of the church tower and the west wall of the church behind it date to this ancient time. The Venerable Bede was born close to Wearmouth and entered the monastery around 679 AD at seven years of age. He is often referred to as 'The Father of English History'.

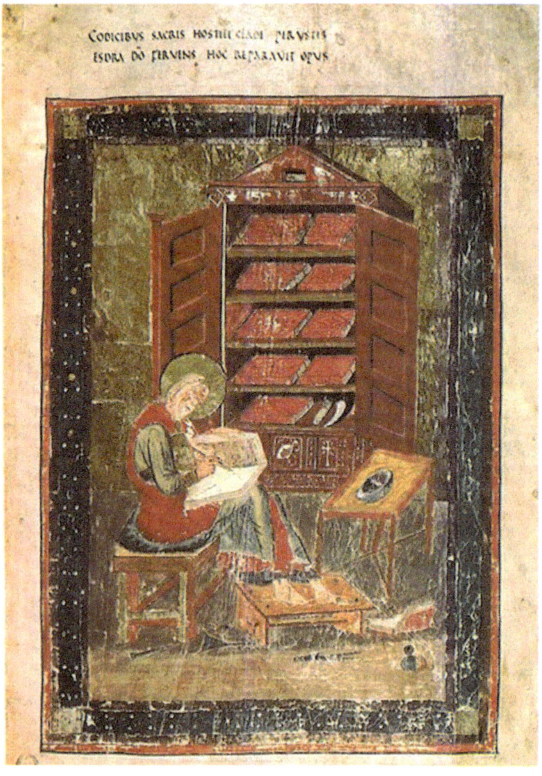

A page from the Codex Amiatinus or 'Wearmouth Bible' at is sometimes known. Three copies of this bible were produced at St. Peter's, Monkwearmouth and its sister monastery St Paul's in Jarrow. In June 716 A.D. Biscop's successor Ceolfrid embarked on a journey to Rome to present one of the bibles to the Pope. Coelfrid died in France whilst on route and what then happened to the bible remains unclear. Almost 1200 years later, however, at the end of the nineteenth century, the Codex Amiatinus housed in the Laurentian Library in Florence was authenticated as the only wholly surviving copy of the ancient Wearmouth Bible.

Monkwearmouth Pageant

A beautifully illustrated handbook printed in 1924 for the Monkwearmouth Pageant, which celebrated the 1,250th anniversary of the building of St Peter's Monastery. The pageant was held in the Victoria Hall between 18 and 21 June. Four episodes in the life of the town and monastery were re-enacted on the Victoria Hall stage.

1. The Consecration of St. Peter's Church, Monkwearmouth, 29 June 674 A.D.
2. The Meeting of the Weremouth Chapter, 2 June 716 A.D.
3. The Departure of Coelfrid 4 June 716 A.D.
4. May Day on Monkwearmouth Green 1497 A.D.

Hymns and psalms accompanied the first three episodes of the pageant.

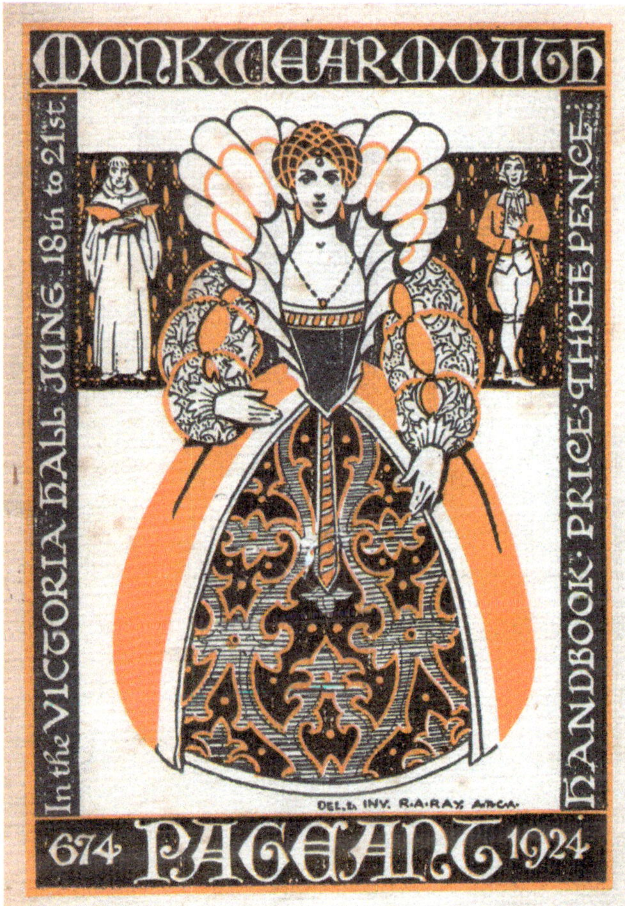

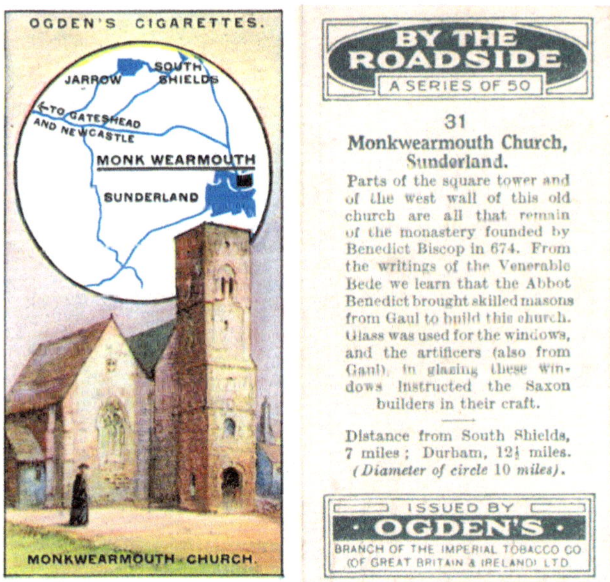

An Ogden's cigarette card released for their 'By The Roadside' series of cards in 1932. Number 31 featured Monkwearmouth Church, Sunderland.

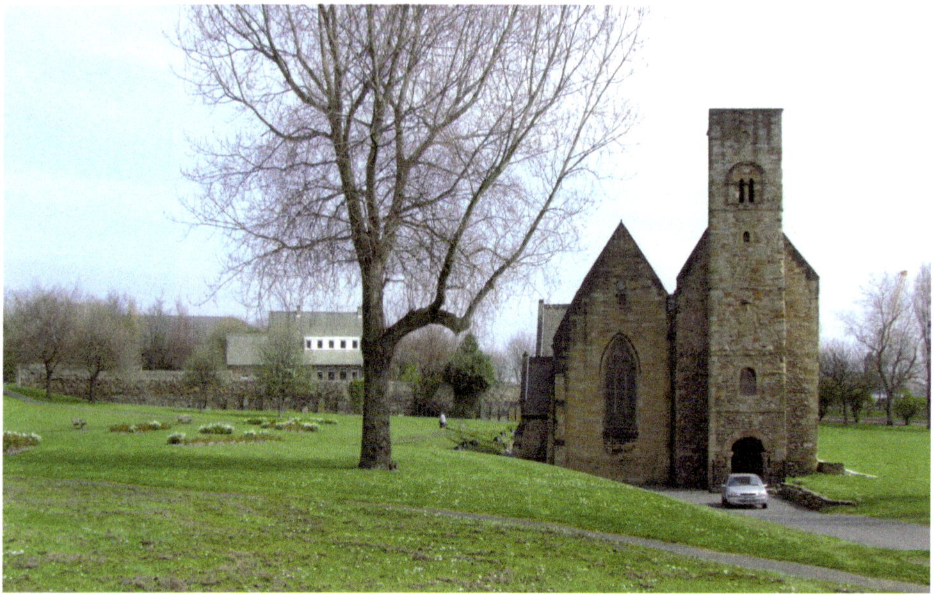

St Peter's Church

A photograph of the church taken in the spring of 2010, looking eastwards towards the sea. The image has been created to emulate the scene below.

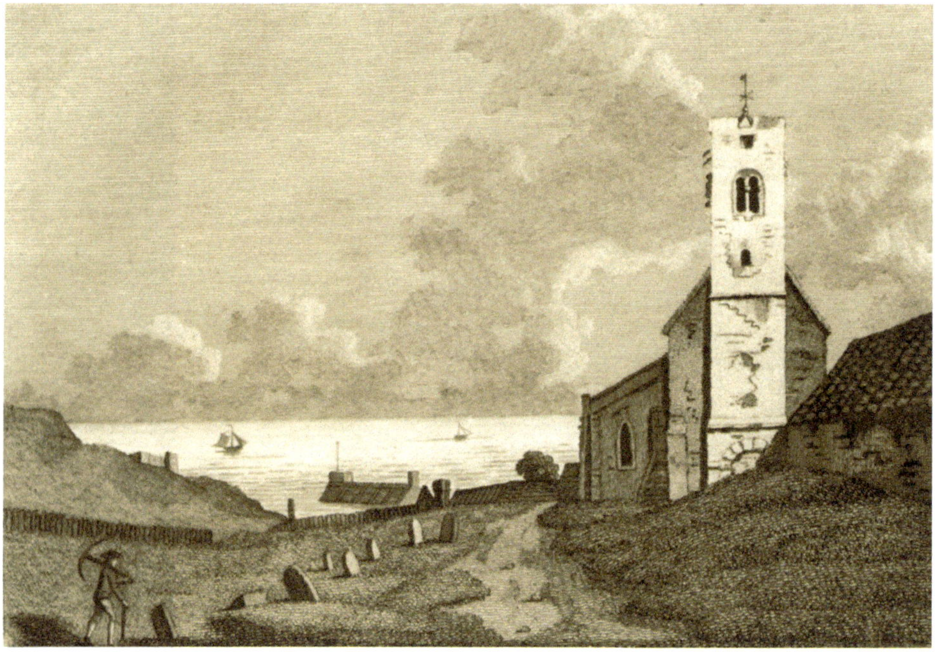

A copper engraving of St Peter's published in London in 1785 by Samuel Hooper. It is entitled "Monks Weremouth Durham" and was produced for Francis Grose's *The Antiquities of England and Wales.* If the topography within the print is accurate for its time, then great changes have taken place to the modern landscape, which is probably attributable to ship's ballast being dumped locally here throughout the eighteenth and nineteenth centuries.

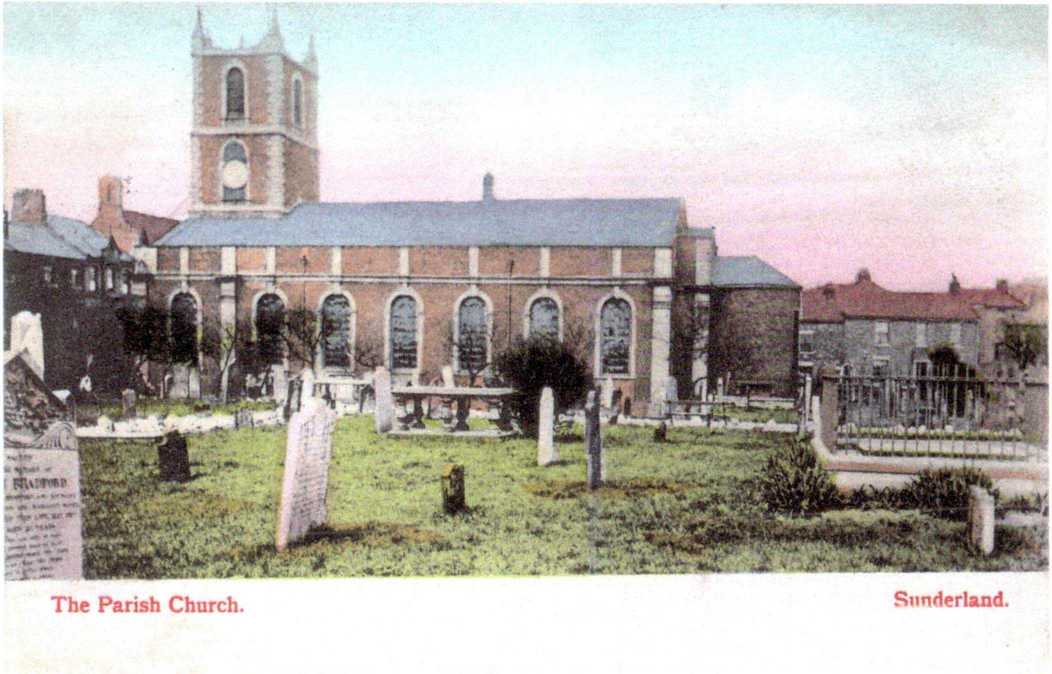

Sunderland Parish Church

The designer of The Church of Holy Trinity is not specifically known, but the first Rector Daniel Newcome and woodcarver William Etty are thought to have been involved. It was the first Parish Church of old Sunderland and also housed the town's Council Chamber and Library. The church (1719) was brick built in a 'baroque' style with stone mouldings around the windows and doors.

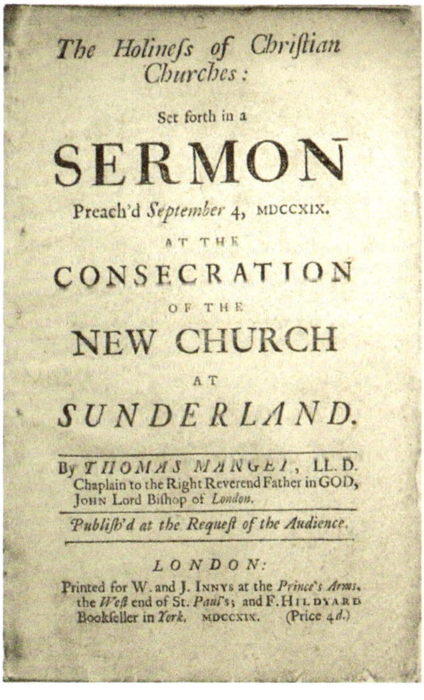

The Holineſs of Chriſtian Churches:

Set forth in a

SERMON

Preach'd *September* 4, MDCCXIX.

AT THE

CONSECRATION

OF THE

NEW CHURCH

AT

SUNDERLAND.

By *THOMAS MANGEY*, LL.D.
Chaplain to the Right Reverend Father in GOD,
JOHN Lord Biſhop of *London.*

Publiſh'd at the Requeſt of the Audience.

LONDON:

Printed for W. and J. INNYS at the *Prince's Arms*, the *Weſt* end of St. *Paul's*; and F. HILDYARD Bookſeller in *York.* MDCCXIX. (Price 4*d.*)

A rare survivor indeed from the early eighteenth century! A twenty-eight-page pamphlet of the sermon preached at the consecration of the 'new church' at Sunderland on 4 September 1719. It was published shortly afterwards (price 4*d*) 'at the request of the audience'. Thomas Mangey, Chaplain to the Right Reverend Father in GOD, John Robinson, Lord Bishop of London, preached the sermon entitled 'The Holiness of Christian Churches'. The Bishop of Durham later rewarded Dr. Mangey with a prebend in the cathedral church.

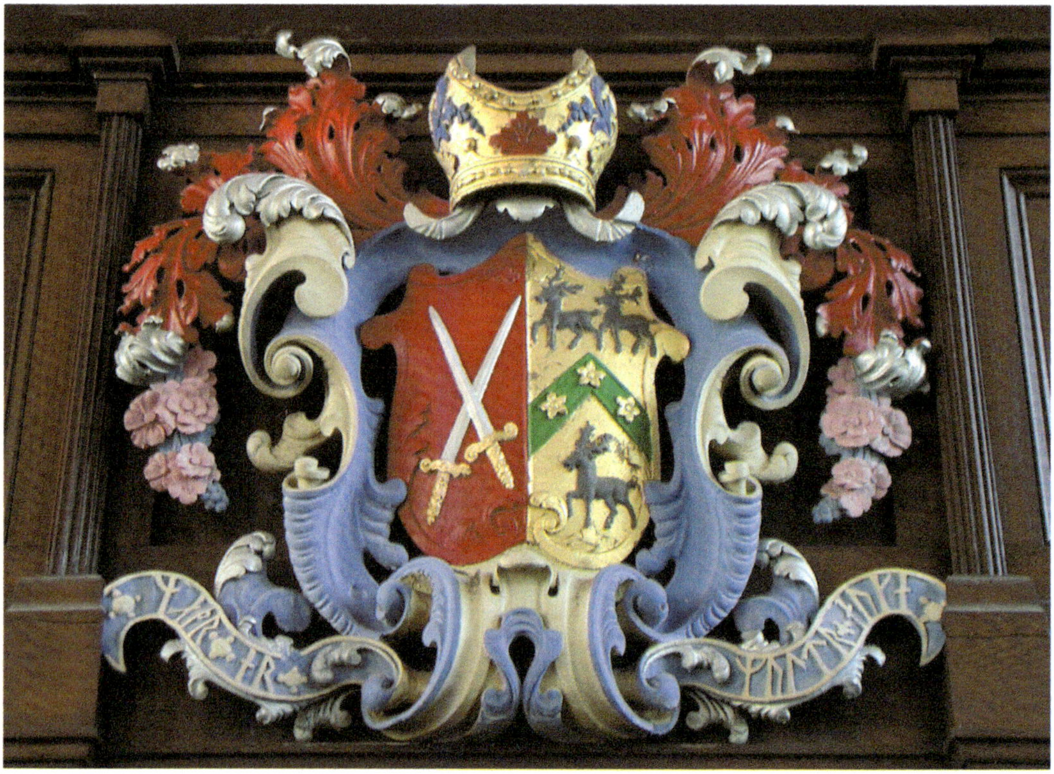

Bishop of London

The coat of arms of the Bishop of London, who performed the consecration ceremony. They are displayed on the panelling of the western gallery in the church.

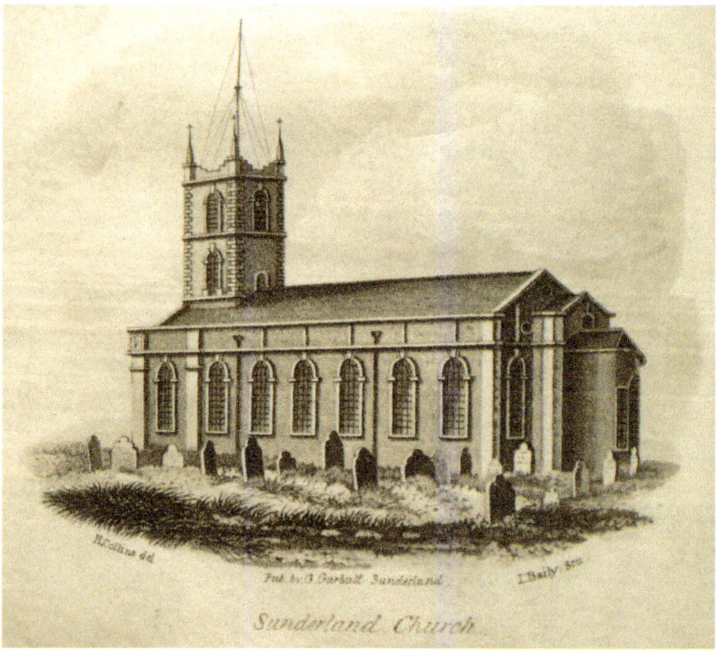

A print of Sunderland Parish Church published by George Garbutt in 1819. The circular apse beyond the chancel arch was added in 1735. In 1803 the church was given a new roof under the direction of Mr Wilson, architect of the cast iron bridge over the Wear. The cost of the roof and nineteen new windows was defrayed by the money obtained for the lead removed from the old roof. Holy Trinity Church is now in the care of the Churches Conservation Trust.

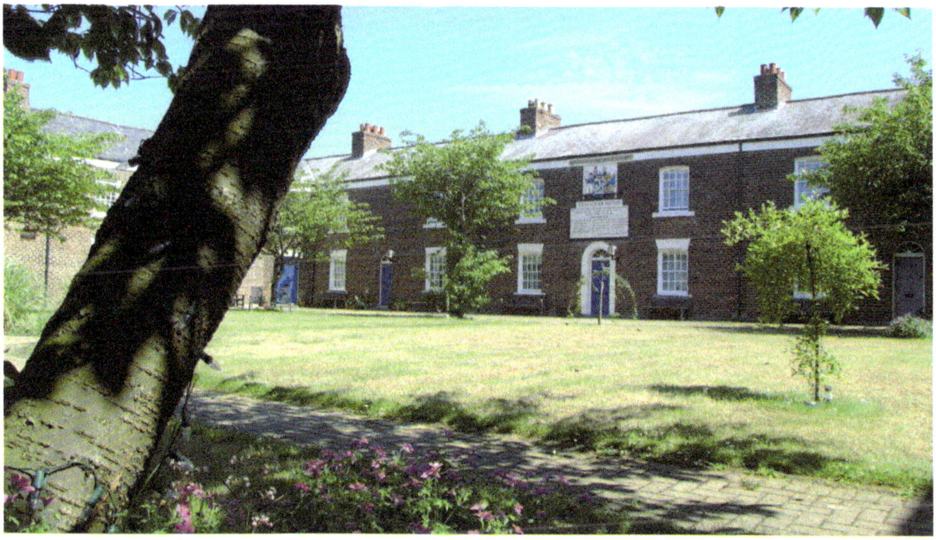

Trafalgar Square

A photograph of the merchant seamen's almshouses in Trafalgar Square Sunderland taken by the author in 2010. The square was erected by the trustees of the muster roll in 1840, some five years before the completion of its namesake in London!

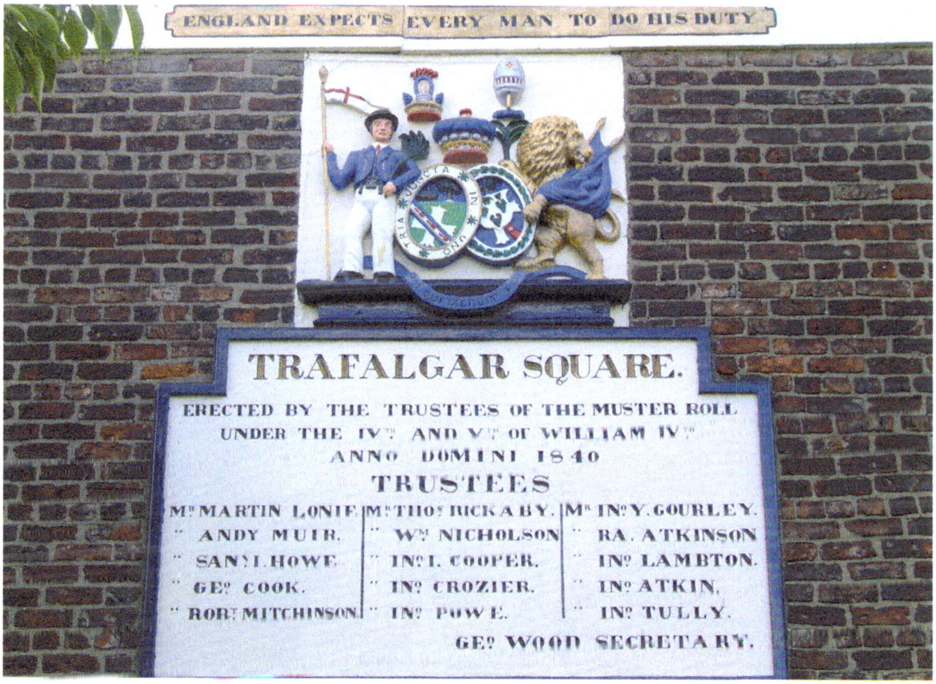

The dedication plaque over the central door of Trafalgar Square. Above it are the words of the signal that Lord Nelson sent from his flagship HMS *Victory* at the commencement of the Battle of Trafalgar in 1805. "England Expects Every Man To Do His Duty". Sixty-six Sunderland sailors served at the Battle of Trafalgar in twenty-five ships of the line and three frigates. The full British fleet totalled thirty-three vessels.

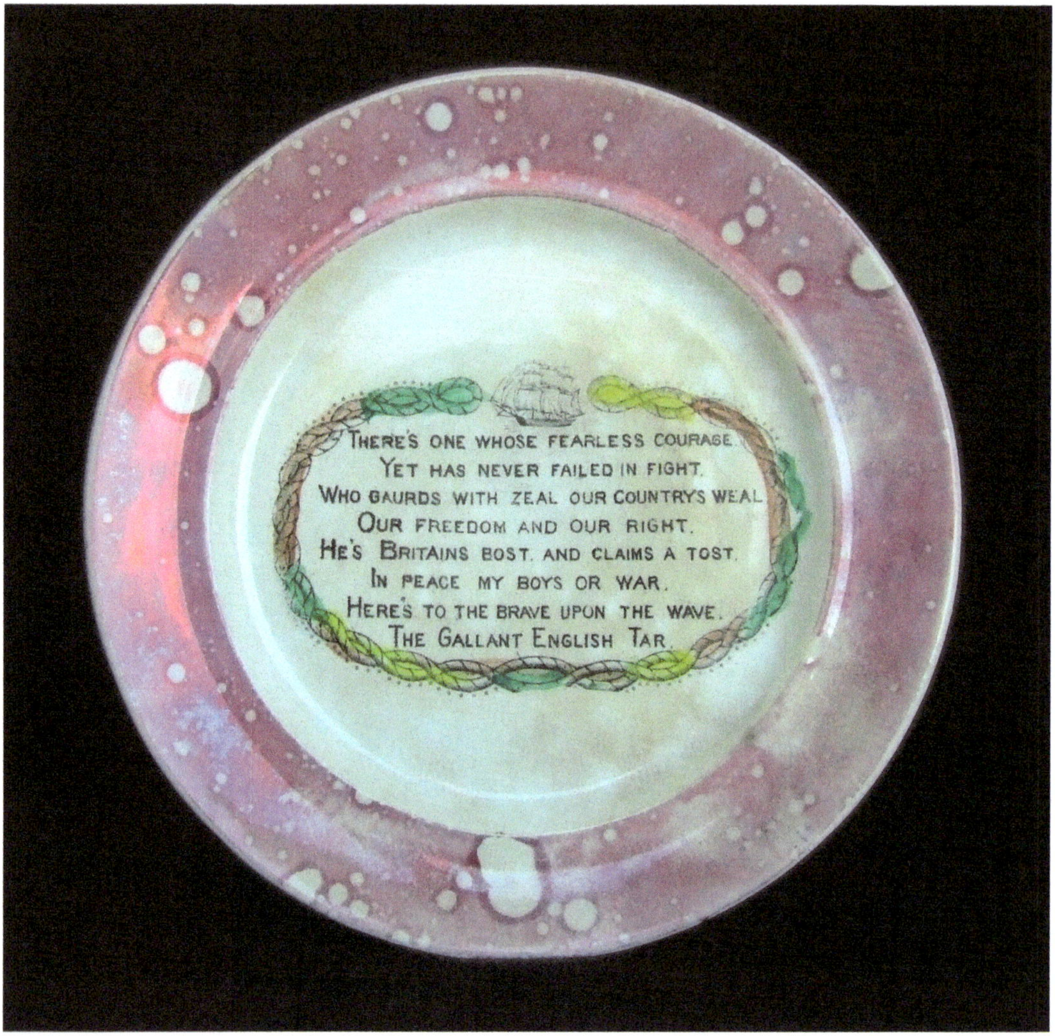

The Battle of Trafalgar

An expression of the high regard held for our country's sailors as displayed on a plate manufactured in mid nineteenth century Sunderland. In 2005, on the bicentenary of the Battle of Trafalgar, Anna Horatia Tribe the great-great-great granddaughter of Lord Nelson and Lady Hamilton said of the sixty-six Sunderland sailors: "My family is proud that our ancestor had such men, for without them, this island would not have kept its freedom".

Trafalgar

The Britons mourn, what else can Briton do
While bleeding Nelson rises to her view
Still is there cause for triumph when she shews
The captured colours of our vanquished foes.
And greater still when Fame was heard to say
All, all was Nelson's on that glorious day.

Verse on a jug manufactured at Phillips Pottery, North Hylton.

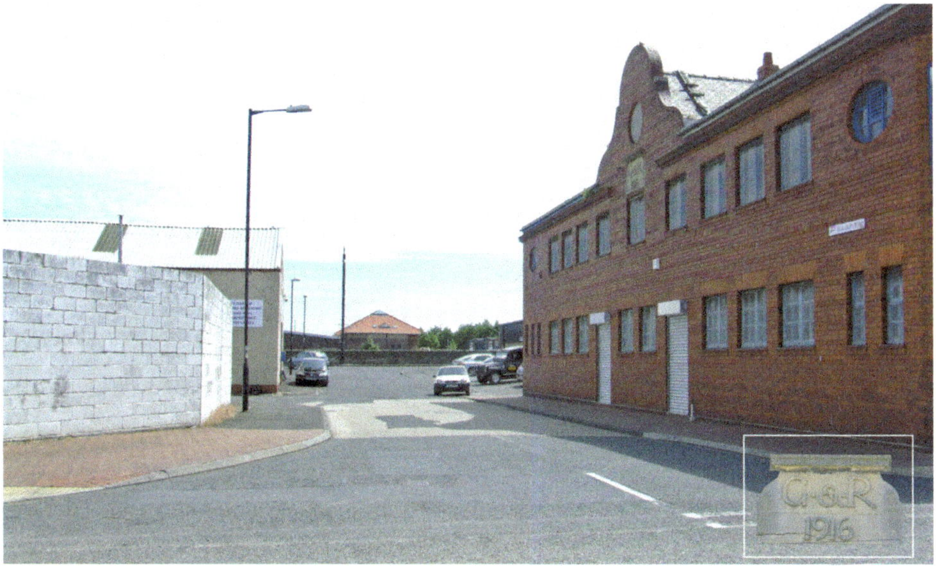

Glaholm & Robson's Ropery

This picture shows the old line of Moor Street in Hendon. In the 1950s, the building to the right (shown as a school on earlier maps) was the social club and canteen of the Glaholm & Robson wire rope works. Little else remains of their wire rope manufactory, which started business here in 1857. Instigator Thomas Glaholm was also a founder member of the *Sunderland Echo*. The above building has a date stone for 1916, with a G&R monogram above it (see inset). The factory closed in 1968 and was demolished thereafter. Two generations of the author's family worked here.

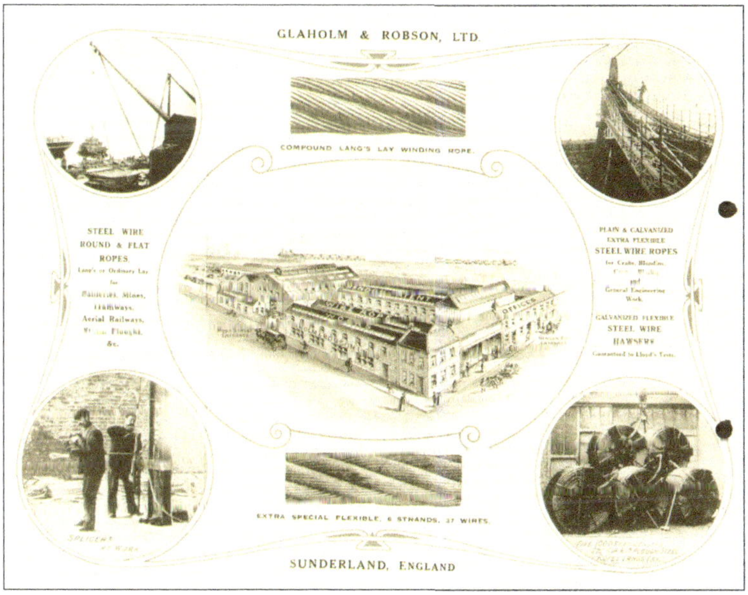

A page from a Glaholm & Robson advertising catalogue printed around 1910 showcasing the range of products, their applications and large factory complex. *Image copyright Beamish Museum Ltd.*

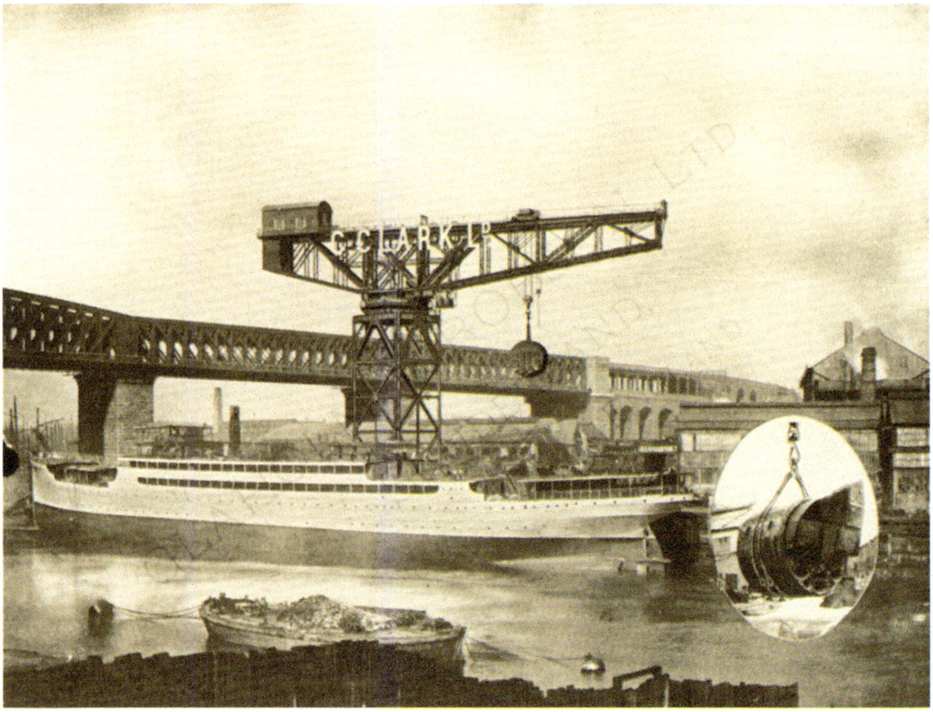

Glaholm & Robson Crane

Another page from the 1910 Glaholm & Robson catalogue. The huge hammerhead crane at George Clark's Marine Engine Works makes use of a of a G&R wire rope to hoist an engine component onto a ship. *Image copyright Beamish Museum Ltd.*

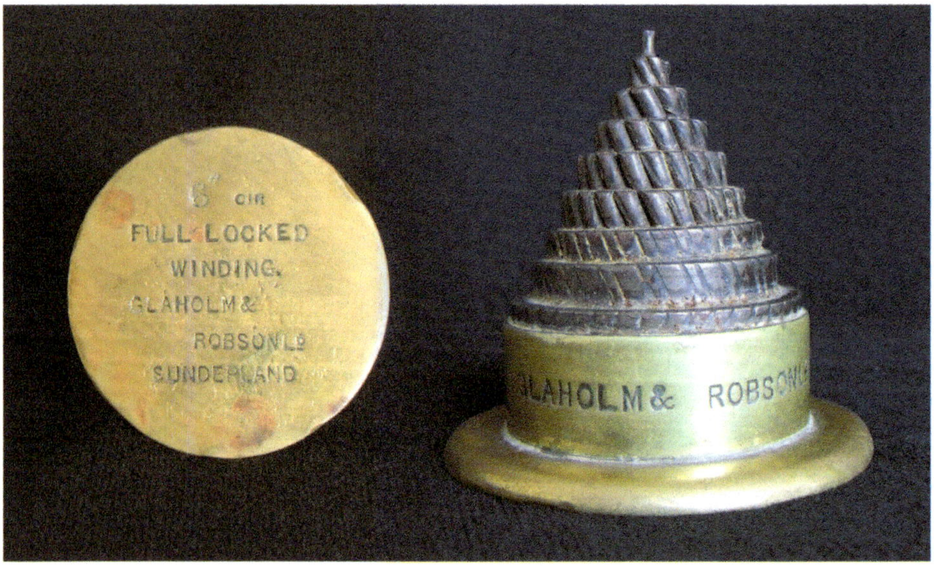

A small sample of a Glaholm & Robson wire rope that has been incorporated into a paperweight. The rope has been pared back and lathe-turned into a conical shape to show the many interwoven steel wires that gave the product its great strength and flexibility.

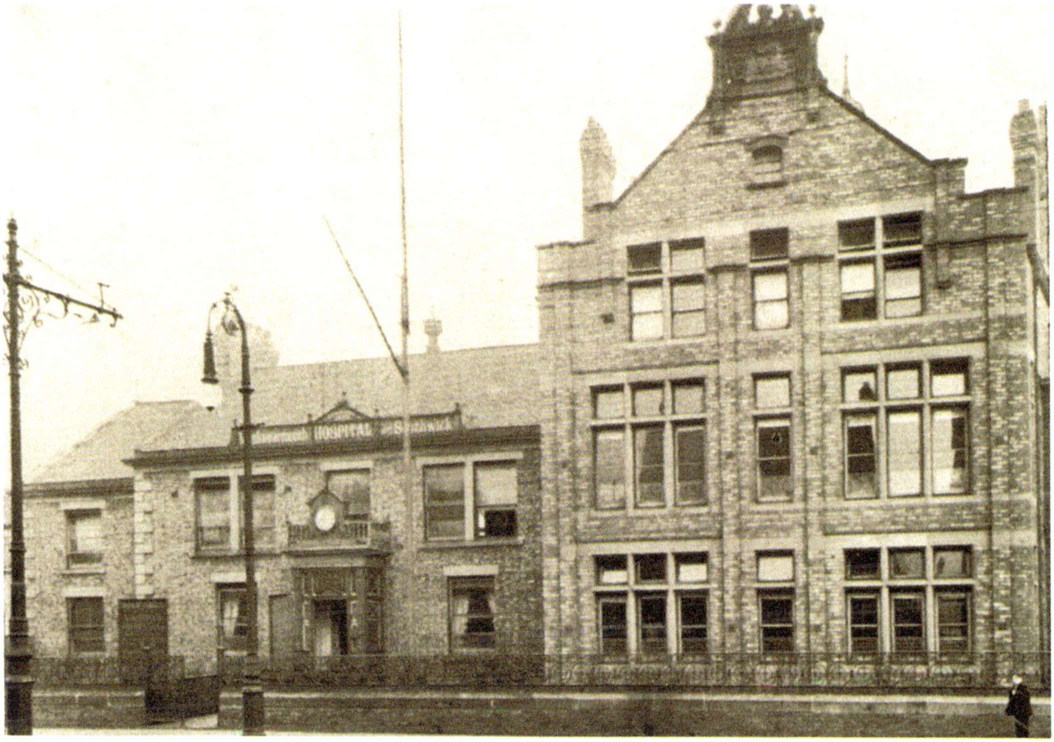

Monkwearmouth and Southwick Hospital

A photograph of Monkwearmouth and Southwick Hospital around 1904. Originally the home of ship owner Ralph Preston in Broad Street, (now called Roker Avenue) it was purchased and transformed by Mr Tyzack, one of the presidents of the dispensary's inauguration. A dispensary had operated from 1873 in the Workman's Hall, but moved to the above premises a year later and it was given the name of 'hospital' in the 1890s. A new purpose built 6-acre site was completed in 1932 at nearby Newcastle Road.

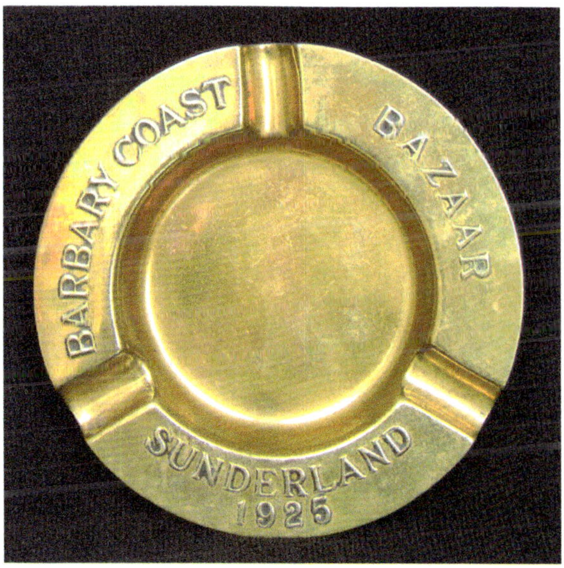

The Duke of York, later George VI visited Sunderland for the first time on 22 October 1925 to open a bazaar in aid of the extension fund for the Monkwearmouth and Southwick Hospital. Sir James Marr had launched the appeal that same year.

The brass ashtray (right) is thought to have been sold during these fund raising activities.

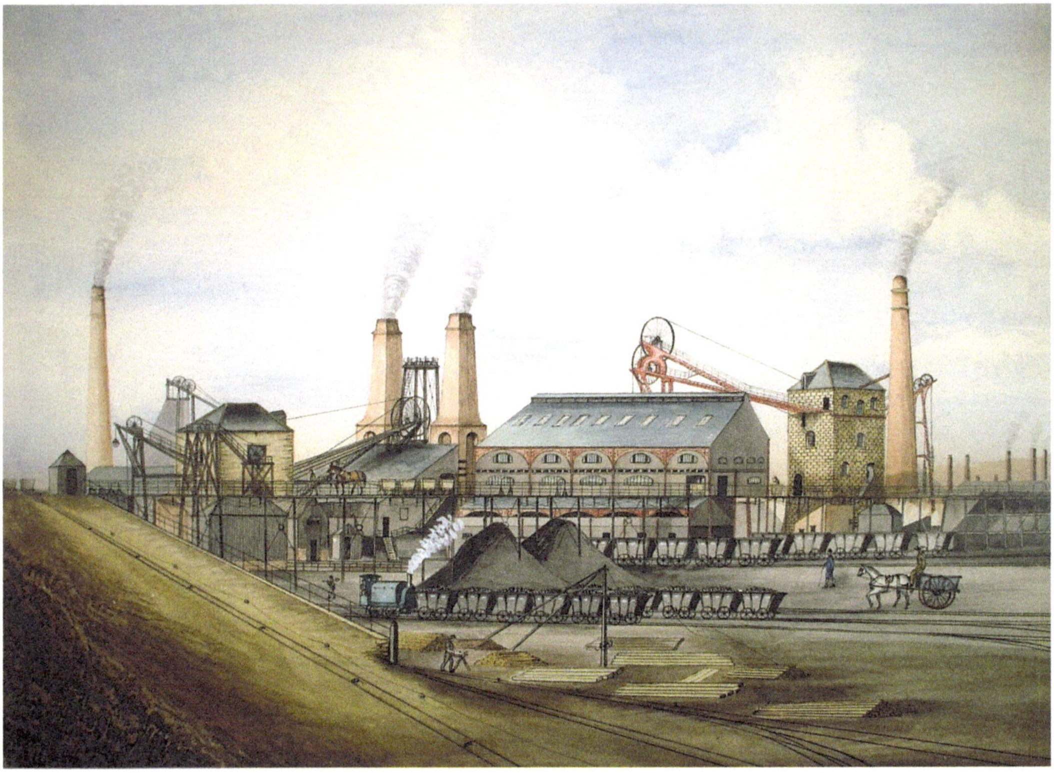

Monkwearmouth Colliery

An 1879 painting of the mine by R. Kane. The sinking of the first shaft began at Pemberton Main Colliery (later known as Monkwearmouth or Wearmouth Colliery) in May 1826. Seven years later, on 12 July 1833 a high quality coal seam was discovered at a depth of 180 fathoms. Seams discovered at 267 and 287 fathoms over the next few years meant it was the deepest working mine in the world. *Image copyright Beamish Museum Ltd.*

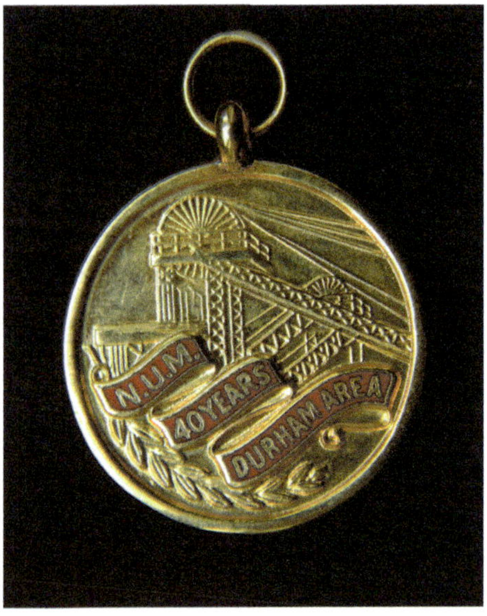

A forty-year NUM medal for the Durham Area. The recipient was miner John Keegan, who worked at Monkwearmouth Colliery for forty-five years.

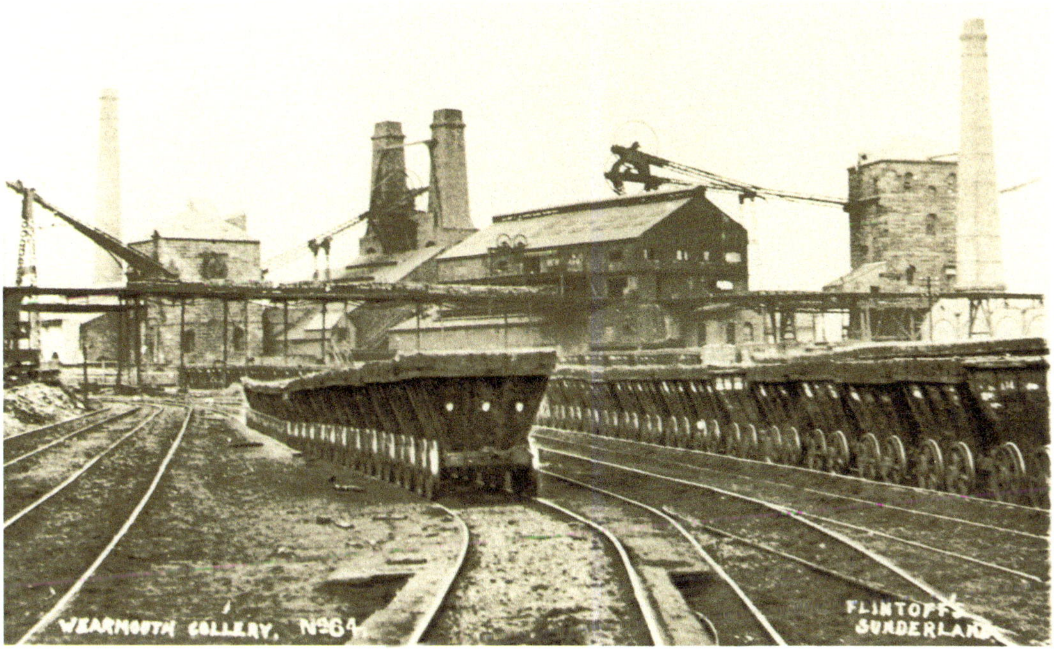

Durham Coalfield

A Flintoff photographic view of the colliery that dates to 1890. It became Sunderland's largest pit and the last mine in the Durham Coalfield to operate, before its closure on 24 November 1993. *Image copyright Beamish Museum Ltd.*

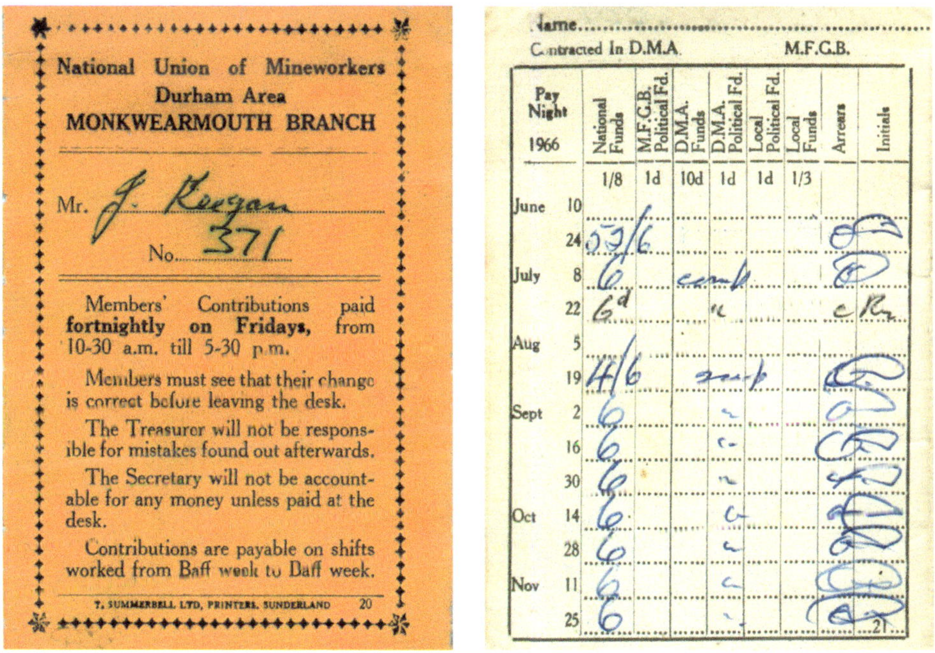

National Union of Mineworkers
Durham Area
MONKWEARMOUTH BRANCH

Mr. J. Keegan

No. 371

Members' Contributions paid **fortnightly on Fridays,** from 10-30 a.m. till 5-30 p.m.

Members must see that their change is correct before leaving the desk.

The Treasurer will not be responsible for mistakes found out afterwards.

The Secretary will not be accountable for any money unless paid at the desk.

Contributions are payable on shifts worked from Baff week to Baff week.

T. SUMMERBELL LTD, PRINTERS, SUNDERLAND 20

Name...

Contracted In D.M.A. M.F.C.B.

Pay Night 1966	National Funds	M.F.G.B. Political Fd.	D.M.A. Funds	D.M.A. Political Fd.	Local Political Fd.	Local Funds	Arrears	Initials
	1/8	1d	10d	1d	1d	1/3		
June 10								
24	53/6							
July 8	6							
22	6d							
Aug 5								
19	4/6							
Sept 2	6							
16	6							
30	6							
Oct 14	6							
28	6							
Nov 11	6							
25	6							

21

A National Union of Mineworkers, Monkwearmouth Branch, union card that belonged to miner John Keegan.

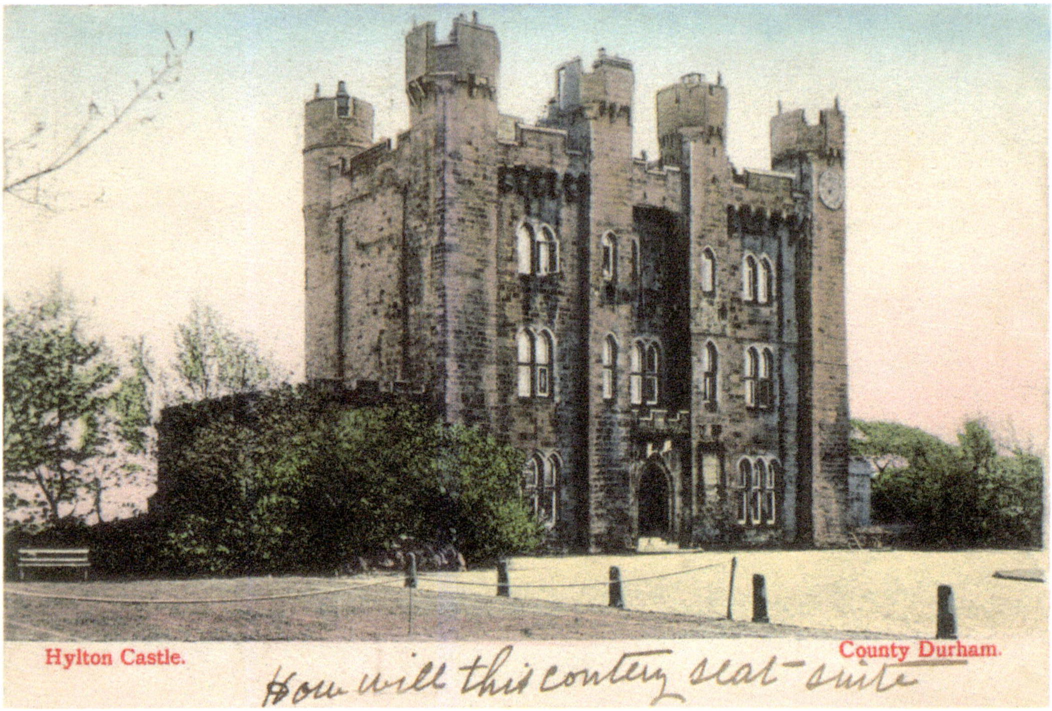

Hylton Castle

An attractive picture postcard of Hylton Castle that dates to around 1903. The stone castle was built in the 1400s by Baron William De Hylton, but a fortified manor house is said to have been on this site after the Norman Conquest. It was the principal seat of the Hylton (or Hilton) family until the demise of the last baron in 1746. The castle is famously known for its ghost called *The Cauld Lad of Hylton.*

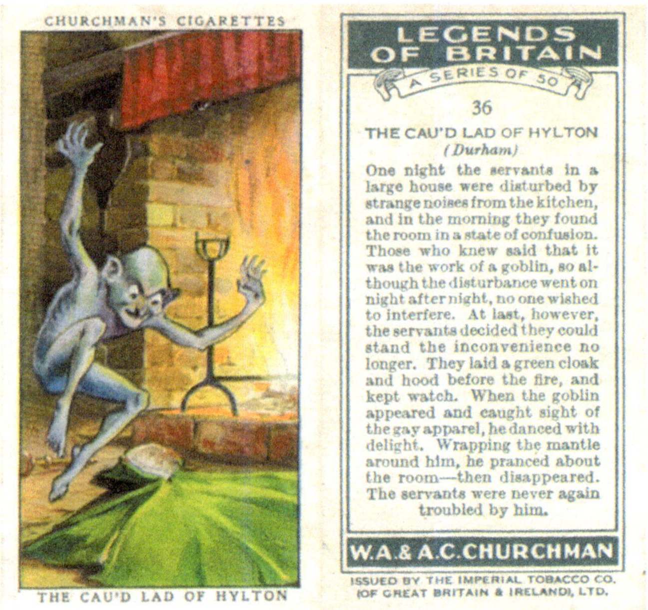

One of a series of fifty cigarette cards issued by the Imperial Tobacco Co. for Churchman's in 1936 called 'Legends of Britain'. In the mid sixteenth century stable lad Robert Skelton was caught sleeping instead of working by Baron Robert Hytlon, who killed him in a fit of rage. It is often said that the Cauld Lad of Hylton is the ghost of Robert Skelton. As the Cauld Lad disappeared (see left) he was heard to say, "Here's a cloak and here's a hood. The Cauld Lad of Hylton will do no more good!"

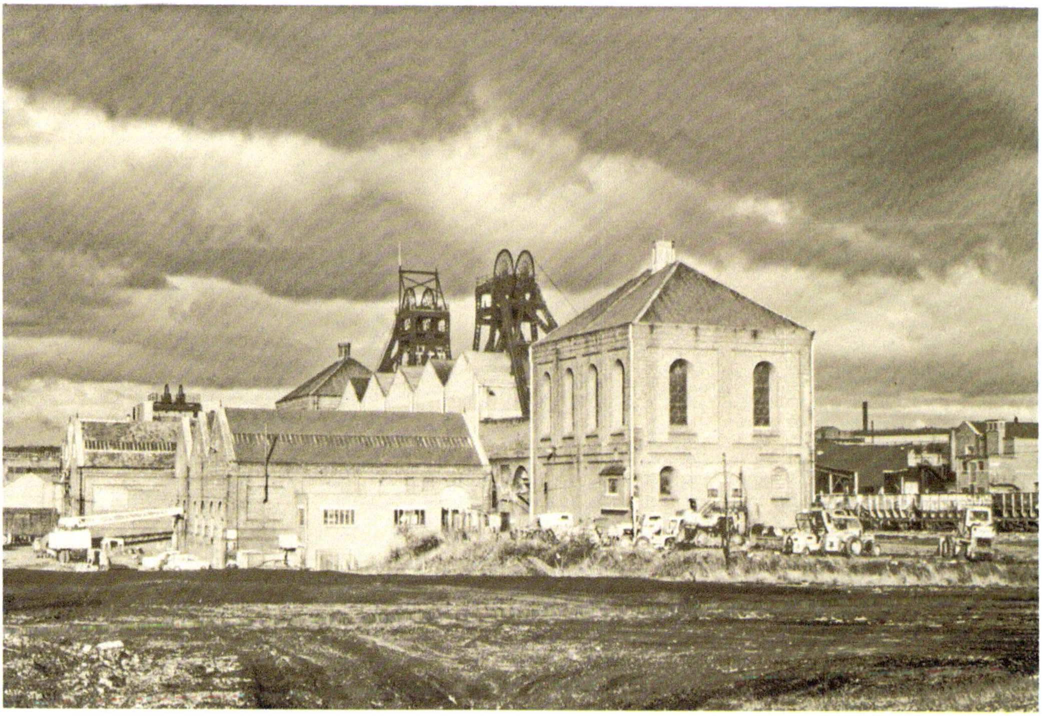

Hytlon Colliery

Sinking began at Hytlon Colliery on 17 May 1897 and the pit opened in 1900. By 1930, over 1800 workers were employed at the mine. The colliery closed on 13 July 1979. *Image copyright Beamish Museum Ltd.*

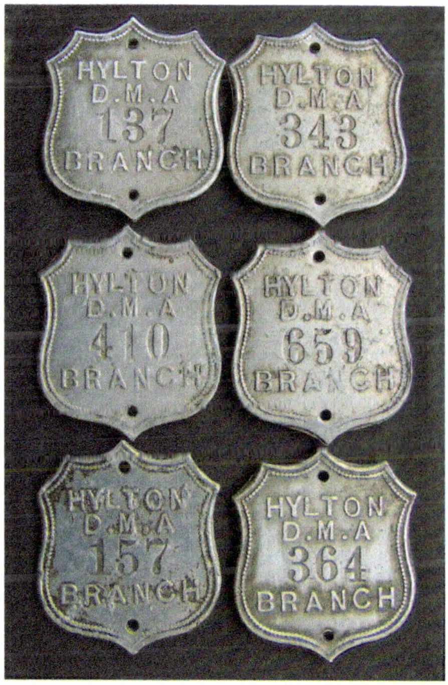

Durham Miner's Association (DMA) tokens for the Hylton Colliery Branch. The first meeting of the DMA took place 20 November 1869 at the Market Hotel, Durham.

Members wore their tokens for lodge meetings so a record of attendance could be kept. The two holes in the tokens were to enable members to stitch them onto their clothing.

The National Union of Mineworkers was formed in January 1945.

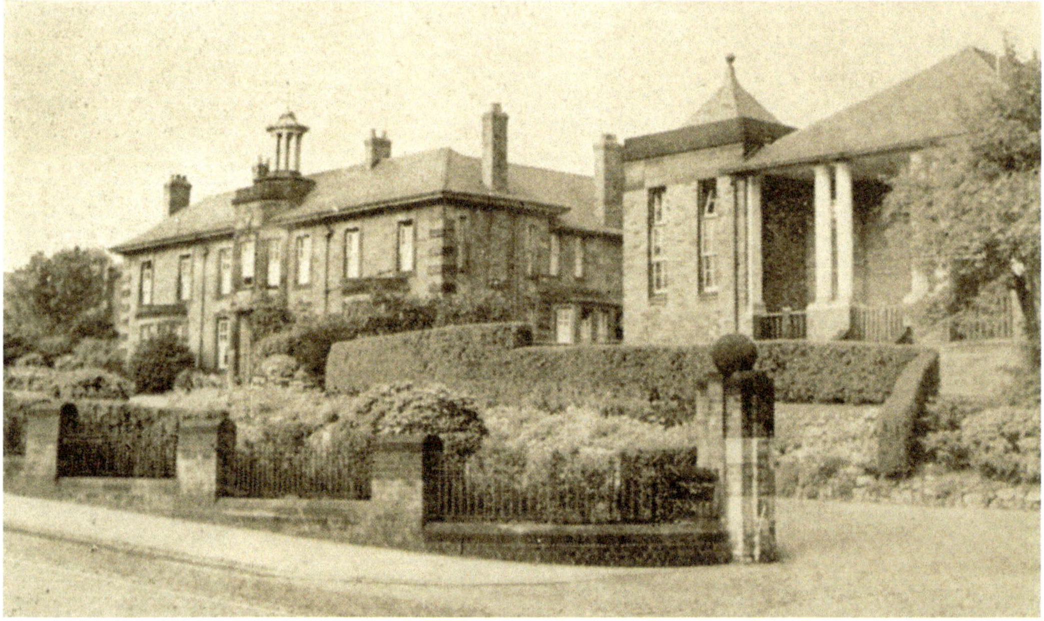

Children's Hospital

A photograph of the new Children's Hospital in Durham Road, which opened on 29 May 1912. It was designed by W. & T. R. Milburn and built by contractor Mr J. Huntley at a cost of £21,000. Mr. John S. G. Pemberton provided two acres of the Barnes Estate for the project, but additional land was also purchased by the committee. The new hospital alleviated the growing problems of a lack of space at the Royal Infirmary for adult care. The two wards in the Children's Hospital were named the Gordon and Priestman Pavilions, after Frederick Gordon JP and Lady Priestman.

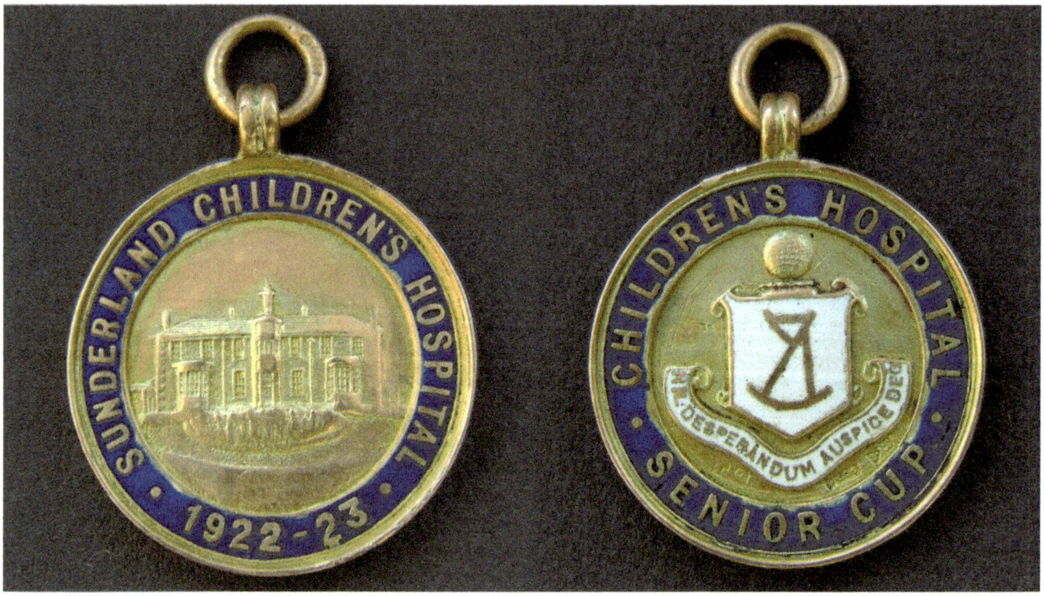

An extremely fine children's hospital senior cup medal presented for the 1922-23 football season. The medal recipient, a great uncle of the author, was Albert Cockerill.

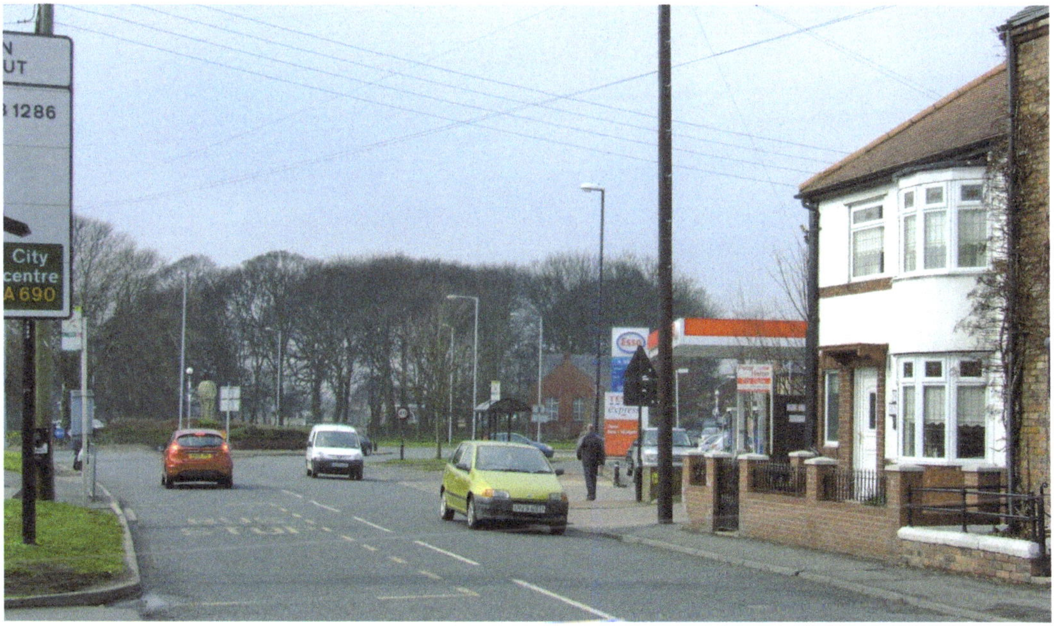

The Crossroads, East Herrington

Looking along Silksworth Road to the crossroads at East Herrington in 2010. The junction is better known today as the 'Board Inn Roundabout', but the villages of East and Middle Herrington are of great age and are marked on Bowen's mid eighteenth century map shown on page 3. This image has been created to replicate the old view below.

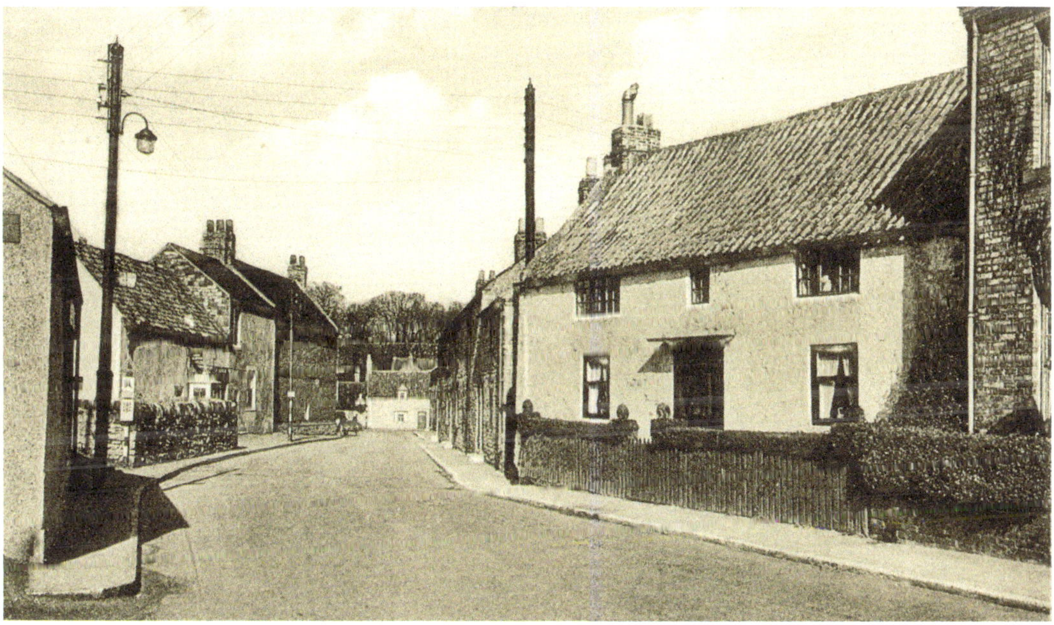

The same view as seen on a 1930s postcard, when the village of East Herrington still retained much of its old character. The butcher's shop and post office are to the left of the picture. The blacksmith's forge and cottage can be seen at the far end of the lane (centre left).

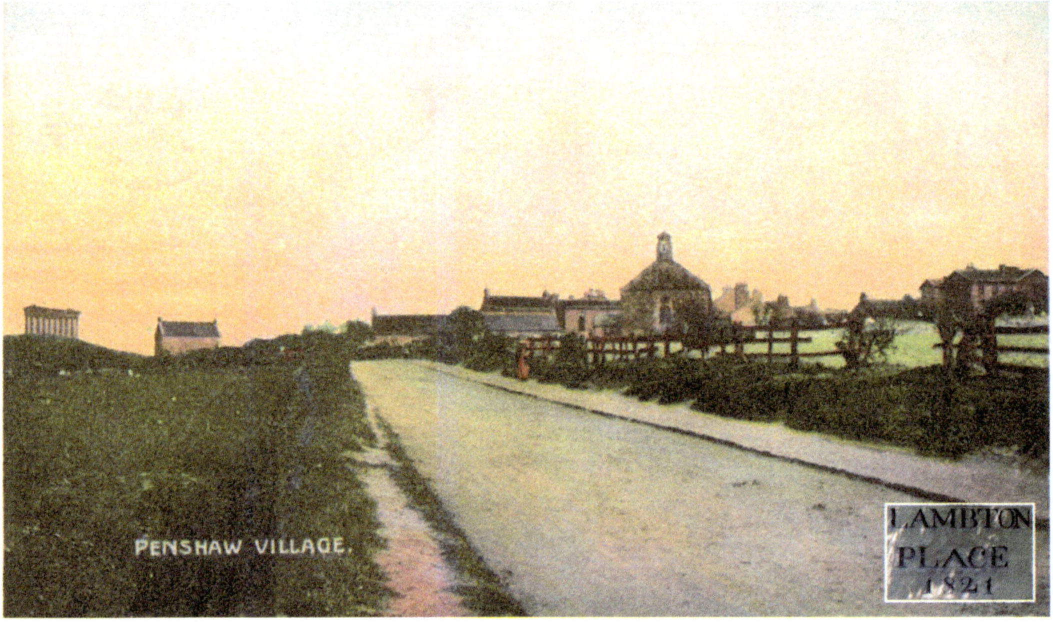

Penshaw Village

An unusual postcard view looking along Back Lane to Old Penshaw Village around 1926. To the left is a glimpse of Penshaw Monument. Centre right is Lambton Place, which leads to All Saints Church (1746) and its burial grounds, which are situated on both sides of the footpath. The date stone for Lambton Place is shown as an inset.

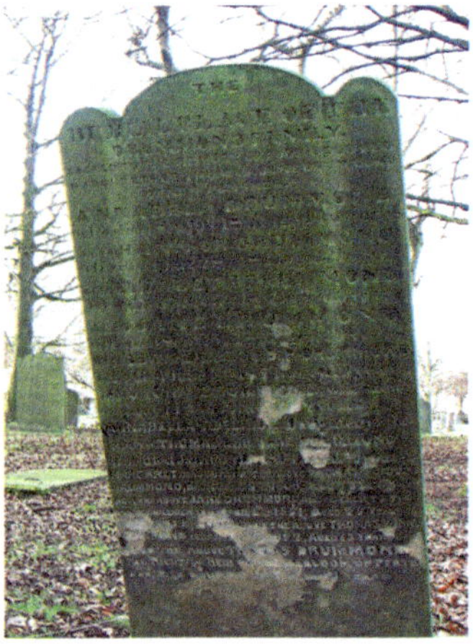

James Drummond third Duke and sixth Earl of Perth died of his wounds after the battle of Culloden in 1746. Or did he? There is a local legend that he survived and took refuge in Biddick on the Wear where he married Elizabeth Armstrong, a local pitman's daughter. Here, he lived and worked in obscurity as a ferryman. Detail on a Drummond family grave residing in All Saints Church graveyard, Penshaw, seems to corroborate this claim. In 1831, in a case heard in the House of Lords, his grandson Thomas was declared "nearest and lawful heir" but failed in his quest to acquire the Perth Estates.

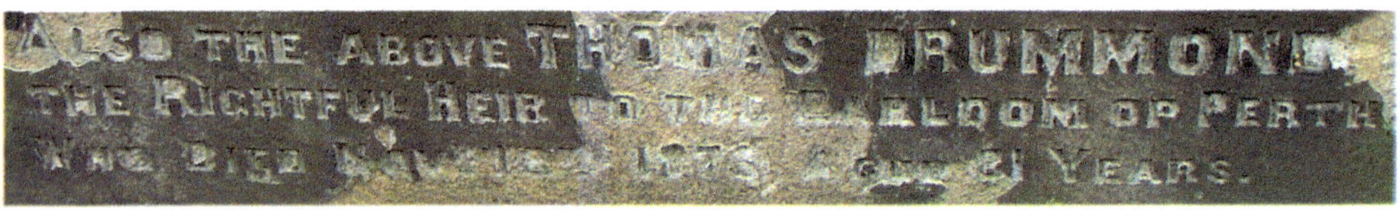

Grandson Thomas Drummond took his claim to be the 'rightful heir to the Earldom of Perth' to his grave with him on 18 November 1873. Today sadly, this headstone lies broken and frost damaged.

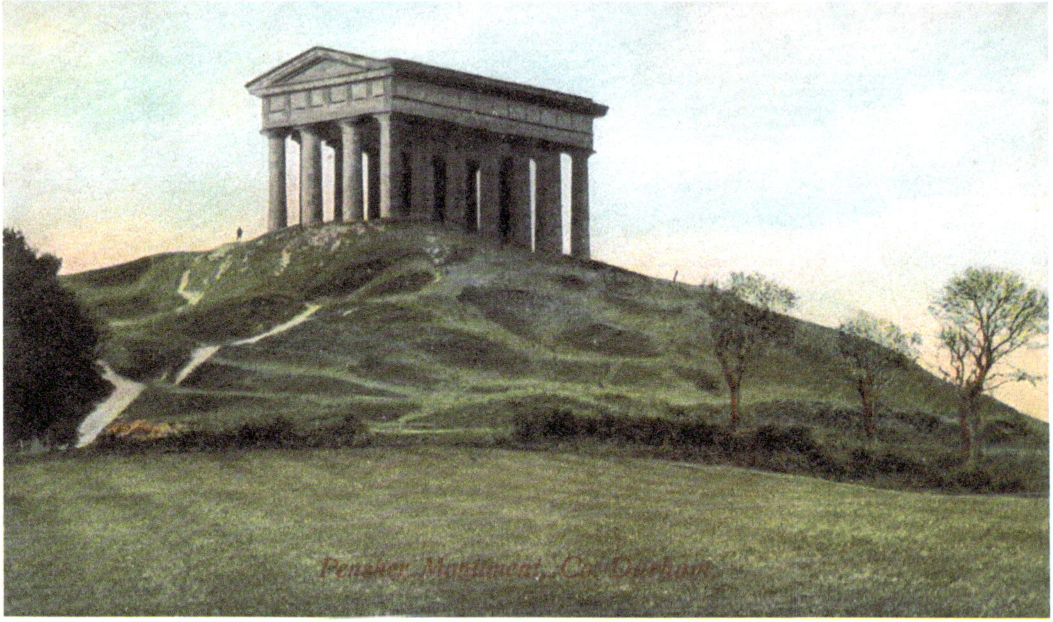

Penshaw Monument

Penshaw Monument or more correctly The Earl of Durham's Monument as seen on a picture postcard that dates to around 1905. The monument was built in 1844, as a half size replica of the *Temple of Hepheastus* in Athens and is dedicated to John George Lambton the first Earl of Durham. It was designed by John and Benjamin Green and the builder was Thomas Pratt of Sunderland. It has been suggested that some of the large base stones of the monument may have come from the ancient river structure Brigg Stones at Hylton, which was dismantled at the beginning of the nineteenth century.

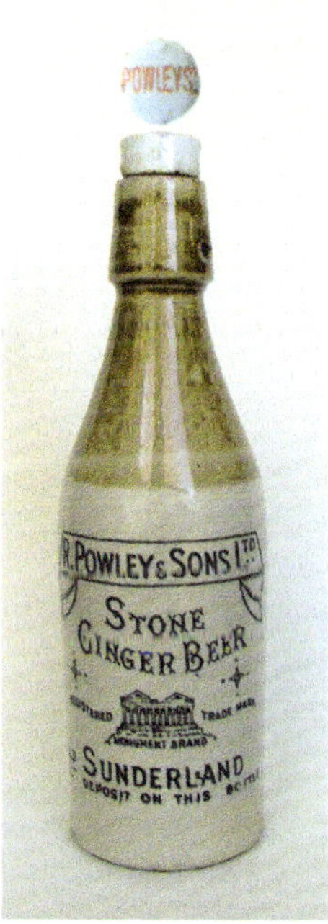

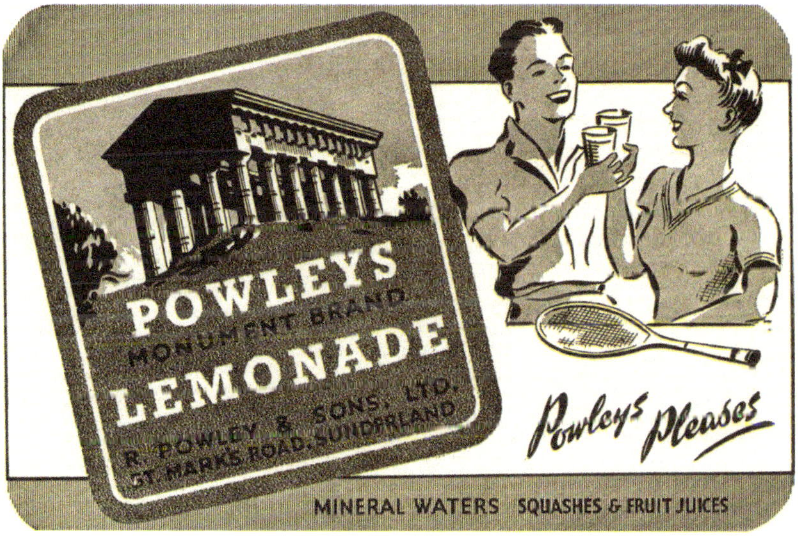

A 'monument brand' stone ginger beer bottle and an advertisement for the company that produced its contents – R. Powley & Sons Ltd. of St. Mark's Road, Sunderland.

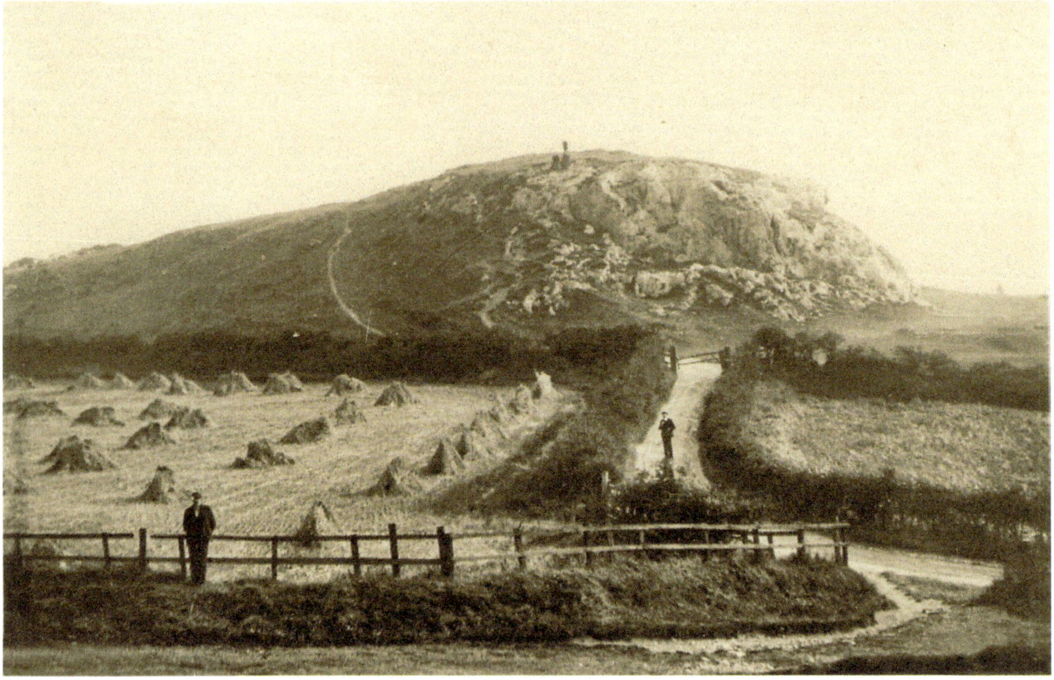

Tunstall Hills

Tunstall Hills, or more accurately, a view of Rocky Hill photographed from the slopes of Green Hill around harvest time in the early 1900s. The hills are an outcrop of magnesium limestone and were once part of an ancient tropical barrier reef that stretched south to Hartlepool. The two hills are one of the most prominent landmarks of the East Durham coastline and were known as the *Maidens Paps* to mariners who worked the coastal trade routes.

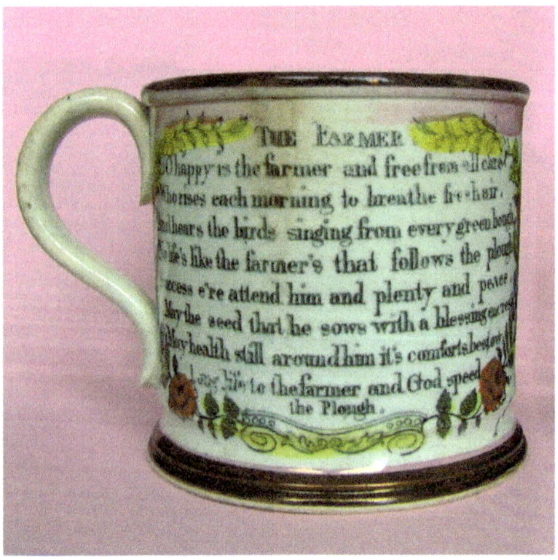

The verse on this mid nineteenth century Sunderland lustre mug could have been written especially for the chap in the above picture!

"Oh happy is the farmer and free from all care, who rises each morning to breathe fresh air. Who hears the birds singing from every green bough, no life's like the farmer's that follows the plough."

A farmer's life style must have seemed a million miles away from the dirt and grime of a working life in the port, shipyards or collieries!

Note the appearance of both pink and copper lustre on the mug. When the gold-based lustre paint solution was applied to white pottery, a pink colour was produced upon firing but when applied to brown earthenware, a copper colour resulted. To produce the copper lustre on the rim and foot of this white-bodied mug therefore, a fine ring coating of brown earthenware slip will have first been applied to the piece.

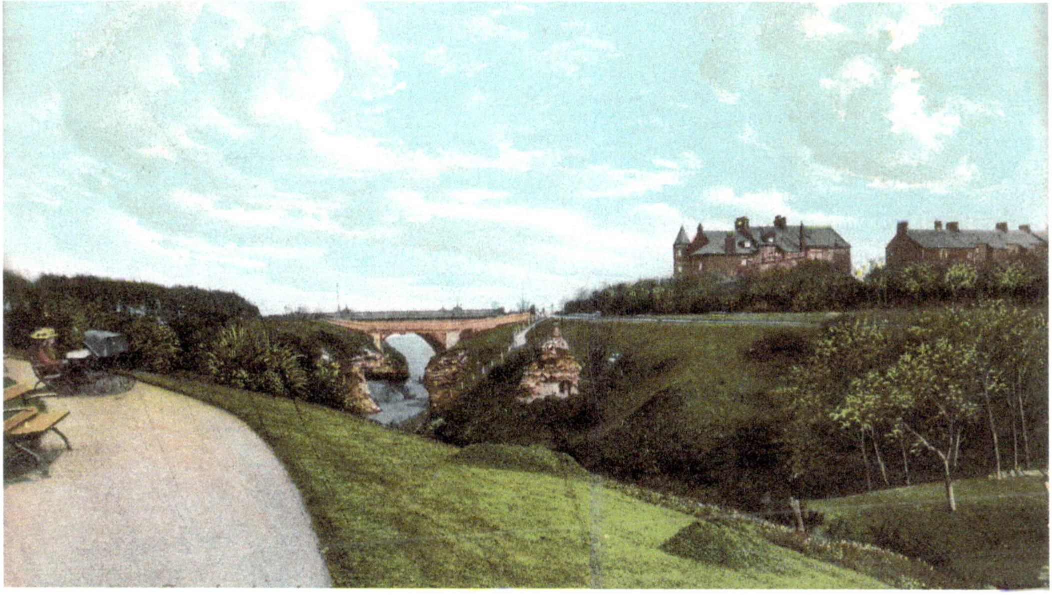

Roker Park

A lovely view of Roker Park taken around 1904. The land for the development of this splendid Victorian park was donated by Sir Hedworth Williamson and the Church Commissioners. Following the opening of the park and the erection of a road bridge across the ravine in 1880, Roker became a popular seaside resort.

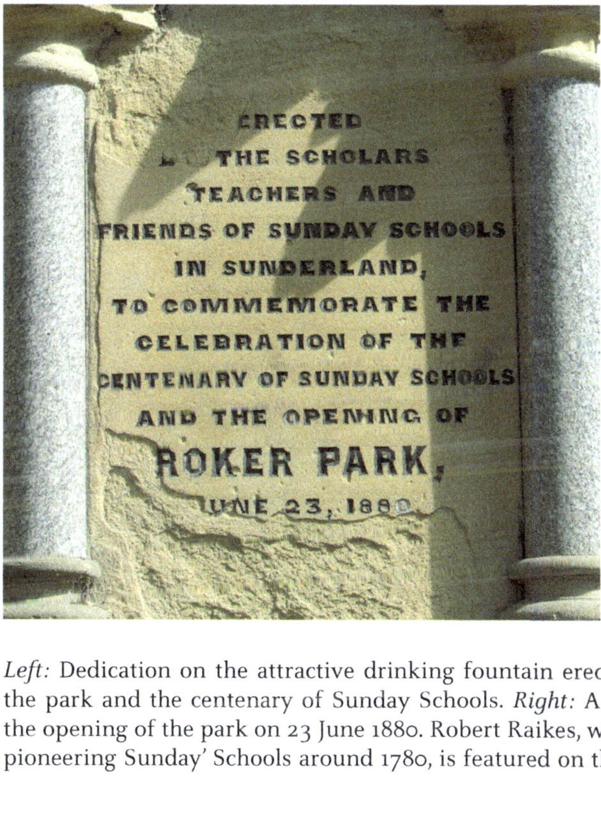

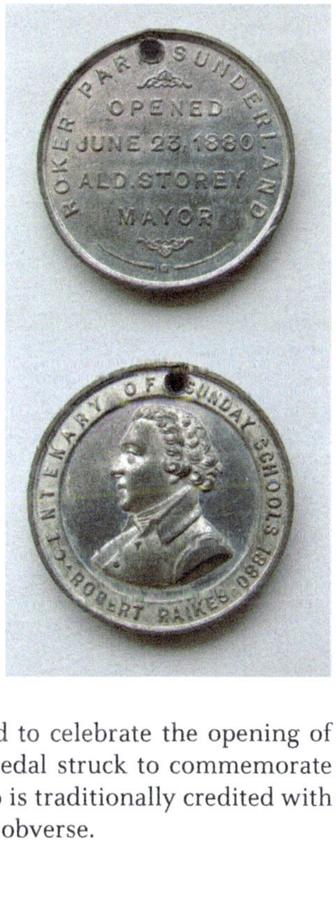

Left: Dedication on the attractive drinking fountain erected to celebrate the opening of the park and the centenary of Sunday Schools. *Right:* A medal struck to commemorate the opening of the park on 23 June 1880. Robert Raikes, who is traditionally credited with pioneering Sunday' Schools around 1780, is featured on the obverse.

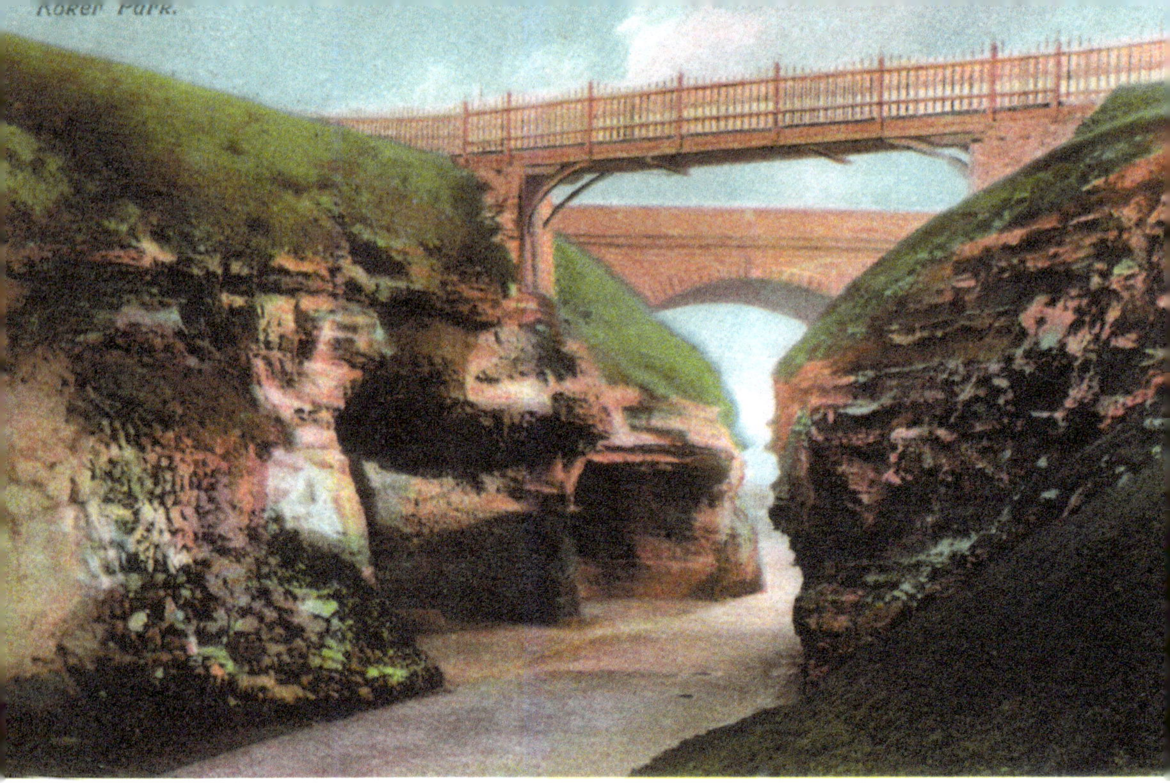

Roker Ravine and the Monk's Cavern or Spotty's Hole

Roker Ravine gives direct access to the beach from the park – a feature that was much admired by visitors to the resort. On the south side of the ravine (right) just beyond the limestone protrusion in the above picture is the entrance to a cave, now sealed, that tradition tells us was the entrance to an underground passageway that wound its way to the ancient monastery of St Peter's at Monkwearmouth.

In his '*History of Sunderland*' published in 1819, author George Garbutt tells us:

"This secret way, which most probably has been wrought by the monks, with a view to alluding their enemies in times of invasion or civil commotion, was some time ago partially explored by the inhabitants of Monkwearmouth. After they had advanced a little way from the entrance, they found the passage perfectly good in general allowing them to walk upright, and entirely hewn out of the limestone rock, with which this place is surrounded. Having proceeded a considerable distance in the direction of the site of the monastery, without meeting any considerable impediment they thought it prudent to return, on account of the danger of coming into contact with foul air, to which they might have been exposed by a further progress".

The cave's later name of Spotty's Hole is said to be attributable to a foreign sailor, who after finding his way to the port of Sunderland in a ship, took up residence there. Historian George Garbutt explains:

"Being unable to speak the English language, his daily subsistence was gained among the farm houses in the neighbourhood, where he endeavoured to make himself understood by means of signs and was known by the name of Spotty, on account of the variegated spots on his upper garment. Having lived for some time in this subterraneous habitation, he suddenly disappeared and was supposed to have either died suddenly, or by advancing too far into the cavern, to have fallen prey to foul air".

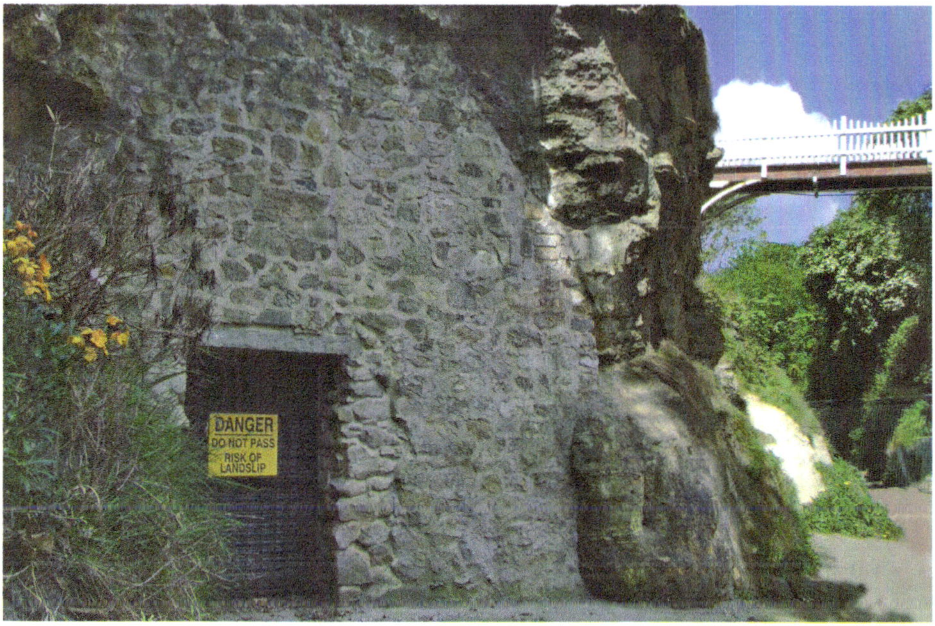

Spotty's Hole

How Spotty's Hole looks today.

Come all ye good people & listen to me,
And a comical jest I will tell unto ye,
Belangin to that Spottee that liv'd on the North Key,
That has neither house nor harbour hee.

The poor auld Wives of the North side dis'nt knaw what
to dee,
For they cannot come to see their husbands when they come
to the key,
For they're fear'd o' their sells & their infants tee :
O ! this Roguish fellow they call Spottee.

But now he's gane away to the sea side,
Where mony a ane wishes he may be wash'd away wi' the
tide ;

For if Flouter's flood come, as it used for to dee,
It will drive his heart out, & where will his midred be ?

Laird Forster was riding alang the sand,
As he or ony other gentleman might dee,
Spottee cam out, his tatter wallups did flee,
His horse took the boggle, & of flew he.

The auld wives of Whitburn does'nt know what to dee ;
They dare not come along the sands, wi' the lang tailed skates in
their hands, to Jacob Spence's landing, as they used for to dee ;
For they com along the sands, wi' their swills in their hands ;
But now they're forced to take a coble, & come in by the sea.

He gathers coals in the day time, as he's weell knawn for to dee,
And makes a fire on i' the night, which casts a light into the sea,
Which garr'd the poor Sloopy cry helm a lee,
And a'back o' the carcasshes com poor she.

Lack & a-well-a day ! says the maister, what shall we dee ?
Trust to Providence, says the mate, & we're sure to get free :
There was a poor little lad on board, that had come a trial
voyage to sea,
His heart went like a pair of bellows, & he swore he wad
never gang mair to sea,

Johnny Ushaw the maister wad a' carried him away,
But the ship's company swore, deel be their feet if they wad
with him stay ;
Wee'll first forfeit our wages for ganging to sea,
Before we'll gang wi' that Roguish fellow they call Spottee.

From the Local Collections of Sir C. Sharp.

The *Ballad of Spotty*

Above: The *'Ballad of Spotty'* from the local collections of Sir Cuthbert Sharp, as published by George Garbutt in 1819. The ballad is thought to have been written by Thomas Clerke.

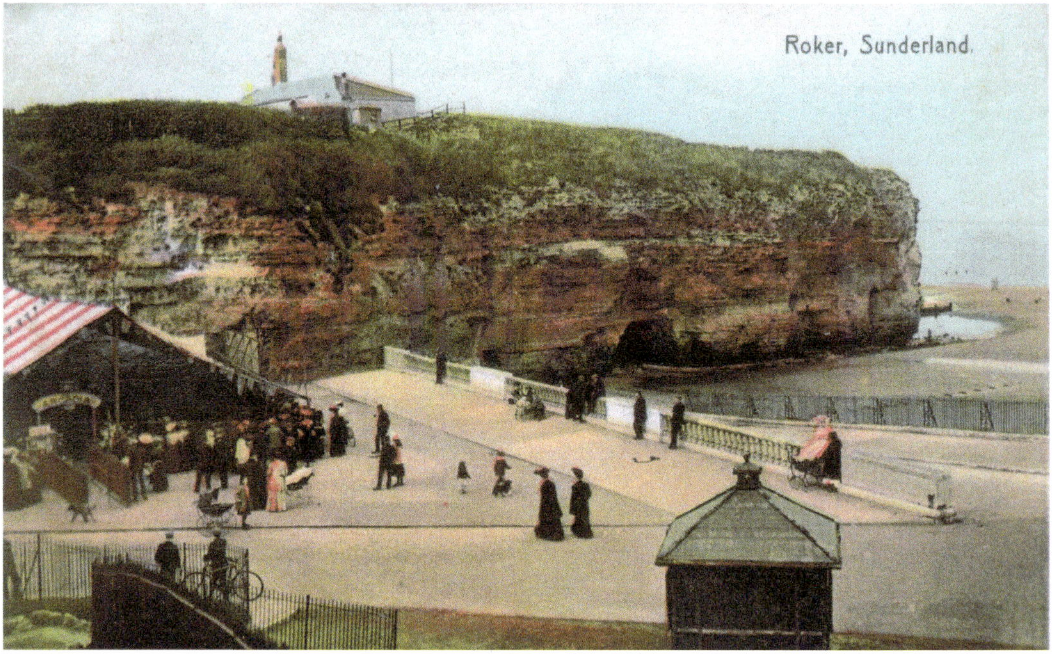

Holey Rock

Holey Rock, Roker around 1910. On the left a Pierrot troupe entertain an audience. The path in the foreground gives access to this beach area via the ravine in Roker Park.

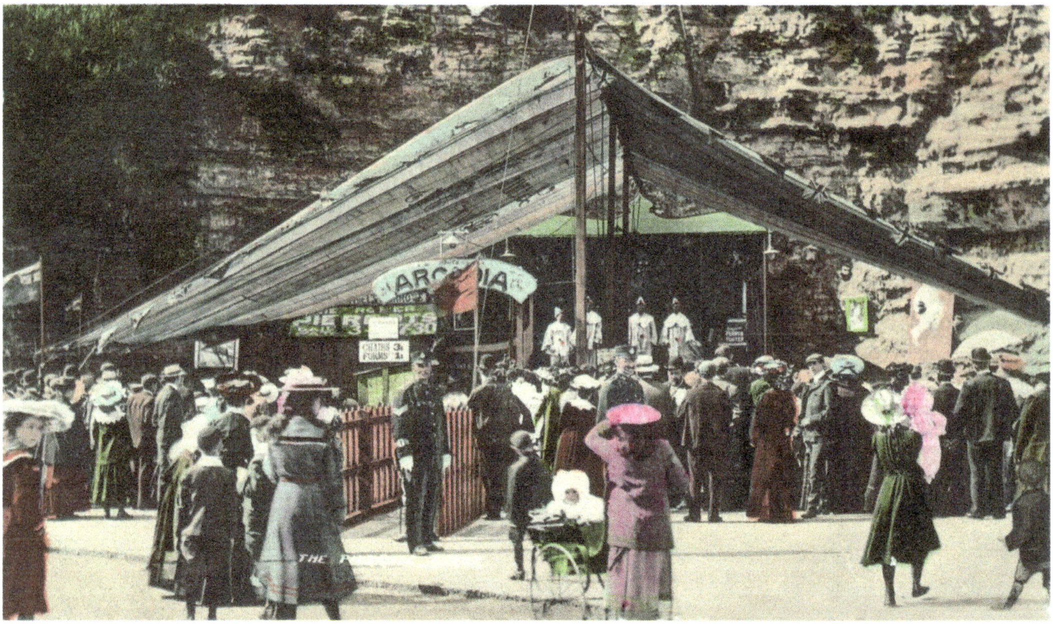

A closer look at the 'Jumbles' who regularly performed their Pierrot show here before the First World War. Daily shows took place on stage between 3.30 and 7.30 and the audience paid 3*d* for a chair or 1*d* for a form. The show could be watched for free however, if you were willing to stand! To the right of the stage is a placard advertising 'Ferry and Foster'.

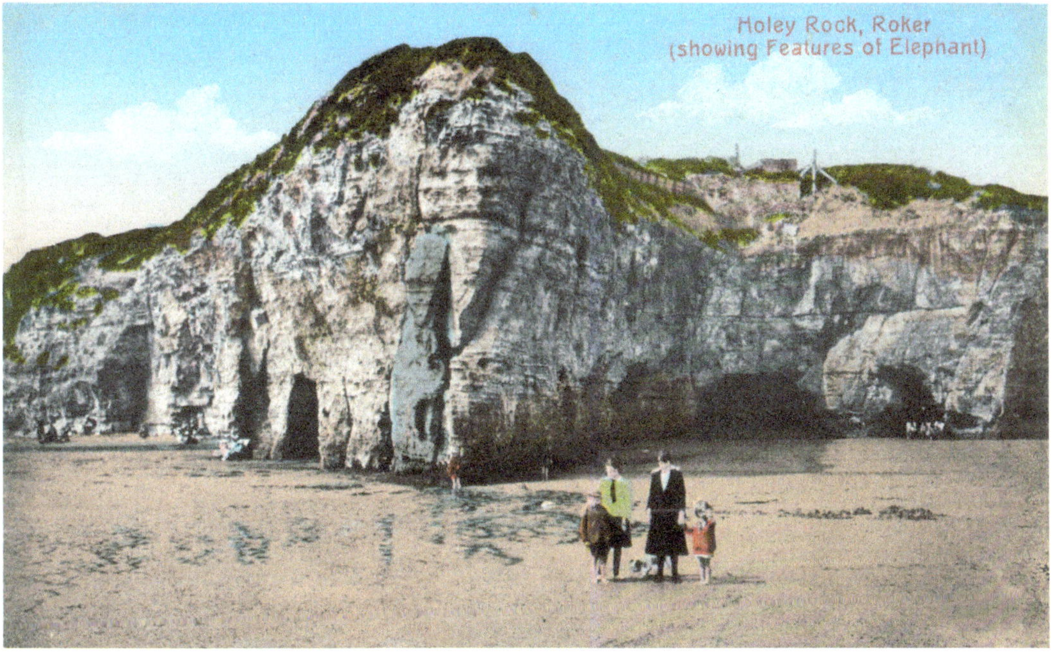

Holey Rock

A postcard view of Holey Rock taken in the 1920s. The rock was said to resemble the features of an elephant. I think I can make out its trunk and rear legs from this angle!

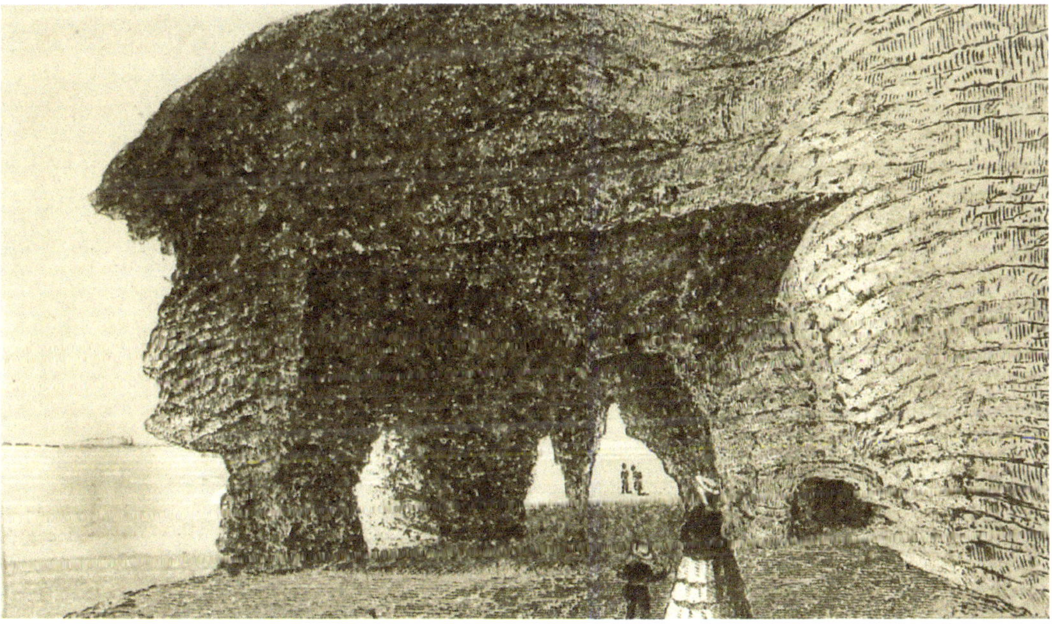

A rare Rock & Co. print of Holey Rock that dates to 1858. The artist drew his picture from a position to the right of the rock as displayed on the above postcard, looking south to face his subject. How fragile the rock and its caves look even in the mid nineteenth century! They were not demolished until June 1936.

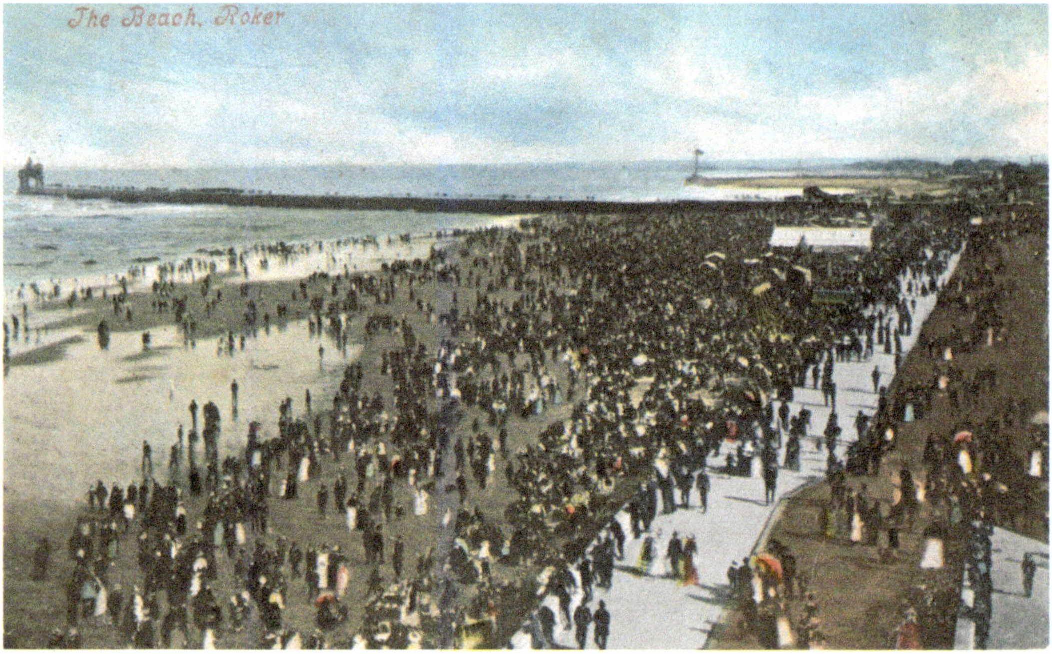

The Beach at Roker

This early 1900s postcard surely confirms the popularity of Roker at this time, when crowds appear to have flocked to the resort in their thousands! The French sender of the card, however, seems to have his doubts as to where the place is. He asks "*Qui est Roker? Savez vous*"*?* Where is Roker? Do you know? Perhaps Spotty could tell him!

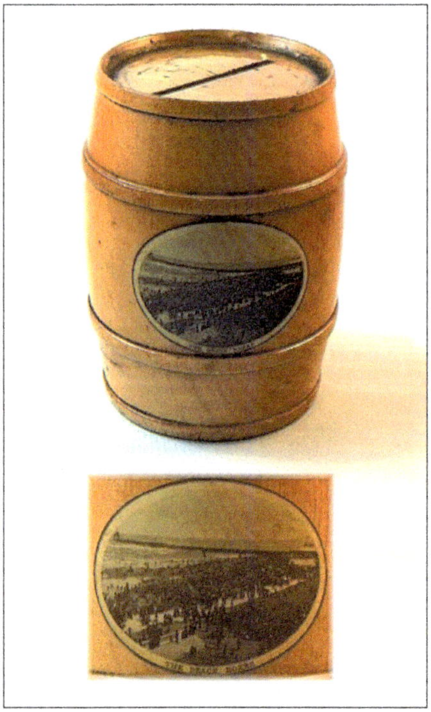

A sycamore wood moneybox souvenir of Roker Beach that dates to the same period as the postcard above. It is known as Mauchline Ware, which was made by three generations of the Smith family of Mauchline in Ayrshire Scotland throughout much of the nineteenth and early twentieth centuries. This factory dominated the wooden souvenir market in the Victorian era.

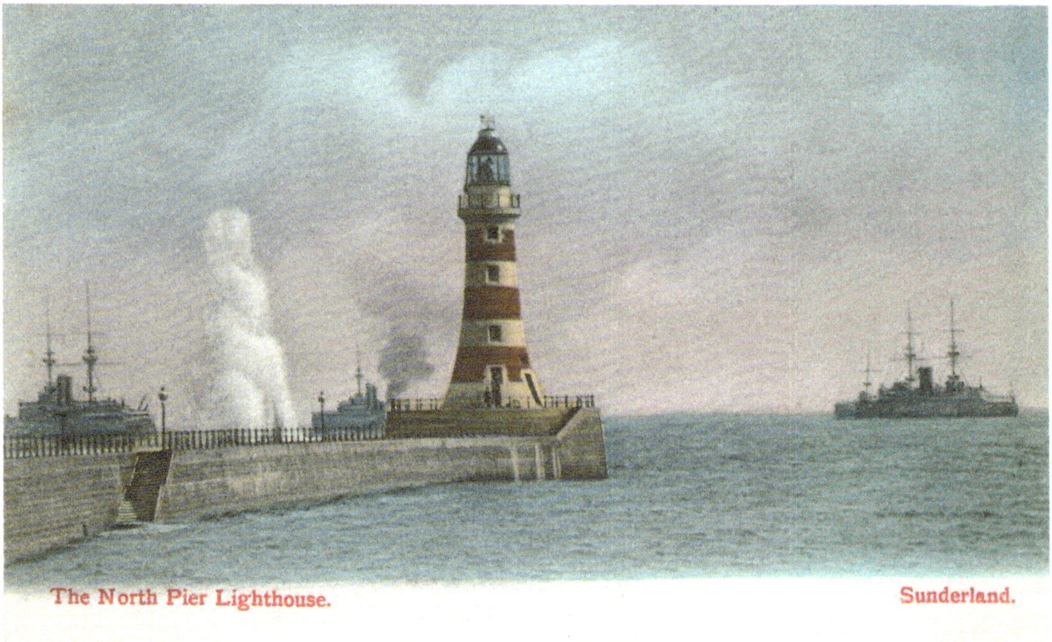

The North Pier of 1903

This postcard features a 'Visit of the Fleet' to Sunderland, shortly after the completion of the new North Pier in September 1903. Work had begun on the breakwater in 1885.

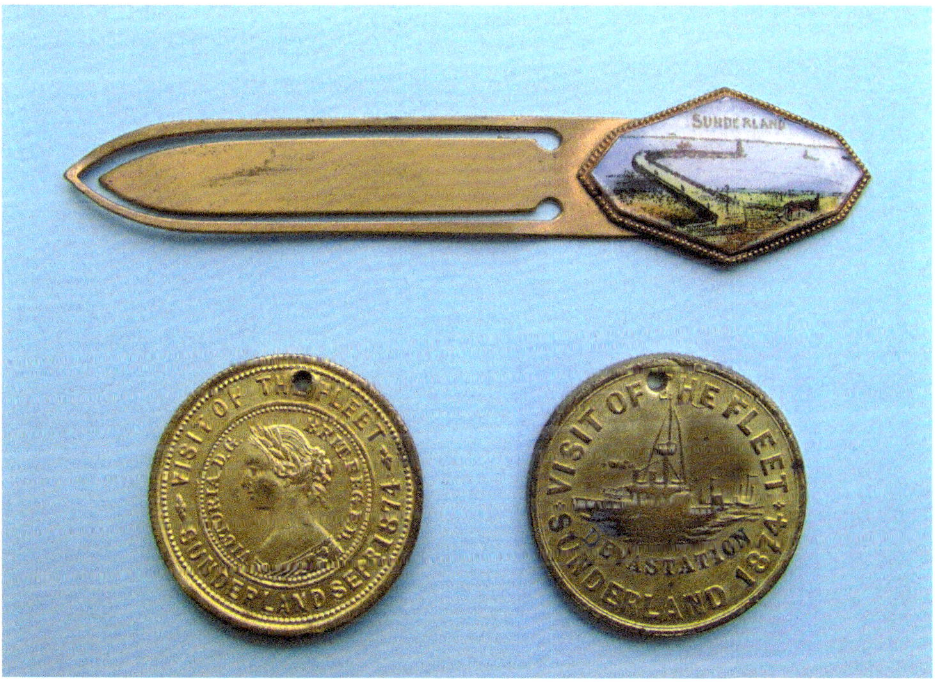

Top: A bookmark featuring an enamelled view of the North Pier, *c.* 1903.
Bottom: A medal commemorating an earlier visit of the fleet in September 1874.

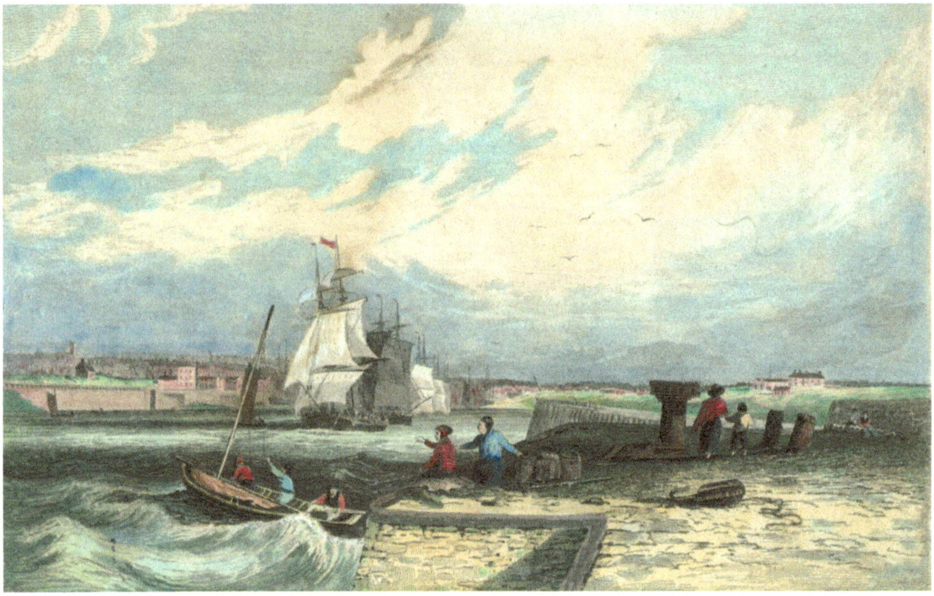

The Old North Pier

A view of Sunderland from the old north pier that was engraved for the *'History of Durham'* and etched by J. Archer. Although plans for a north pier were first proposed in 1748, construction work did not start until thirty-eight years later. Its timber framework was faced with masonry in the last years of the eighteenth century and an octagonal lighthouse was completed in 1802. A remarkable feat of engineering took place in 1841 after the pier was further extended in length.

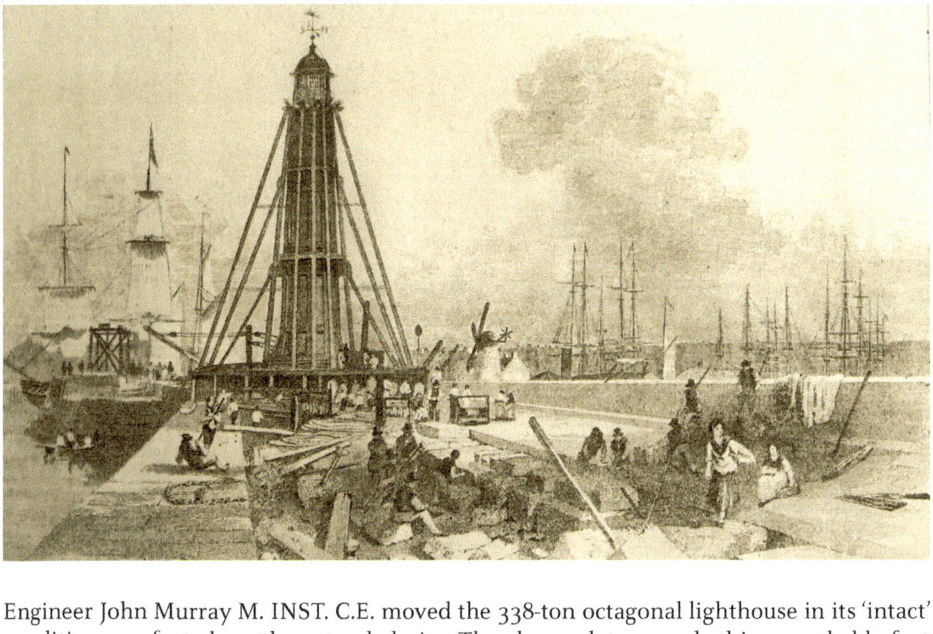

Engineer John Murray M. INST. C.E. moved the 338-ton octagonal lighthouse in its 'intact' condition 450 feet along the extended pier. The above plate records this remarkable feat and it was presented by Mr Murray to author Jeremiah Summers for his book the *History and Antiquities of Sunderland,* which was published in 1858.

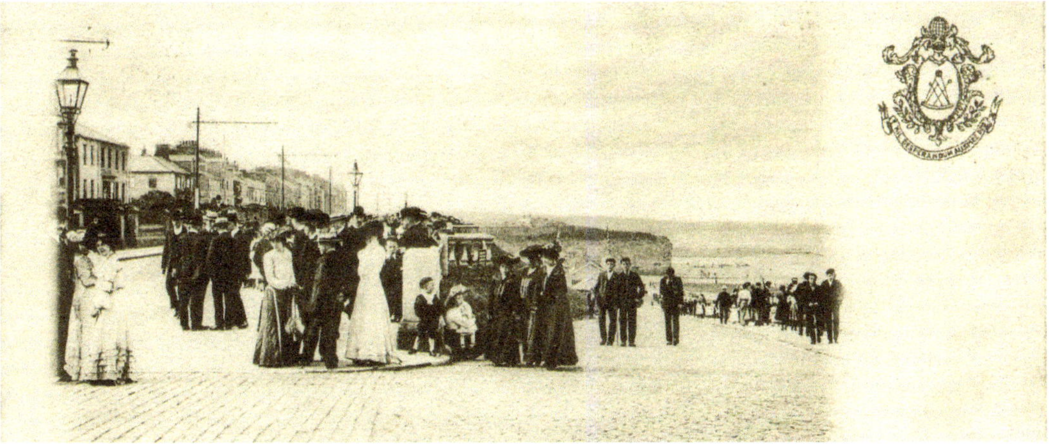

The Ladies of Sunderland

What better pastime could there be for the ladies of the town, but to walk along the upper promenade at Roker dressed in their finery. In 1785, comedian and theatre manager James Cawdell penned a 'Song on the Ladies of Sunderland'. It features in his book *The Miscellaneous Poems of James Cawdell,* which was published in that year by James Graham of Sunderland.

SONG
ON THE LADIES OF SUNDERLAND

GREAT Jove call'd a council in heav'n of late
Some ills to prevent, that impended;
The Virtues, obedient, the summons await;
But none of the Graces attended.
When slighted his mandate the deity saw,
He roll'd his impetuous thunder;
And fill'd the whole senate, assembled, with awe
And ev'ry immortal with wonder

Then, calling for Mercury, bade him in haste,
Explore the wide regions of heav'n—
But all to no purpose those mansions he trac'd
No tidings of them could be giv'n
'Till Truth, stepping forward, with wisdom profound,
Gave thus her unerring opinion:
That to earth they had rambled, as none could be found
In Jupiter's boundless dominion.

The Genius of Britain, escorted by Fame,
Arose and the mystery ended;
Declaring that lately to England they came,
And he them from dangers defended.—
The god then enquir'd in what part of the isle
They resided;- (his warmth gently ceasing.)
At Sunderland, answer'd fair Fame, with a smile,
And their numbers are daily increasing

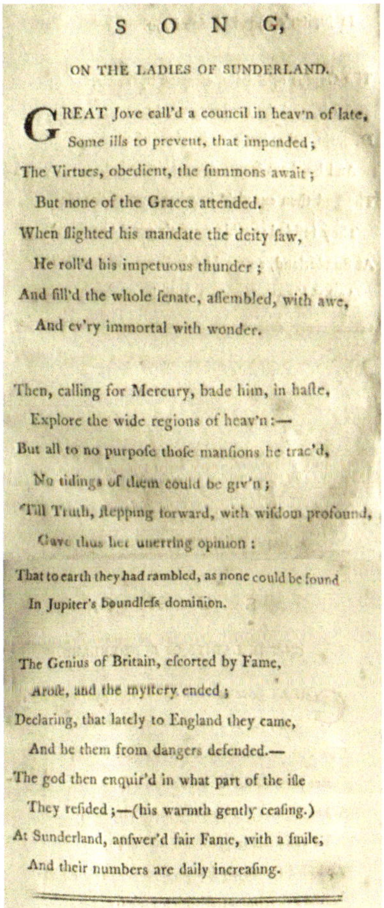

S O N G,

ON THE LADIES OF SUNDERLAND.

GREAT Jove call'd a council in heav'n of late,
Some ills to prevent, that impended;
The Virtues, obedient, the ſummons await;
But none of the Graces attended.
When ſlighted his mandate the deity ſaw,
He roll'd his impetuous thunder;
And fill'd the whole ſenate, aſſembled, with awe,
And ev'ry immortal with wonder.

Then, calling for Mercury, bade him, in haſte,
Explore the wide regions of heav'n:—
But all to no purpoſe thoſe manſions he trac'd,
No tidings of them could be giv'n;
'Till Truth, ſtepping forward, with wiſdom profound,
Gave thus her unerring opinion:
That to earth they had rambled, as none could be found
In Jupiter's boundleſs dominion.

The Genius of Britain, eſcorted by Fame,
Aroſe, and the myſtery ended;
Declaring, that lately to England they came,
And he them from dangers defended.—
The god then enquir'd in what part of the iſle
They reſided;—(his warmth gently ceaſing.)
At Sunderland, anſwer'd fair Fame, with a ſmile,
And their numbers are daily increaſing.

Right: An original print of the song from Cawdell's 1785 book.

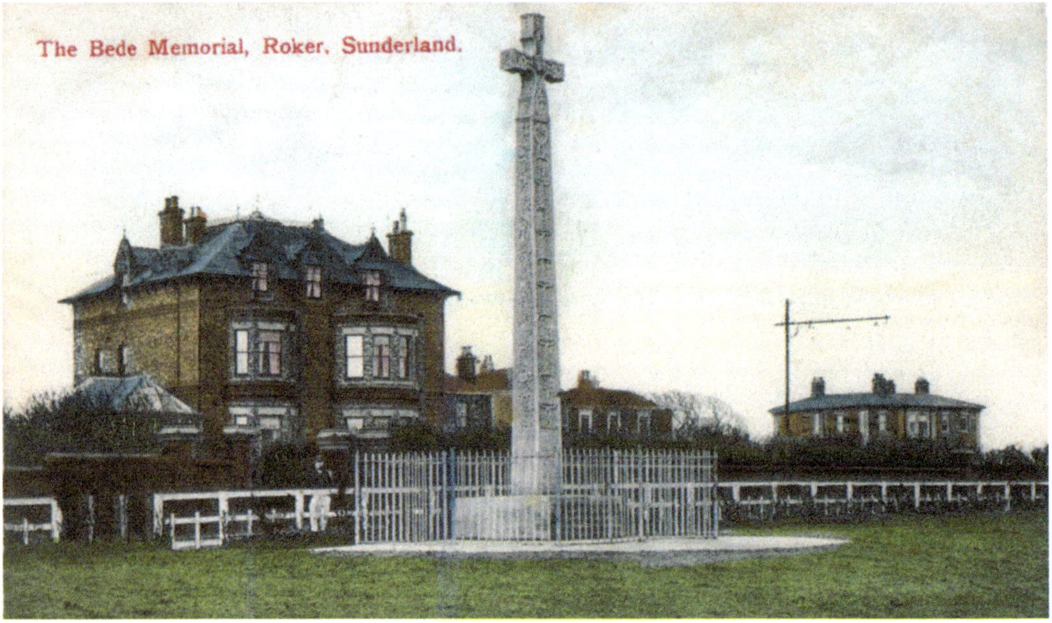

The Bede Memorial Cross, Roker

The handsome Bede Memorial Cross pictured in around 1906. The cross was the work of Charles Clement Hodges and its four intricately carved faces recorded some of the remarkable events in the life of the Venerable Bede. The Archbishop of York unveiled the work on 11 October 1904. It was temporarily removed from site during the two World Wars for protection. Unfortunately its condition deteriorated whilst in storage and attempts to restore it took place when re-assembled on site.

south side north side

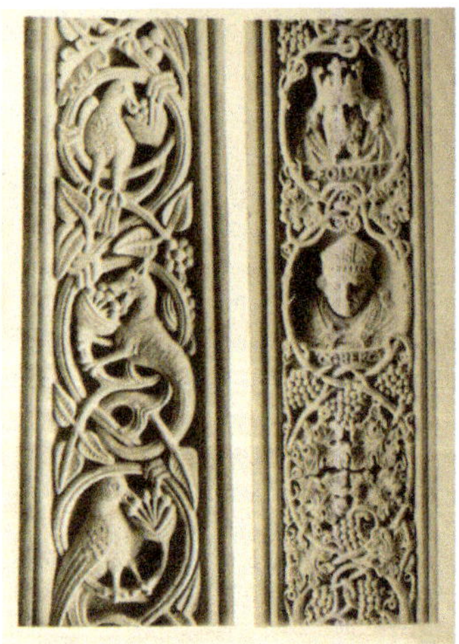

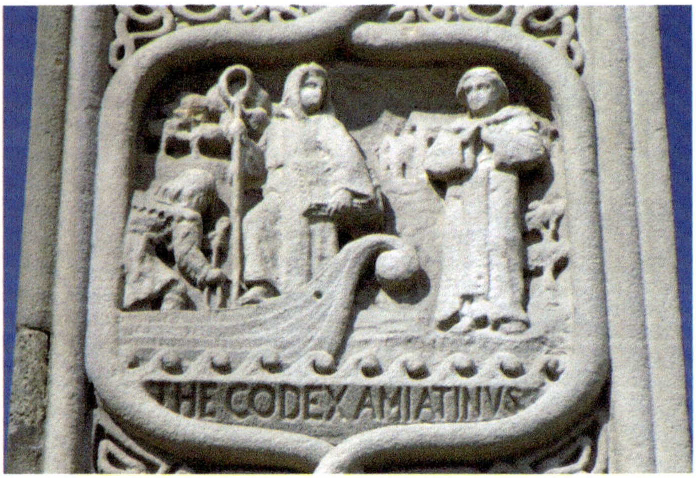

Above left: The fine sculptural detail of the cross when photographed in 1904, shortly after its creation.

Above right: worn detail on the cross today (east side). Ceolfrid embarks on his journey to Rome in 716 A.D. to present one of three bibles produced at the monastery to the Pope.

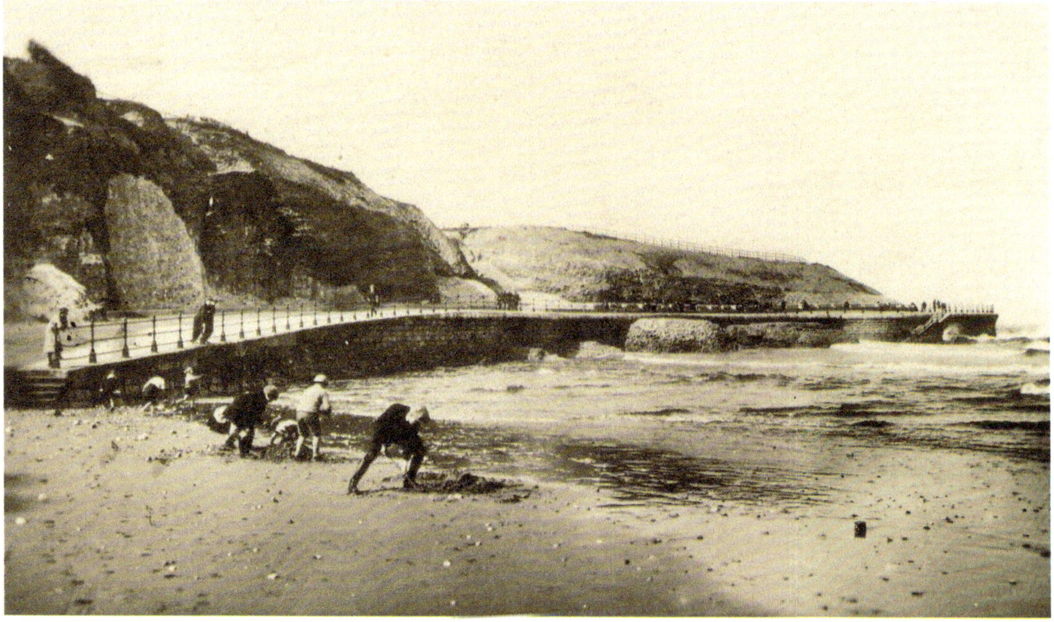

New Promenade & Cannonball Rocks, Seaburn

A view of the new promenade and cannonball rocks in an area commonly known as 'The Cat and Dog Steps'. The steps, which are located at the centre of the view, bring the visitor down to the beach level from the upper promenade in Cliffe Park. The author spent many happy family days out here in the 1950s and '60s!

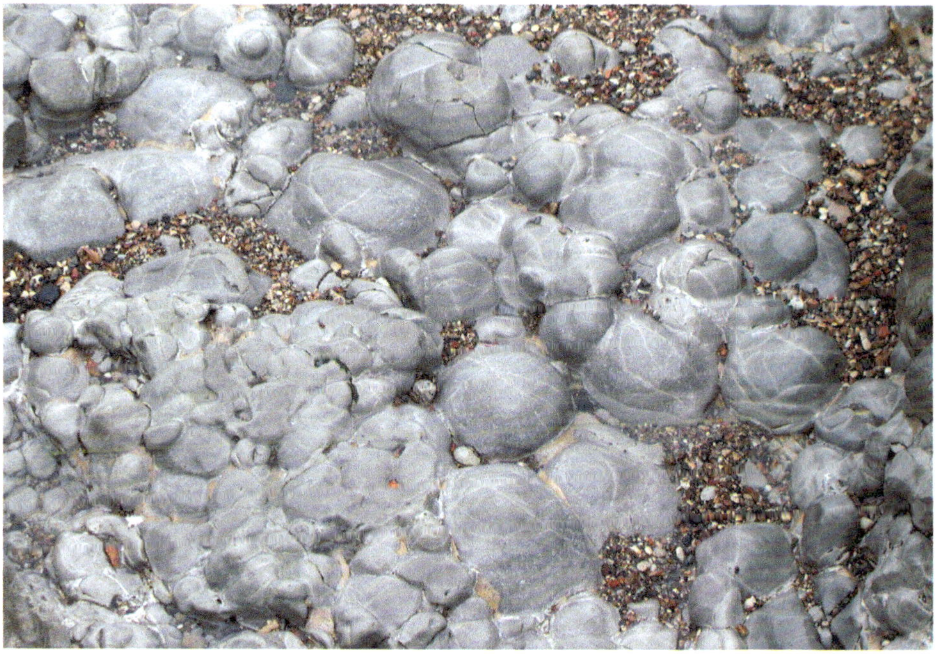

A close up view of the cannonball rocks. A concretionary limestone rock formation that is unique to Sunderland.

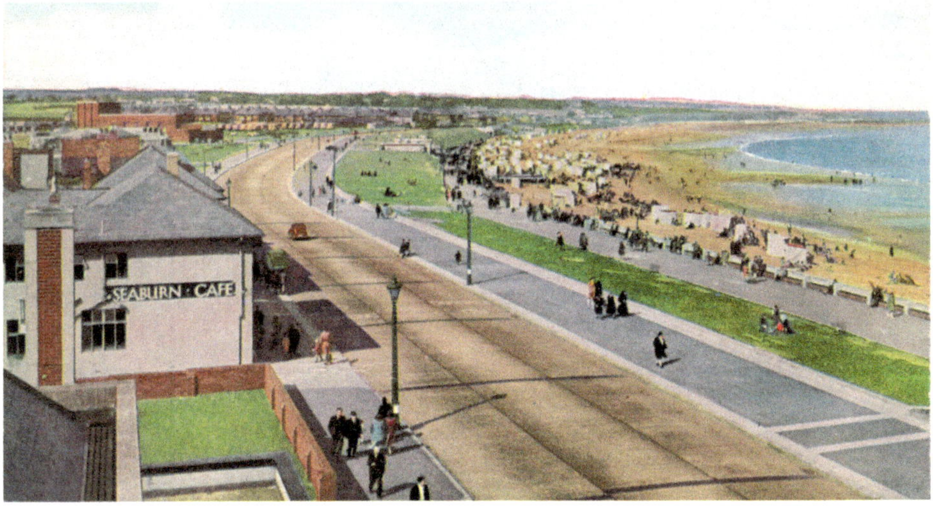

Promenade and Beach, Seaburn

An early 1950s view along Seaburn beach and promenade. The photographer must have been staying at the Seaburn Hotel and popped his head out of the window to get this shot!

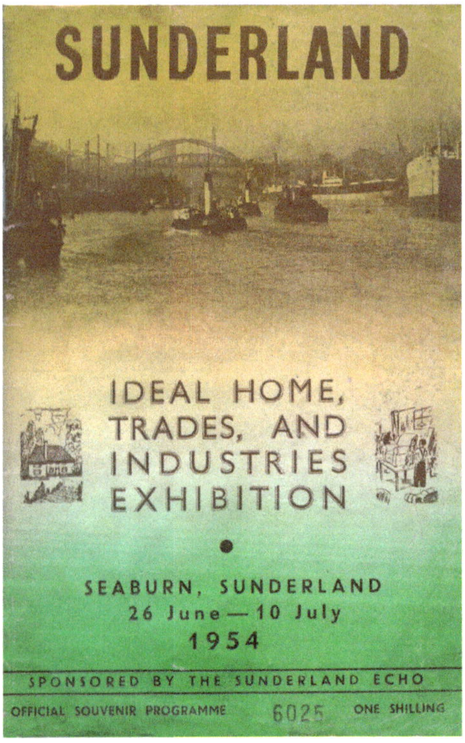

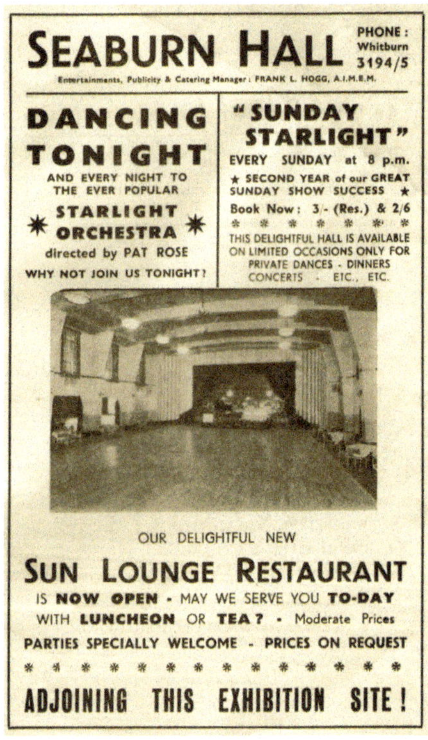

Above left: A souvenir programme for the Ideal Home, Trades and Industries Exhibition held at Seaburn in June/July 1954 – one year after the above the card was posted.

Above right: An advert for Seaburn Hall in the souvenir programme. The exhibition site was adjacent to the hall.

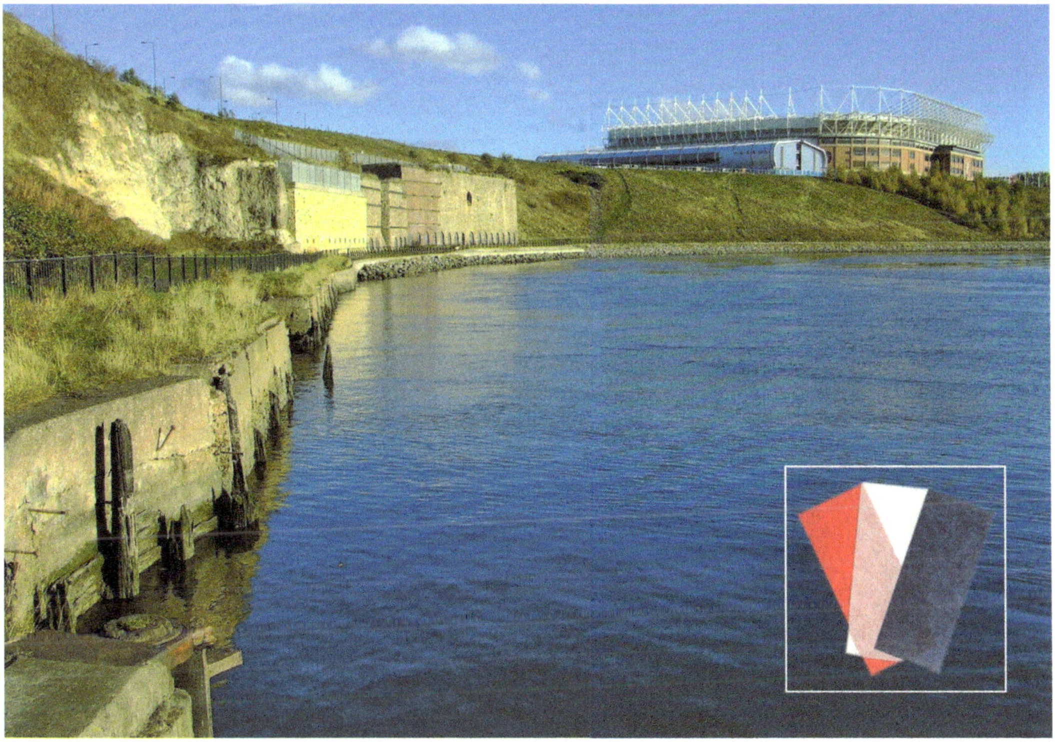

Stadium of Light and Sunderland AFC

The Stadium of Light as photographed by the author in November 2007. Faced with the prospect of converting Roker Park into an all-seater reduced capacity ground by August 1994, then Chairman Bob Murray opted to build a new stadium. The first site considered was on land adjacent to the Nissan car plant, but in 1995, the club put forward plans to build a stadium on the former site of Wearmouth Colliery. In November of that year their plans were approved. The stadium opened on 30 July 1997 with a friendly against Dutch club Ajax. Prince Andrew, Duke of York officially opened the stadium and pop group Status Quo performed a set before kick off. *Inset*: Some of the red, white and black bunting that filled the air at the spectacle.

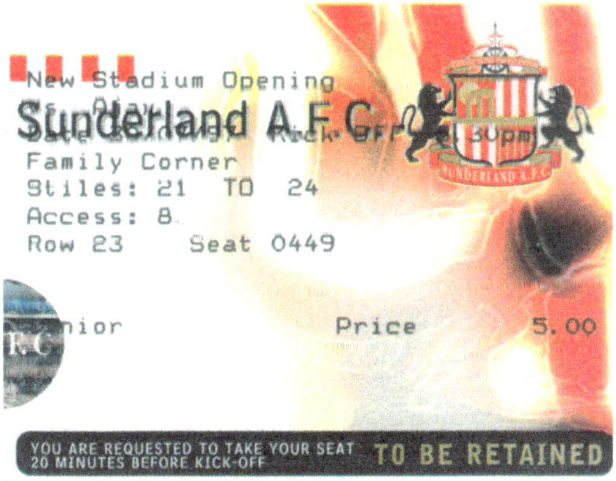

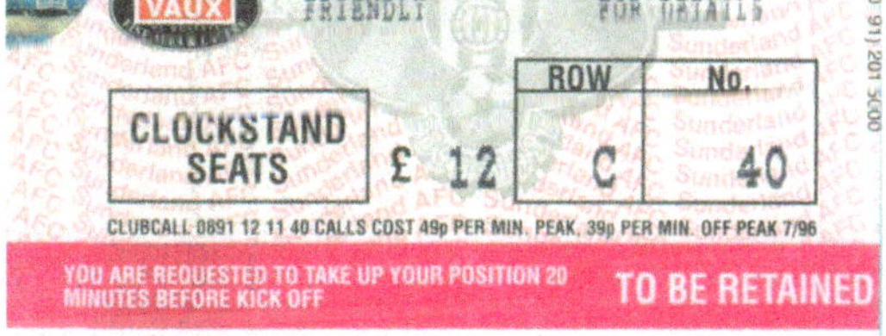

Tickets to the first game at the Stadium of Light against Ajax (left) and the last game at Roker Park (right) in which Sunderland beat Liverpool 1-0 in a friendly.

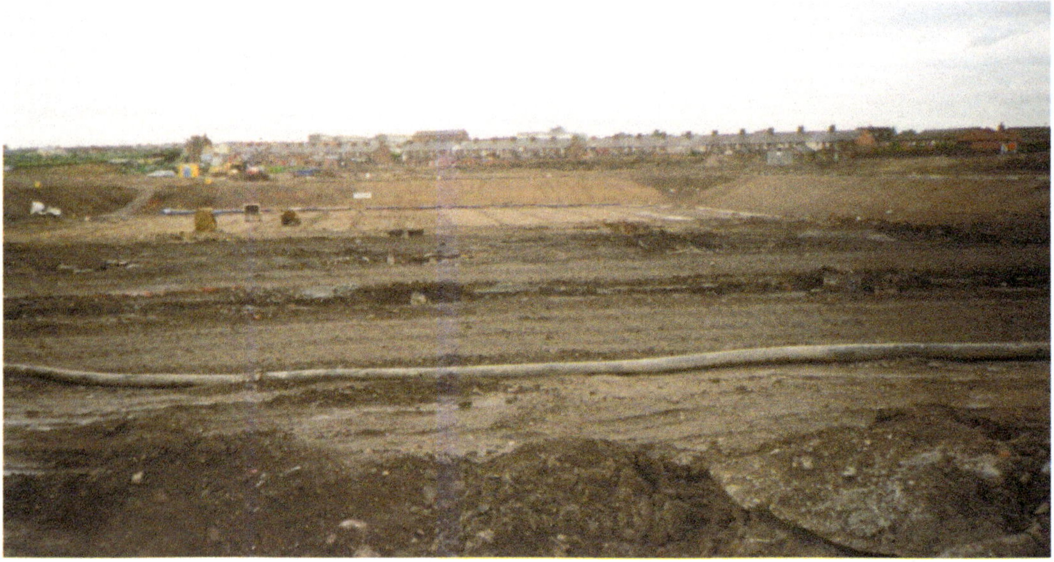

The New Stadium

The laying out of the new stadium begins in 1996. Ballast Wiltshier plc, who had constructed the Amsterdam Arena for AFC Ajax were contracted to build the arena. By the time building work had started, the planned seating capacity had risen from 34,000 to 42,000. In the year 2000 the North Stand was extended to further raise the official stadium capacity to 49,000.

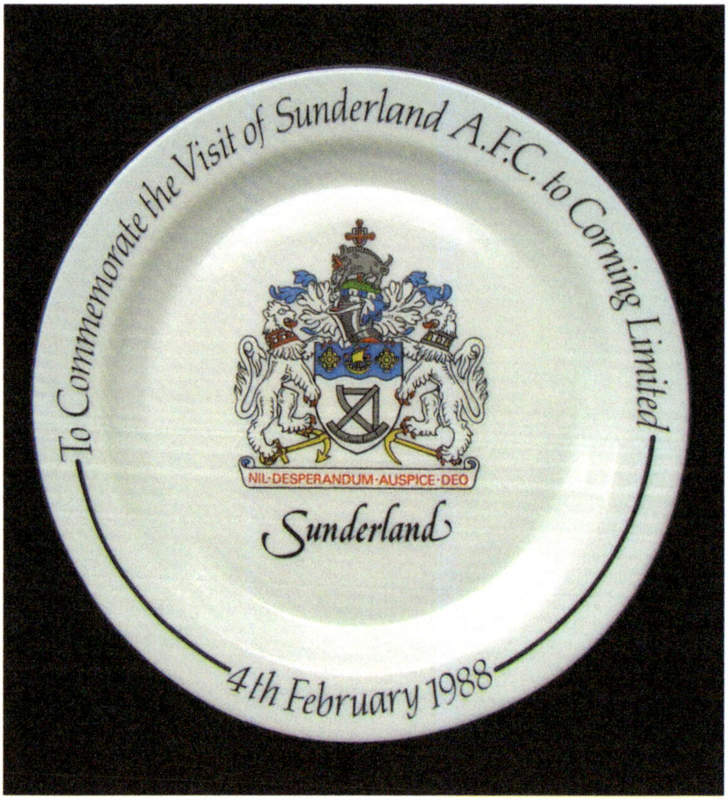

A plate manufactured at Corning Glassworks of Sunderland to commemorate a visit there on 4 February 1988 by Sunderland AFC. The factory of James A Jobling first acquired a licence to manufacture 'Pyrex' heat resistant glassware here in 1921. Sadly the factory closed in September 2007.

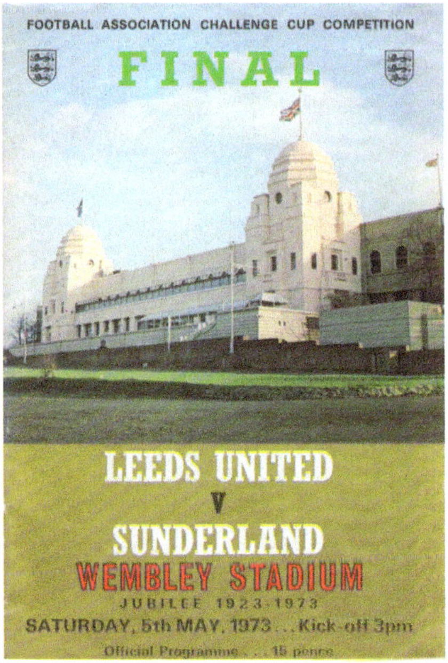

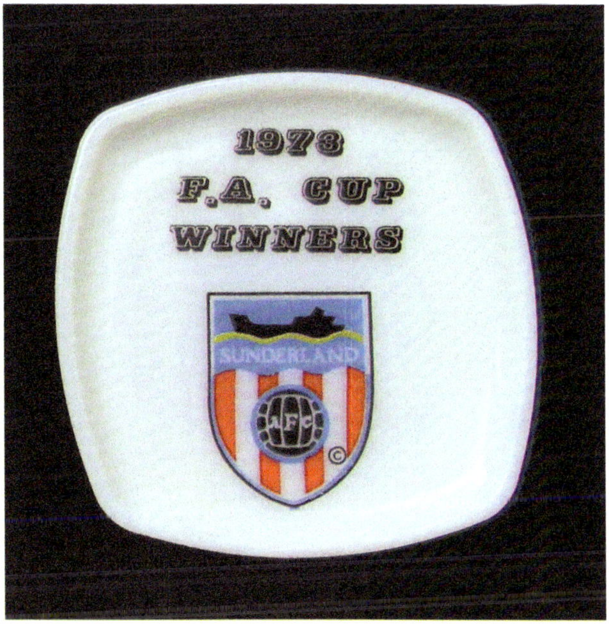

The 1973 Cup Final

Left: A programme for the 1973 cup final against the mighty Leeds Utd. The outcome was a famous and well-deserved victory for the lads! On the right is a small cup winner's ashtray by James A Jobling that commemorates that much-celebrated victory.

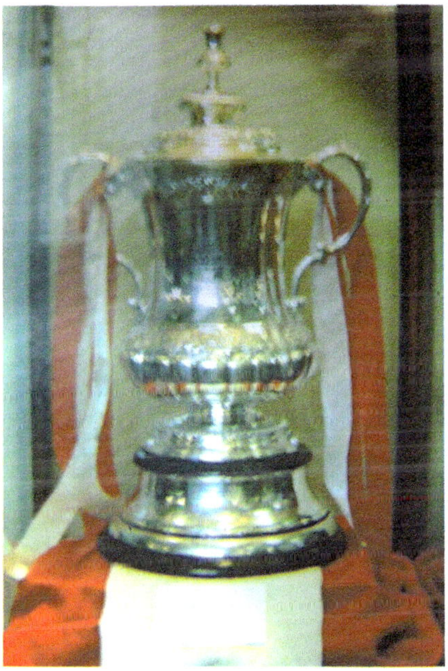

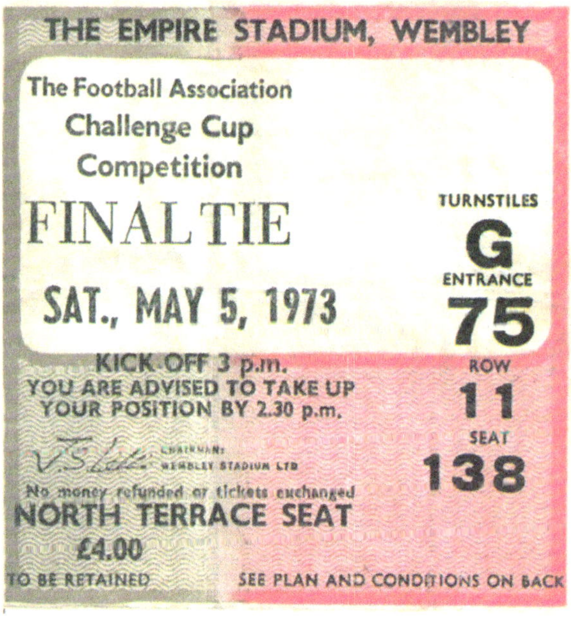

THE EMPIRE STADIUM, WEMBLEY

The Football Association
Challenge Cup
Competition

FINAL TIE

SAT., MAY 5, 1973

KICK-OFF 3 p.m.
YOU ARE ADVISED TO TAKE UP
YOUR POSITION BY 2.30 p.m.

CHAIRMAN:
WEMBLEY STADIUM LTD

No money refunded or tickets exchanged

NORTH TERRACE SEAT

£4.00

TO BE RETAINED

SEE PLAN AND CONDITIONS ON BACK

TURNSTILES G

ENTRANCE 75

ROW 11

SEAT 138

Above left: The FA cup draped in red and white ribbons on public display in Sunderland after the victory.

Above right: A ticket for the 1973 cup final.

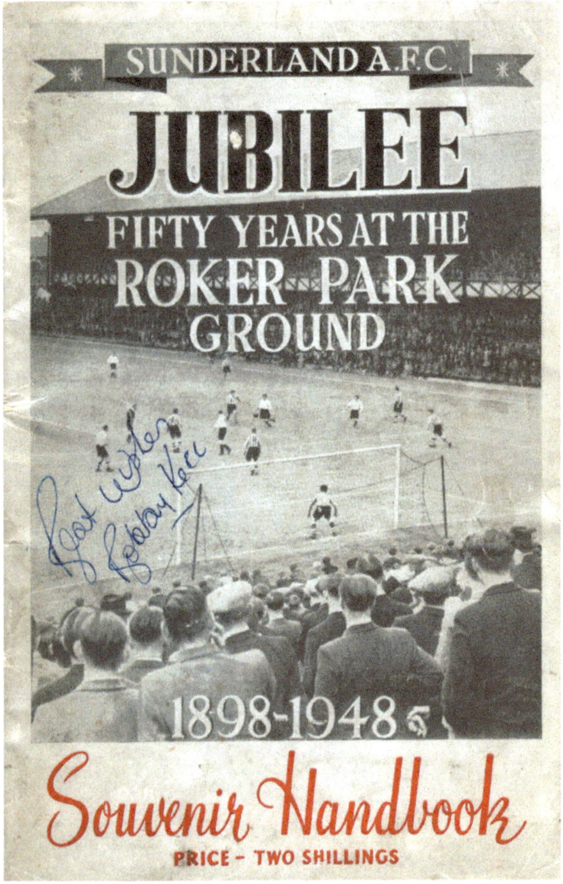

Roker Park

A souvenir handbook commemorating fifty years at the Roker Park ground from 1898 to 1948. It has been signed at some later date by the captain of the 1973 cup winning team, Bobby Kerr.

Roker Park was opened 10 September 1889 by the president of the club, the Marquis of Londonderry. It was built on farmland in the occupation of a Mr Tennant but the overall building scheme also included plans for surrounding housing.

The ground took twelve months to complete and as in the last ever game at Roker Park, Sunderland's very first opponents were Liverpool FC.

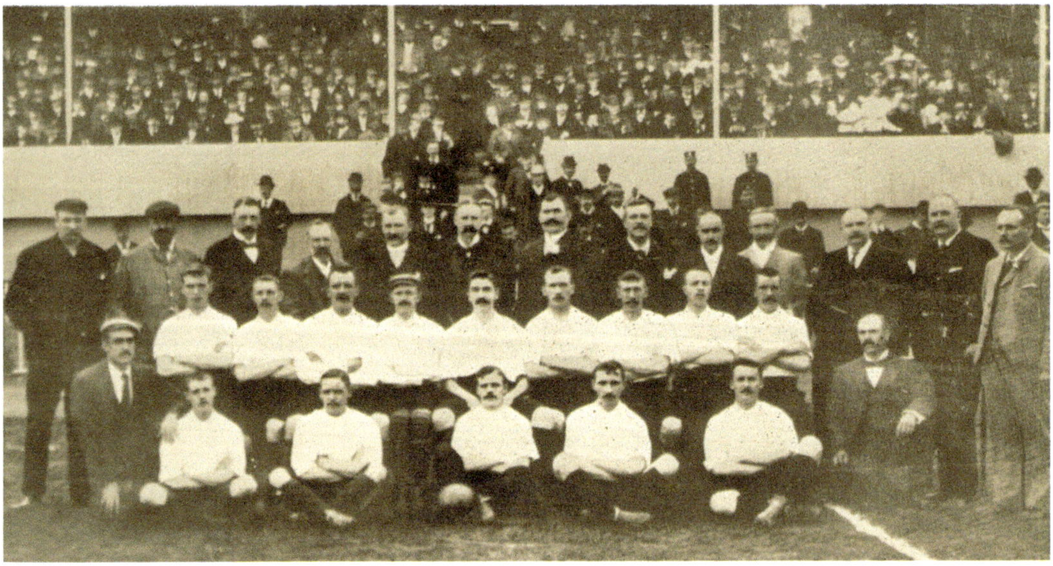

The Sunderland team (in white) and officials at the opening fixture at Roker Park on 10 September 1898.

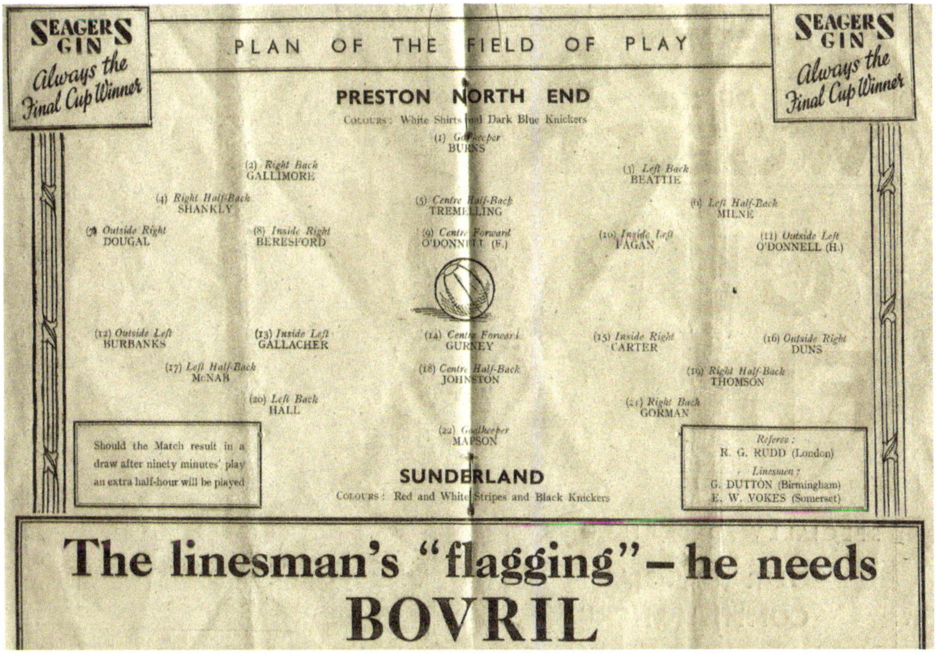

The 1937 Cup Final

The centre pages of the official 1937 cup final programme showing the two opposing teams, Preston North End and Sunderland. The Wearsiders won the cup for the first time by 3 goals to 1.

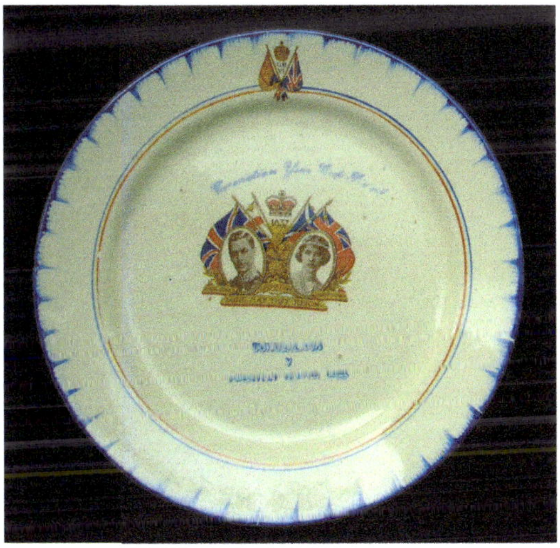

Right: A plate commemorating the 1937 'Coronation Year Cup Final'. It would appear that a Coronation commemorative plate has been overprinted with the cup information and sold as a 'special issue' souvenir. The Cup Final was played on the 1st May and the Coronation took place eleven days later.

Below: A plaque commemorating the 1937 victory made by a great uncle of the author, Albert Cockerill.

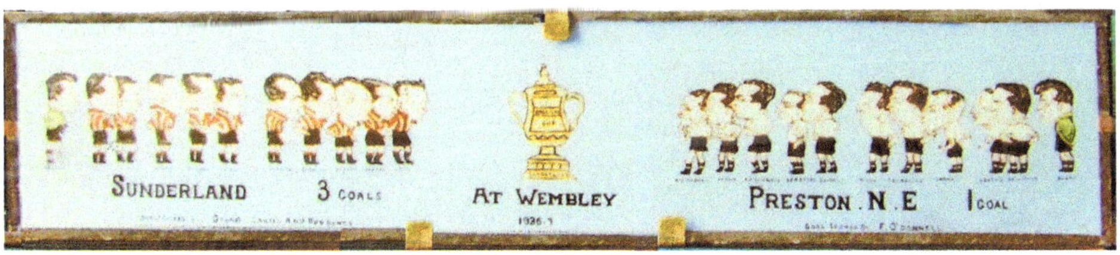

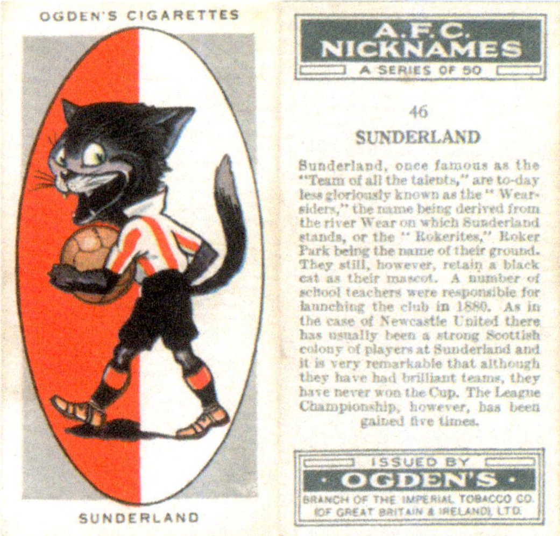

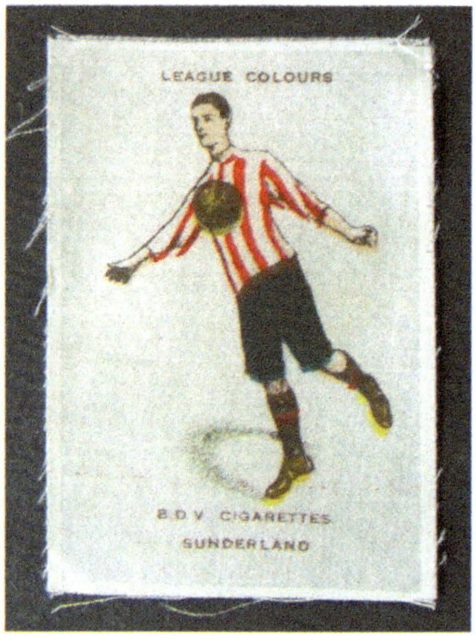

Cigarette Cards

Above left: A cigarette card (No 46) issued by Ogden's in 1933 for a series called 'A.F.C. Nicknames'. Note the reference to Sunderland never having won the Cup. We would have to wait another four years to rectify that situation!

Above right: a cigarette silk issued by Godfrey Phillips Cigarettes in the 1920s as part of a series called 'League Colours'. Two sizes of each silk were released, the larger being the rarer of the two.

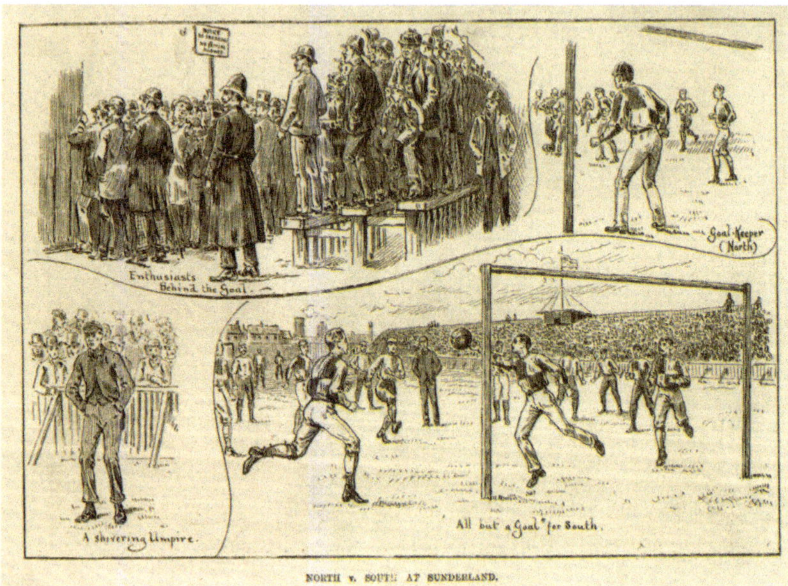

An illustration of a North *v.* South game played at Sunderland. A date of 1889 has been hand-written onto the sheet, which is likely to come from one of the 'illustrated' papers that were popular at that time. If this date is accurate, then the pitch featured would be the Newcastle Road ground. Sunderland played here from around 1885 to 1898. The final Sunderland game at Newcastle Road was against Notts. Forest on 23 April 1898.

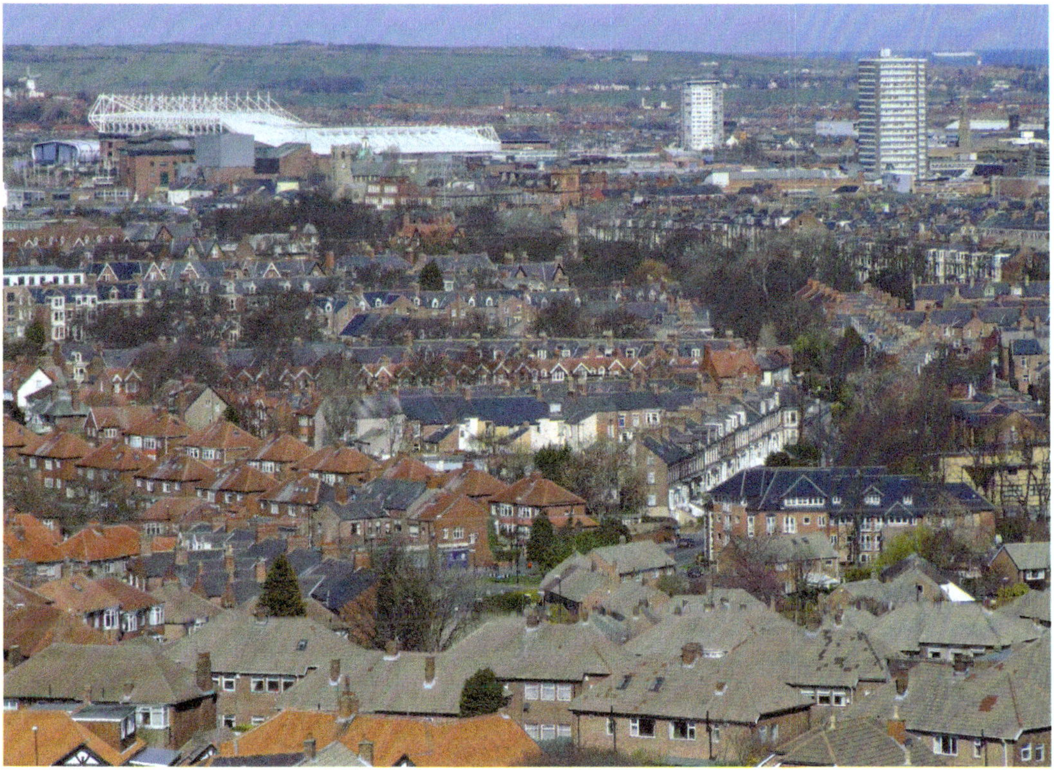

And Finally, The Modern City of Sunderland

The modern City of Sunderland in March 2009, as seen through a telephoto lens from the top of Tunstall Hills. Many of the city's landmarks and well known buildings can be seen on this shot.

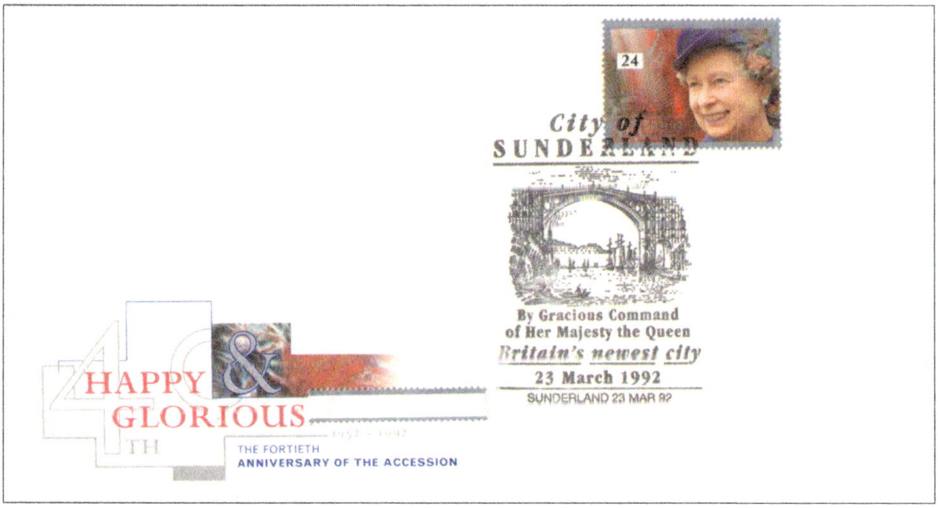

A first day cover of 23 March 1992 commemorating the city status granted to Sunderland by gracious command of the Her Majesty the Queen on the fortieth anniversary of the accession.

Bibliography

The Miscellaneous Poems of James Cawdell, Comedian, 1785
Sermons on Several Subjects by Revd William Paley, DD, 1806
A Historical and Descriptive View of the Parishes of Monkwearmouth & Bishopwearmouth and the Port & Borough of Sunderland by George Garbutt, 1819
History of the Town and Port of Sunderland by James Burnett, 1830
The History and Antiquities of Sunderland Volume 1 by Jeremiah W. Summers, 1858
The Life of Jack Crawford – Sunderland Sailor by Capt, Edward Robinson, 1866
Sunderland: A History of the Town, Port, Trade and Commerce by Taylor Potts, 1892
The Opening of the South Dock Sunderland 1850 compiled by Robert Hudson, 1900
St Peter's Church, Monkwearmouth by James Patterson, 1912
History of Sunderland by William Cranmer Mitchell, 1919
The Tramways of Sunderland by S.A. Staddon, 1964
Some Chapters in the History of Sunderland, edited by Helen G. Bowling, 1969
Sunderland Pottery by Tyne and Wear County Council Museums, 1984
Railways of Sunderland by Tyne and Wear County Council Museums, 1985
Sunderland – River Town and People edited by Geoffrey E Milburn & Stuart T Miller 1988
Sunderland A Century of Shopping by Phillip Curtis, 1999
Chester-le-Street and its Place in History by Raymond Selkirk, 2000
The Mystery of the Duke of Perth – A Historical Enigma by Arthur Appleton, 2001
Sunderland The Largest Shipbuilding Town in the World by Alan Brett and Andrew Clark, 2005
The Sundered-Land: The Story of a Seaport and its Township by Robert Moon, with a trilogy by Lily Firmin and Anne Howdon, 2008

Printed and bound by CPI Group (UK) Ltd, Croydon, CR0 4YY
17/03/2026
02073003-0003